DATE DUE

LOUISE ERDRICH

Critical Companions to Popular Contemporary Writers
Kathleen Gregory Klein, Series Editor

Rudolfo A. Anaya
by Margarite Fernández Olmos

V. C. Andrews
by E. D. Huntley

Maya Angelou
by Mary Jane Lupton

Tom Clancy
by Helen S. Garson

Mary Higgins Clark
by Linda C. Pelzer

Arthur C. Clarke
by Robin Anne Reid

James Clavell
by Gina Macdonald

Pat Conroy
by Landon C. Burns

Robin Cook
by Lorena Laura Stookey

Michael Crichton
by Elizabeth A. Trembley

Howard Fast
by Andrew Macdonald

Ken Follett
by Richard C. Turner

Ernest J. Gaines
by Karen Carmean

John Grisham
by Mary Beth Pringle

James Herriot
by Michael J. Rossi

Tony Hillerman
by John M. Reilly

John Irving
by Josie P. Campbell

John Jakes
by Mary Ellen Jones

Jamaica Kincaid
by Lizabeth Paravisini-Gebert

Stephen King
by Sharon A. Russell

Barbara Kingsolver
by Mary Jean DeMarr

Dean Koontz
by Joan G. Kotker

Robert Ludlum
by Gina Macdonald

Anne McCaffrey
by Robin Roberts

Colleen McCullough
by Mary Jean DeMarr

James A. Michener
by Marilyn S. Severson

Toni Morrison
by Missy Dehn Kubitschek

Anne Rice
by Jennifer Smith

Tom Robbins
by Catherine E. Hoyser and Lorena Laura Stookey

John Saul
by Paul Bail

Erich Segal
by Linda C. Pelzer

Amy Tan
by E. D. Huntley

Anne Tyler
by Paul Bail

Leon Uris
by Kathleen Shine Cain

Gore Vidal
by Susan Baker and Curtis S. Gibson

LOUISE ERDRICH

A Critical Companion

Lorena L. Stookey

CRITICAL COMPANIONS TO POPULAR CONTEMPORARY WRITERS
Kathleen Gregory Klein, Series Editor

Greenwood Press
Westport, Connecticut • London

Library of Congress Cataloging-in-Publication Data

Stookey, Lorena Laura.
    Louise Erdrich : a critical companion / Lorena L. Stookey.
       p. cm.—(Critical companions to popular contemporary
writers, ISSN 1082–4979)
    Includes bibliographical references (p.) and index.
    ISBN 0–313–30612–5 (alk. paper)
    1. Erdrich, Louise—Criticism and interpretation. 2. Women and
literature—United States—History—20th century. 3. Indians in
literature. I. Title. II. Series.
PS3555.R42Z87   1999
813'.54—dc21   99–21709

British Library Cataloguing in Publication Data is available.

Library of Congress Catalog Card Number: 99–21709
ISBN: 0–313–30612–5
ISSN: 1082–4979

First published in 1999

Greenwood Press, 88 Post Road West, Westport, CT 06881
An imprint of Greenwood Publishing Group, Inc.
www.greenwood.com

Printed in the United States of America

The paper used in this book complies with the
Permanent Paper Standard issued by the National
Information Standards Organization (Z39.48–1984).

10 9 8 7 6 5 4 3 2 1

Contents

Series Foreword *by Kathleen Gregory Klein*   ix

1. The Life of Louise Erdrich   1

2. Louise Erdrich's Fiction: Community and Storytelling   13

3. *Love Medicine* (1984, 1993)   29

4. *The Beet Queen* (1986)   51

5. *Tracks* (1988)   69

6. *The Bingo Palace* (1994)   91

7. *Tales of Burning Love* (1996)   109

8. *The Antelope Wife* (1998)   127

Bibliography   143

Index   163

Series Foreword

The authors who appear in the series Critical Companions to Popular Contemporary Writers are all best-selling writers. They do not simply have one successful novel, but a string of them. Fans, critics, and specialist readers eagerly anticipate their next book. For some, high cash advances and breakthrough sales figures are automatic; movie deals often follow. Some writers become household names, recognized by almost everyone.

But, their novels are read one by one. Each reader chooses to start and, more importantly, to finish a book because of what she or he finds there. The real test of a novel is in the satisfaction its readers experience. This series acknowledges the extraordinary involvement of readers and writers in creating a best-seller.

The authors included in this series were chosen by an Advisory Board composed of high school English teachers and high school and public librarians. They ranked a list of best-selling writers according to their popularity among different groups of readers. For the first series, writers in the top-ranked group who had received no book-length, academic, literary analysis (or none in at least the past ten years) were chosen. Because of this selection method, Critical Companions to Popular Contemporary Writers meets a need that is being addressed nowhere else. The success of these volumes as reported by reviewers, librarians, and teachers led to an expansion of the series mandate to include some writ-

ers with wide critical attention—Toni Morrison, John Irving, and Maya
Angelou, for example—to extend the usefulness of the series.

The volumes in the series are written by scholars with particular ex-
pertise in analyzing popular fiction. These specialists add an academic
focus to the popular success that these writers already enjoy.

The series is designed to appeal to a wide range of readers. The general
reading public will find explanations for the appeal of these well-known
writers. Fans will find biographical and fictional questions answered.
Students will find literary analysis, discussions of fictional genres, carefully organized introductions to new ways of reading the novels, and
bibliographies for additional research. Whether browsing through the
book for pleasure or using it for an assignment, readers will find that
the most recent novels of the authors are included.

Each volume begins with a biographical chapter drawing on published
information, autobiographies or memoirs, prior interviews, and, in some
cases, interviews given especially for this series. A chapter on literary
history and genres describes how the author's work fits into a larger
literary context. The following chapters analyze the writer's most important, most popular, and most recent novels in detail. Each chapter
focuses on one or more novels. This approach, suggested by the Advisory Board as the most useful to student research, allows for an in-depth
analysis of the writer's fiction. Close and careful readings with numerous
examples show readers exactly how the novels work. These chapters are
organized around three central elements: plot development (how the
story line moves forward), character development (what the reader
knows of the important figures), and theme (the significant ideas of the
novel). Chapters may also include sections on generic conventions (how
the novel is similar to or different from others in its same category of
science fiction, fantasy, thriller, etc.), narrative point of view (who tells
the story and how), symbols and literary language, and historical or
social context. Each chapter ends with an "alternative reading" of the
novel. The volume concludes with a primary and secondary bibliography, including reviews.

The alternative readings are a unique feature of this series. By dem-
onstrating a particular way of reading each novel, they provide a clear
example of how a specific perspective can reveal important aspects of
the book. In the alternative reading sections, one contemporary literary
theory—way of reading, such as feminist criticism, Marxism, new his-
toricism, deconstruction, or Jungian psychological critique—is defined in
brief, easily comprehensible language. That definition is then applied to

the novel to highlight specific features that might go unnoticed or be understood differently in a more general reading. Each volume defines two or three specific theories, making them part of the reader's understanding of how diverse meanings may be constructed from a single novel.

Taken collectively, the volumes in the Critical Companions to Popular Contemporary Writers series provide a wide-ranging investigation of the complexities of current best-selling fiction. By treating these novels seriously as both literary works and publishing successes, the series demonstrates the potential of popular literature in contemporary culture.

Kathleen Gregory Klein
Southern Connecticut State University

1

The Life of Louise Erdrich

As she has often remarked in interviews, Louise Erdrich grew up in a family of storytellers and thus learned very early to appreciate the world of possibilities invoked by a storyteller's voice. She must, too, have been attracted to the sounds and rhythms of the stories—as she puts it, to their "rise, break and fall" (Schumacher 175)—for in her own telling of tales, she has striven to position her readers to "hear" a "story told" (Chavkin and Chavkin 231). "There's something particularly strong," she claims, "about a *told story*" (Bruchac 103). Encouraged by her parents, Erdrich began writing stories when she was a small child; her father supported this early stage of her literary life with a nickel a story, and her mother made the covers for her daughter's first books. Erdrich, then, began early to experiment with a writer's voice, but she also spent her childhood observing and listening: As she reveals to Hertha D. Wong, "I was . . . the one who listened in on everything else" (Wong, "An Interview," 46).[1]

Karen Louise Erdrich was born June 7, 1954, in Little Falls, Minnesota, and grew up in Wahpeton, the small town in North Dakota's Red River Valley where her parents taught in a school run by the Bureau of Indian Affairs. The eldest of Ralph Louis and Rita Joanne (Gourneau) Erdrich's seven children, she experienced within her closely knit family circle the strong sense of connection to community that emerges as a theme in each of her novels. Erdrich indeed remains especially close to her family, and mentions in *The Antelope Wife*'s acknowledgments that her father copyedited her book. Two of her sisters, Heid and Lise, are also writers of poetry and fiction, and, in fact, Heid Erdrich has written in collaboration with her older sister.

Erdrich has many fond memories of childhood visits with her grandparents, and some of these memories surface in her writing. For example, her father's German parents ran a butcher shop in Little Falls, Minnesota, the town where she was born; in *Jacklight*, her first published collection of poems, Erdrich describes the world of a small-town butcher shop in a section of the volume entitled "The Butcher's Wife." (She dedicates these poems to her Polish step-grandmother, Mary Korll.) Readers of *The Beet Queen* find a butcher shop featured prominently in that novel. The same butcher shop also appears in *Tracks* and *Tales of Burning Love*. In *The Antelope Wife*, the notion of the family store takes the form of a bakery shop.

Erdrich's Ojibwa and French grandparents on her mother's side of the family lived on North Dakota's Turtle Mountain Reservation, where her grandfather Patrick Gourneau served as tribal chair. Gourneau, a beader and powwow dancer, was also a fine storyteller, and Erdrich particularly recalls his stories of the Great Depression and his accounts of his experiences as a Wobbly, a member of the international labor organization called the International Workers of the World. Family stories of life during the hard times of the 1930s made a strong impression on Erdrich, and she readily acknowledges that "there's a lot of Depression" (Jones 6) in the settings of *Love Medicine* and *The Beet Queen*.

During her years as a teenager Erdrich listened to Joan Baez and experimented with "dressing funny" (Cryer 81) when she acquired from her father articles of his leftover Army clothes. (She was also, however, a cheerleader for her high school wrestling team, and perhaps that is where she learned about the "windshield-wiper wave" [BQ 331] that Dot Adare employs during the Beet Queen Parade.) Erdrich read poetry while she was in high school, and she also continued to write, recording her observations and experiences in a series of journals. When she decided, in 1972, to enroll at Dartmouth College, she had never before been away from her family, and she had never traveled very far from her home.

The year Erdrich entered Dartmouth marked significant changes on the college's Hanover, New Hampshire, campus. On one hand, Erdrich was among the first group of women admitted to the college, and, on the other, it was during that year that Dartmouth introduced a new program in Native American Studies. Founded in 1769, Dartmouth had originally defined its mission as serving the "education of Indian youths and others" (Trueheart 116), but since its founding it had in fact numbered only twelve Native American students among its graduates. It was at Dartmouth that Louise Erdrich met Michael Dorris, the man she would later marry—and who would in 1997 take his own life. Dorris, a young anthropologist from Yale, was hired to head the college's new Native American Studies Program, and so 1972 was also his first year at Dartmouth. Although Erdrich majored in English and Creative Writing during her college years, she took some courses as well in Native American Studies and began to become interested in her own Ojibwa background. As she later observed, Dartmouth's program emphasized "the importance of keeping your heritage" (Wong, "An Interview," 33).

After her graduation from Dartmouth, Erdrich spent a couple of years acquiring work experience before she enrolled in the graduate school at Johns Hopkins University. In her home state, she worked for the North Dakota Arts Council as a visiting poet and teacher. Erdrich traveled about the state, presenting workshops in schools, prisons, and hospitals while using her free time to work on her own writing. In these early years she also worked as a waitress, a lifeguard, a sugar beet weeder, a cucumber picker, and a construction worker—and all of these jobs, in one way or another, provided experience that she could later draw upon while writing her novels. During the summer of 1977 she worked in Lincoln, Nebraska, on a public television documentary about the Northern Plains Indians, and found in this experience an occasion to further pursue her growing interest in Native American peoples.

Erdrich knew, by the time that she was twenty, that she wanted to be a writer. Her work experiences had taught her that she had little tolerance for "authority" in the workplace, and she realized that if she "were to have any chance at all for happiness in work" (Chavkin and Chavkin 233), she would find it doing what afforded her the greatest satisfaction. The first public recognition of her work came while she was still an undergraduate at Dartmouth; when she was a senior, *Ms.* accepted one of her poems for publication. In 1978 she entered the M.A. program in Creative Writing at Johns Hopkins University, and she was awarded her degree in 1979. While in the graduate program, Erdrich worked on many of the poems that would later be published in *Jacklight*, and she also began to try her hand at fiction in the form of a novel-in-progress that she entitled *Tracks*. For many years Erdrich carried with her the manuscript of *Tracks*, occasionally borrowing sections to use in other works.

Finally, after she had published *Love Medicine* and *The Beet Queen*, she returned to her first novel and reworked its design. *Tracks* was at last published in 1988.

After graduate school, Erdrich moved to Boston, where she became the communications director and the editor of *The Circle*, a newspaper published by the Boston Indian Council. In Boston she worked within an urban Indian community and found this experience to be quite different from her earlier experiences with Native American life in reservation communities. She encountered many people who were, like her, of mixed blood, and she realized that her own Native tradition was an important part of her life and something that she wanted to write about. In fact, she reports, she began to find herself *"forced"* to write about her experience as a mixed-blood Native American. As she tells Michael Schumacher, "I didn't choose the material; it chose me" (Schumacher 175).

In 1979 Erdrich returned to Dartmouth to give a poetry reading, and on that occasion she renewed her acquaintance with Michael Dorris. After the reading, she and Dorris talked, and then later they began to write to one another. Their correspondence continued through 1980, the year Dorris spent lecturing at Auckland University in New Zealand and Erdrich spent as a fellow at the MacDowell Colony in New Hampshire. In early 1981 Erdrich once again returned to Dartmouth, this time as writer-in-residence, and later in that year, on October 10, she and Dorris were married. After their marriage, Erdrich became adoptive mother to Abel, Sava, and Madeline (Birdie), the three Native American children whom Dorris had adopted as a single man.

Erdrich's marriage soon became a literary partnership as well, and for many years the couple worked in collaboration with one another. The collaboration began when, to earn some extra money, the two together penned romance fiction under the pseudonym Milou North. As they later explained, "Milou" was a genderless combination of their names, Michael and Louise, and "North" referred to the location of their New Hampshire home. These stories were particularly popular in Britain, where they were printed in *Woman;* in the United States, a few were published in *Redbook*. Erdrich remembers Milou North with affection and adds that "writing to spec" (Trueheart 115) afforded her useful practice in the early days of her writing career.

With respect to the writing she cared more about, Erdrich was at first reluctant to share her work-in-progress with another. Gradually, however, she grew to trust Dorris's judgments, and over the years the two became accustomed to reviewing and editing each other's work. Inspired by his wife, Dorris began to write as well: He is perhaps best known for *The Broken Cord*, his study of Fetal Alcohol Syndrome, and his novel, *A Yellow Raft in Blue Water*. Erdrich and Dorris often discussed the characters in their books, and Erdrich credits Dorris with helping her arrange *Love Medicine*'s sequence of narratives. In fact, she notes that it was Dorris who first saw that her independently published short stories, "Scales" and "The Red Convertible," might indeed be part of a longer work. Long after the days of Milou North, Erdrich and Dorris once again collaborated directly; together they wrote *The Crown of Columbus*, the only novel upon which both of their names appear.

The Crown of Columbus, published in 1991, just before the year of Columbus's quincentenary, is in part historical fiction and in part a mystery-adventure and a tale of romance. At the heart of the plot is the love story of Dartmouth professors Vivian Twostar and Roger Williams, who, like Columbus, set out on a voyage of discovery and, as Columbus did, end up in the Bahamas. Vivian and Roger are in search of a missing page of Columbus's diary and a golden crown that he is said to have brought to the New World. The intrepid adventurers risk life and limb in the course of their quest, but their search for treasure eventually leads each of them to significant discoveries about themselves and each other. For Vivian and Roger, the search for Columbus's artifacts is also the search for an understanding of the voyager himself, and through their readings of his character readers are invited to consider the mysteries surrounding Columbus the man. In *The Crown of Columbus*, Vivian and Roger do find "Europe's gift to America" (*CC* 490), the crown that Columbus carried, but instead of a golden crown, it is "the Crown of Thorns" (*CC* 492) that Christ wore during the Crucifixion. Columbus's gift to the New World thus serves as an emblem of the suffering of Native American peoples after contact with the Christians of Europe.

Erdrich and Dorris enjoyed sporting with one another while writing *The Crown of Columbus*. Each would write a section of the novel and then pass the manuscript on to the other. Although they both had in mind the agreed-upon design of the book, specific details of the plot evolved as the novel was being written. Erdrich describes, for example, a particularly challenging twist of plot she presented to Dorris: She wrote a scene wherein Roger jumps into shark-infested waters from the sinking rubber raft that holds his baby daughter. Dorris, she later reported, met his challenge with aplomb. Reviewer Sybil Steinberg describes *The Crown of Columbus* as a "light-hearted romantic mystery" (Steinberg 60); in writing it, Erdrich and Dorris returned to the collaborative style that had served them when they wrote their early romances under the name Milou North.

Dorris not only acted as Erdrich's trusted collaborator, but, shortly after their marriage, he also declared himself her agent. (He even prepared suitable letterhead stationery for this purpose.) He worked earnestly on Erdrich's behalf, and his first important breakthrough came in 1983 when Henry Holt and Company accepted *Jacklight* for publication. A couple of years earlier, he had also encouraged Erdrich, who was then mainly writing short stories, to compete for the Nelson Algren Fiction Award. The couple heard about the award only days before the submission deadline, but Erdrich barricaded herself in the kitchen and wrote "The World's Greatest Fishermen," the story that she would later use as the opening chapter of *Love Medicine*. Erdrich indeed won the prestigious award in 1982, and it was with this prize that she truly launched her writing career.

Holt, the publishers of *Jacklight*, also published *Love Medicine* in the fall of 1984, and that first novel, notes Kenneth Lincoln, "garnered more literary awards . . . than any other book in printing history" (Lincoln 209). Among its other prizes, *Love Medicine* was awarded the National Book Critics Circle Award for Best Fiction, and, when *The Beet Queen*, Erdrich's second novel, was published two years later, it too was nominated for that same award. In addition to the prizes awarded her novels, Erdrich has received recognition for both her poems and short stories. She has, for example, been awarded the Pushcart Prize in Poetry and the O. Henry Prize for her short fiction. Several of her stories have been printed as well in *The Best American Short Stories* series. Erdrich has been the recipient of a Guggenheim Fellowship, and in 1992 she was recognized with the Western Literary Association Award.

In 1995 Erdrich published a memoir, *The Blue Jay's Dance*, that offers readers a glimpse of her life as both mother and writer during the busy years of the 1980s and early 1990s. During this period Erdrich published six novels (one every two or three years) while raising six children—in addition to their three adopted children, Erdrich and Dorris had three daughters, Persia, Pallas, and Aza. Dedicated to the three daughters to whom she gave birth, *The Blue Jay's Dance* conflates the passage of many years into a description of one. It begins with the winter birth of a child and then moves through the seasons of that child's first year of life. Amidst the bustle of domestic activity, Erdich finds moments of solitude to contemplate the larger setting of the natural landscape outside the family house and to meditate upon correspondences between the vocations of parent and writer.

The decade of the 1990s opened with a tragedy within the Erdrich-Dorris household. In 1991, their oldest child, Abel, was struck and killed by a car. Abel, who suffered from the mental and physical disabilities characteristic of severe instances of Fetal Alcohol Syndrome, was twenty-three years old at the time of the accident. (In *The Broken Cord* [1989], Dorris had written an account of his son's lifelong struggle with the problems engendered by his medical condition.) A few years later, in 1996, Erdrich and Dorris separated after fifteen years of marriage, and, in April of the following year, Dorris committed suicide.

While there is some mystery surrounding the circumstances of Dorris's death and, of course, many rumors as well, for Erdrich and Dorris were a well-known literary couple, Erdrich later revealed that her husband had for many years suffered from bouts of depression and sleeplessness and had, in fact, been "suicidal from the second year" (Jones and Stone 82) of their marriage. During the last years of their marriage Erdrich and Dorris were troubled by disputes with their older children Sava (Jeffrey) and Madeline, and during the couple's separation there were charges of child abuse filed against Dorris. Since his death, police files on the investigation of those charges have been permanently sealed, and Erdrich has reestablished her family ties to Sava and Madeline. *The Antelope Wife*, published after Dorris's death, is dedicated to Louise Erdrich's five children and also contains a prefatory note for her readers: In it Erdrich states that her novel, whose plot indeed depicts a suicide, was written before her husband's death—and that he is now "remembered with love" by his family.

Erdrich and her three young daughters now live in Minneapolis, just a few hours away from her parents' North Dakota home. Madeline also lives in the city, and she and her mother often get together. Erdrich continues to write, and she also studies the piano and takes lessons in Ojibwa. (A recent short story, "Naked Woman Playing Chopin," speaks to Erdrich's fascination with the piano.) In addition to her other writing projects, she is now working on her second children's book; the first, *Grandmother's Pigeon*, was published in 1996. Erdrich has long been interested in beading and quilling, traditional Ojibwa arts; she enjoys spending time on Manitoulin Island in Ontario, where a colony of artists produces traditional porcupine quill work.

ERDRICH'S BACKGROUND AS REFLECTED IN HER WORK

Erdrich began her mature literary career as a poet, and the evidence of her origins can be found in her lyrical prose, in her deft use of imagery and metaphor, and in her employment within her fiction of patterned designs and recurring motifs. She began to move from poetry to fiction in 1980, when she became conscious of the narrative elements at work in her poems and realized "that there was not enough room in a poem unless you are a John Milton" (Coltelli 23) to tell her stories fully. From writing poems, Erdrich moved to writing short stories, for, as she says about the narratives that she eventually linked together in *Love Medicine*, she did not see at first "that the bunch of episodes was really a long, long story." When Erdrich could clearly see how her independent tales "meshed" (Grantham 16) to give shape to a larger narrative design, she moved from the form of the short story to that of the novel—and here too Erdrich found a larger design at work, for five of her novels are interconnected with one another.

Readers of all Erdrich's fiction can readily see the patterns of her books' references to one another and note the changing shapes of the tales retold in them. This intertextuality is most apparent in the first five novels, but even *The Antelope Wife*, which introduces a setting and a group of characters different from those of the earlier novels, mentions the North Dakota books' Pillager family. In one instance, intertextuality in Erdrich's work extends beyond her own fictional world, for *The Bingo Palace* contains a brief allusion to Ida, a character from Michael Dorris's novel, *A Yellow Raft in Blue Water*. The only book not at all linked to the others is *The Crown of Columbus*, which Erdrich wrote in collaboration with Dorris.

Kenneth Lincoln and numerous other critics describe Erdrich's work as a literature of "homing" (Lincoln 209), which is to say that it is fiction wherein a sense of home and place plays a central role. With the exception of *The Crown of Columbus*, all of Erdrich's novels are set in the midwestern plains states where she grew up. Although she lived for many years in the eastern United States, Erdrich's attraction to the flatness and openness of North Dakota and Minnesota remained firmly rooted in her blood. "To experience . . . flatness," she once remarked in an interview, is "very good for the soul" (Wong, "An Interview," 53). "Homing" is indeed a central theme throughout Erdrich's work, one that is repeatedly expressed in characters' quests to find or to return to the place where they belong, the place that is home. Within Erdrich's literary imagination, that place is clearly the wide and flat spaces of the American Great Plains. Her fiction, as she says, is "informed by . . . nostalgia or longing . . . for openness" (Jones 6).

Louise Erdrich was raised as a Catholic, and this tradition too is reflected in her work, where many of her Native American characters are portrayed as missionized Catholics who also participate in the religious belief systems of their traditional culture. Indeed, Erdrich found a model for this kind of practice of religious belief in the person of her grandfather Patrick Gourneau, who "observed both Catholicism and his traditional Chippewa religion" (Cryer 81). For her grandfather, as Erdrich reports, Catholicism and Ojibwa belief were so thoroughly intertwined that "he would do pipe ceremonies for [church] ordinations" (Bruchac 99). Like Gourneau, Erdrich's characters live within two religious traditions, and in *Tracks* she finds occasion to consider certain of the implications of this historical circumstance.

Not only does Erdrich figure into her novels the landscape she knew as a child, she also writes about the people who live there—the Native Americans whose ancestral lands became Minnesota and North Dakota, and the Scandinavian, German, Polish, and Scots immigrants who migrated to the region. Indeed, the names of her characters represent all of these ethnic identities, including, of course, her own German, Ojibwa, and French ethnic roots. In reference to Erdrich's Native American heritage, readers of her novels encounter three different names used to designate her people. In *Tracks*, Old Nanapush refers to his people as the *Anishinabe*, and, indeed, this is the name (meaning "original or spontaneous people") that the Algonquian speakers living in the Great Lakes region before contact with Europeans used among themselves. After contact, Europeans began to call the Anishinabe the *Chippewa* (those people who lived south of Lake Superior) or the *Ojibwa* (the northern branches of the Anishinabe), and the French fur traders called them the Saulteur. In her early novels, set in North Dakota, Erdrich often uses the term Chippewa, and later, when she shifts her setting to Minnesota, she refers to the people as Ojibwa.[2]

Although Erdrich represents ethnic groups in her novels' characters, she sees as part of her writer's work the task of countering common stereotypical images of both Native Americans and other people. She hopes that readers will perceive her characters as figures they can understand and with whom they can sympathize—even when those characters have, as Malcolm Jones observes, "more warts than haloes" (Jones 6). In an interview with Laura Coltelli, Erdrich makes explicit her desire to confront stereotypical images of Native Americans when she states: "I want to be able to present Indian people as sympathetic characters, nonstereotypes, characters that any non-Indian would identify with" (Coltelli 26).

While the characters that people Erdrich's fiction are unquestionably memorable, "warts" and all, they are all part of the landscapes of community depicted in her books. In other words, Erdrich's novels never focus upon the single story of a central character, but instead offer readers a vision of community wherein many characters' lives and stories are interconnected with one another. Indeed, as more than one critic has noted, for Erdrich it is the community that serves as "protagonist" (Wong, "Louise," 173) in the novels. The strong sense of community expressed in all her work obviously reflects features of the writer's own experiences and background: her upbringing in a small town and her own commitment to family and community.

For Louise Erdrich, who has been telling her stories since she was a child, writing has been a lifelong preoccupation. She has published poems, essays, short stories, and novels—indeed she has worked in all the genres except drama (though when she was a child she enjoyed staging skits with her sisters and brothers). She tries to write each day and generally has several projects underway at once. It is important to her, she says, to find a first sentence or a telling image or significant title, and she jots down her inspirations when they occur to her: She scribbled the first sentence of "Scales" on a Travelhost napkin, and her father's story of his first ride in a barnstormer's airplane provided the image from which *The Beet Queen* grew. Erdrich writes her novels in sections, not necessarily in the order in which they will later appear, and often interesting connections suggest themselves as she works on the sections. For example, she had almost finished writing *The Beet Queen* before it occurred to her that the character Wallacette was in fact *Love Medicine*'s Dot Adare. With this discovery, Erdrich strengthened the connections among her five North Dakota novels that are themselves all sections of a "long, long story."

NOTES

1. The listener/observer is a recurring figure in Erdrich's fiction, and various critics or reviewers have suggested that in such characters as *Love Medicine*'s

Albertine Johnson or *The Antelope Wife*'s Cally Roy, readers might catch a glimpse of the writer herself.

2. Because *Ojibwa* has come to be used as the generic term that signifies all branches of the Anishinabe, that is the name used throughout this discussion of Erdrich's fiction.

2

Louise Erdrich's Fiction: Community and Storytelling

Louise Erdrich thinks of herself as a "citizen" (Moyers 144) of two nations, and, indeed, her literary art has roots in both Euro-American and Native American narrative traditions. Like many other contemporary fiction writers, she both works from and experiments with the Euro-American tradition of the novel, but she also incorporates within that genre features of other genres and elements of an oral storytelling tradition. Her use of the form of the novel lies in the tradition of William Faulkner, for she too situates multiple narrators within the mythic landscape of a regional community. In her hands, however, the novel as genre is transfigured; as Nan Nowick aptly observes, Erdrich "specializes in a hybrid genre, fiction with the intensity and lyricism of poetry, short story sequences that transcend themselves to become novels" (Nowick 74). Erdrich's own experiences with both family narrative and the Ojibwa oral tradition have shaped her desire to present her stories in the voices of storytellers, and through her representation of characters as storytellers, she transforms her readers into listeners.

Erdrich moved from the form of the narrative poem to that of the short story when she perceived that she needed room to tell her tales more fully. Similarly, when she saw a larger design within the patterns of her short fiction, she began to work with the form of the novel. Her use of that form is always experimental, however, and readers find that she employs different narrative strategies in each of her books: She changes her use of narrative point of view, and she shapes new designs for her structuring of plot. Erdrich's plots, comprised of multiple, interconnected stories, do not necessarily unfold through a chronologically linear progression but rather serve as the threads whereby characters' stories are woven together. Her technique of weaving stories together quickly drew the attention of reviewers and narrative theorists when *Love Medicine* was first published, and it indeed engendered a debate about the genre of that book. Several critics in fact suggested that *Love Medicine* be regarded as a short story collection rather than a novel.

Although Erdrich experiments idiosyncratically with the form of the novel, features of her work resemble those of other writers. Like William Faulkner, she creates a fictional world and peoples it with multiple narrators whose voices commingle to shape her readers' experience of that world. As Hertha D. Wong points out, she also shares Faulkner's interest in examining the "effects of race, miscegenation, the haunting power of the past, and the ironic intersections of the comic and the tragic" (Wong, "Louise," 183). Like Flannery O'Connor, Erdrich invokes elements of Catholic tradition and mysticism in her work, and she often imbues her representation of Catholicism with the aura of the grotesque (as in, for example, her depiction of the nun Sister Leopolda). Erdrich shares with Toni Morrison a predilection for incorporating myth, allegory, and characteristics of an oral tradition in her fiction, and she also shares Morrison's interest in portraying features of women's lives and experiences. Like Morrison and other contemporary women writers, she offers scenes of childbirth, domestic activity, and family life; her characters—female and male alike—not only nurture children but also cook, sew, and peel potatoes.

Erdrich's fiction also resembles the work of other contemporary Native American writers, particularly in its focus on the homecoming theme that is first introduced in *Love Medicine* and then played out in variations through her other novels. As Robert Silberman has pointed out, the theme of the "troubled homecoming" is firmly established in a "well-known group of works by Native American authors: D'Arcy McNickle's *The Surrounded*, N. Scott Momaday's *The House Made of Dawn*, Leslie Marmon Silko's *Ceremony*, James Welch's *Winter in the Blood* and *The Death of Jim Loney*" (Silberman 101). While Erdrich's treatment of the homecoming theme draws upon a tradition shaped by other Native American writers, writers also interested in exploring the experience of a return to the reservation and in searching out a definition of home, it nonetheless refashions conventions of that tradition. For example, whereas McNickle,

Momaday, Silko, and Welch all depict the return of male characters, in Erdrich's fiction the experience of coming home is shared by male and female characters: Not only does Lipsha Morrissey make his return, but so do June Kashpaw, Albertine Johnson, Lulu Nanapush, Dot Adare, and Fleur Pillager.

Not only can Erdrich's fiction be seen in relation to that of an earlier generation of Native American writers, but it also shares many of the concerns of Native American writers who began publishing in the 1990s. Like Erdrich, whose 1998 novel, *The Antelope Wife*, is set in the city of Minneapolis, Greg Sarris and Sherman Alexie are interested in the contemporary Native American's search for identity off the reservation, in an urban setting. Sarris's 1995 novel, *Grand Avenue*, is set in Santa Rosa, California, and Alexie's *Indian Killer* (1997) is set in Seattle. Like Erdrich as well, who often addresses the plight of the orphan in her work, both Sarris and Alexie present portraits of Native American characters as orphans. Erdrich's work can also be compared to that of two other recently published writers, David Treuer, who shares her Ojibwa heritage, and Susan Power, whose 1994 novel, *The Grass Dancer*, resembles Erdrich's fiction in its uses of humor. Both Treuer and Power are reported to be working on novels that feature Native Americans in an urban setting.

Erdrich's readers frequently encounter instances of the marvelous depicted in her fiction. In *Tracks*, for example, when a tornado sweeps through Argus, North Dakota, one of the narrators describes the objects carried in the wind: A whole herd of cattle flies through the sky, and a candle sails by, still burning brightly. In both *Love Medicine* and *The Bingo Palace*, ghosts make appearances, and in several of the novels miracles occur. While some critics suggest that Erdrich employs features of magical realism in her work, she comments that she does not regard her own use of the marvelous incident as playing the role it serves in the work of Gabriel García Márquez or other magical realists. Indeed, Erdrich's presentation of the magical episode is generally ambiguous or suggestive, inviting an allegorical or psychological reading as well as a literal interpretation.[1] If, "in a magical realist story there must be an irreducible element, something that cannot be explained by logic, familiar knowledge, or received belief" (Young and Hollaman 4), then Erdrich's use of the marvelous is characteristically different from that of the magical realists, for her magic is typically grounded in familiar knowledge or received belief.

In various published interviews Erdrich addresses questions about the magical elements in her fiction and suggests that her use of exaggeration, coincidence, and the unpredictable arises from her early exposure to her own family's telling of "you'll-never-believe-this kinds of stories" (Caldwell 67). She further explains that because she was raised in the tradition of Catholic symbolism, where the occurrence of the miraculous is not an unusual event, her rendering of the marvelous can often be read in the context of religious mysticism. In the account of the tornado in *Tracks*, Erdrich elaborates upon North Dakota folklore, and in several of *The Beet Queen*'s scenes she draws inspiration from fairy-tale tradition. Other magical episodes, including characters' experiencing of visions or Fleur Pillager's transmogrification into the bear can be interpreted in the context of Ojibwa custom and belief. Generally speaking, Erdrich's use of the marvelous incident can be recognized as one of the strategies she employs to incorporate elements of oral tradition into her work.

Although Erdrich characteristically shapes a plot from the connections among a book's several interrelated stories, plot does not circumscribe the storytelling that takes place in her novels. In other words, her fiction commonly features the telling of stories within stories in what might be regarded as arrangements of narratives that resemble Chinese boxes.[2] The stories within stories serve a variety of purposes, for through them Erdrich characterizes the figures who populate her novels, unfolds the designs of her books' recurring motifs, and repeatedly shows, through her characters' different versions of stories, that "reality" (Chavkin and Chavkin 224) must always be understood in respect to point of view. In a review of Erdrich's 1998 novel, *The Antelope Wife*, Michiko Kakutani comments on this narrative technique, noting that Erdrich's use of "multiple viewpoints and surreal tales within tales" is "what she does best" (Kakutani, "*The Antelope Wife*," C18).

All of Erdrich's novels present instances of stories embedded in other stories; indeed, *Tales of Burning Love*, the fifth book in her series of North Dakota novels, is in fact plotted around the use of this device. In that novel four women characters who are trapped together during a blizzard tell one another stories of their lives with another character, the man who has been husband to each of them. In other novels the embedded stories are not necessarily implicated in the development of plot but serve other significant purposes. In *The Antelope Wife*, for example, a character named Klaus Shawano seemingly digresses when he tells the entertaining tale of how he came to acquire a German man's name. While Klaus's story is delightful in itself, it is by no means the digression that it at first appears to be. *The Antelope Wife* is deeply interested in names and in the act of naming, and Klaus's tale therefore elaborates upon this important motif. Furthermore, Klaus's story is relevant to the novel's characterization of his brother, for it explains the origin of Frank Shawano's abiding obsession with the recipe he spends his life attempting to perfect.

Critics of Erdrich's novels have responded, for the most part, to the individual texts that comprise her work. With the exceptions of *The Crown of Columbus* and *The Antelope Wife*, however, her novels are connected to one another, sharing a setting in the North Dakota landscape and a community of characters whose lives frequently intersect. When the five North Dakota novels are considered in relation to one another, a new pattern of the story within a story begins to emerge, for very often a tale recounted in one of the books is indeed retold in another. When a story from one novel is retold in another—in a changed context or in a different version—readers are inevitably offered a new angle from which to consider Erdrich's fictional world. When, for example, readers hear again in *Tales of Burning Love* the story with which *Love Medicine* opens, they are presented with surprising revelations about June Kashpaw's encounter with Andy on the last day of her life.

As critic Geoffrey Stokes wryly observes, Erdrich's fiction is far removed from the fashionable novelistic style he describes as "wan, attentuated minimalism" (Stokes 60). On the contrary, Erdrich's richly textured, lyrical prose is occasionally criticized for being overwrought, and indeed the writer herself has acknowledged that she is well aware of a temptation to overwrite. Erdrich quite obviously brings both the poet's eye and ear and the poet's love of language to the craft of fiction; in incorporating poetic rhythms and imagery in her storytelling, she finds yet another means to link a written text to an oral tradition—for poetry, ultimately, is always meant to be heard.

Erdrich employs characteristics of the poetic in her prose fiction in a variety of ways. For example, she uses recurring images and metaphors as unifying devices, as elements of the stitching whereby she weaves her novels' stories together. In *Love Medicine*, where water imagery is dominant, the novel opens with June Kashpaw crossing the snow, walking "over it like water" (*LM* 7) and closes with Lipsha Morrissey's crossing the water to make his way home. In between its opening and closing scenes, *Love Medicine* draws upon repeated instances of images of water to shape a motif that resonates throughout the book. Similarly, *The Beet Queen* uses air imagery as a unifying device, and *Tracks* repeatedly invokes images of earth. Both *The Bingo Palace* and *Tales of Burning Love* offer repeated images of fire and ice, and *The Antelope Wife* weaves its stories together through its use of the metaphor of beading.

Erdrich also uses repeated metaphors in her depiction of characters. Members of the Pillager family, for example, are frequently associated with the wolf, and when Fleur or another character with Pillager blood smiles a wolfish grin, readers are reminded that the members of this family possess extraordinary shamanistic powers. Indeed, the appearance of the grin signals the exercising of Pillager power. In *The Beet Queen*, where the dominant imagery is that of air, and where many of the characters are portrayed as subject to airy flights of fancy, one character is depicted in sharply contrasting terms: From the first page of the novel, when readers are told about this character that "her name was square and practical as the rest of her" (*BQ* 1), Mary Adare is shown to be solid and grounded, a character for whom the promise of airy expanses offers no attraction.

In addition to associating characters with recurring images, Erdrich also uses her characters' sensations of the physical world as a means of portraying their natures or their states of mind. *Love Medicine*'s Nector Kashpaw, for example, experiences his life as though it were swirling about him, and he therefore thinks of himself as adrift in a river's current, sometimes moving swiftly through rapids and sometimes bobbing more slowly with the water's flow. Nector's image of himself as moving through water is extended when, after he has passed into senility, Lipsha Morrissey envisions him floating atop a lake, fishing for his thoughts. In *The Beet Queen*, Karl Adare likewise sees his own life in terms of the landscape that surrounds him. As he contemplates a scene of desolation whose emptiness is lit by flashing neon signs, he realizes that he too is "part of the senseless landscape. A pulse, a strip, of light" (*BQ* 318).

Erdrich's poetic passages are embedded in an otherwise distinctly colloquial literary style. She often distinguishes her characters through their idiosyncratic uses of language or dialect (in *Love Medicine*, for example, Lipsha occasionally utters malapropisms), and, in some of the novels (*Love Medicine*, *The Bingo Palace*, and *The Antelope Wife*) narrative voices speak directly and intimately to readers, addressing a story's listener as "you." Erdrich's informal, colloquial style obviously serves her desire to render her stories as though they were being told in a speaking voice, and several critics have indeed remarked on her success in this endeavor. Kathleen Sands, for example, sees at work in *Love Medicine*'s storytelling "the secular anecdotal narrative process of community gossip" (Sands

14), and Robert Silberman praises the same novel for its success in "capturing just plain talk—kitchen-table talk, bar talk, angry talk, curious talk, sad talk, teasing talk" (Silberman 112).

In addition to incorporating in her fiction elements from the genre of poetry and features that evoke oral storytelling traditions, Erdrich shapes some of her novels from her work in another literary genre, that of the short story. Indeed, sections or chapters from almost all of her novels have been published independently as short stories. In *Love Medicine*, which Erdrich was inspired to write when she began to see connections between short stories she had already published, the form of the short story is perhaps especially apparent. In that first book each of the chapters possesses the strong sense of closure that is particularly characteristic of short fiction, and, although all the narratives are artfully linked together, each of the chapters is shaped by its own self-contained action or plot. Because Erdrich is ultimately interested in representing the life of a community, and therefore in the many separate stories that are part of that life, it is indeed fitting that her novels are structured around several strands of plot; in *Love Medicine* she clearly begins to experiment with the techniques whereby she characteristically weaves her novels' multiple stories together.

Erdrich has commented on her incorporation of short stories in longer works of fiction, noting that while the stories often seem to her to gain resonance when they are linked to other stories, she nevertheless misses the satisfying integrity of the short story that stands alone. Like the narrative poem, however, the short story is itself too limited a form to appropriately contain the complexities of Erdrich's fictional communities, and she therefore willingly relinquishes the sense of the solitary story as a self-contained form when she joins stories together to construct a novel. She continues to write and publish short fiction ("Naked Woman Playing Chopin" was printed in the July 27, 1998, edition of *The New Yorker*), and it is likely that other short pieces of hers will indeed appear in future novels. Erdrich, after all, is a writer who begins her work with the solitary image, word, or title that serves as the focal point for the telling of stories and for the shaping of narrative designs that link stories together. In other words, she is an artist who constructs a fictional world through a process of accretion.

Like Toni Morrison's work, Erdrich's attracts the interests of both readers of popular fiction and students of literature. Several of her novels have been listed among best-sellers, and both *Love Medicine* and *Tracks* have become part of the canon in American Literature classes. Erdrich's experimentation with the form of the novel has drawn the attention of narrative theorists, and her representation of her fictional world as the site of community has particularly interested feminist critics. Erdrich, who acknowledges that her novels are not "easy reading," has been somewhat surprised by her readers' attention to work that is, as she says, not "commercial writing" (Frenkiel 76), and she has been particularly heartened by the favorable responses of many Native American readers, including "people who have lived similar lives to" (Frenkiel 78) those of the characters in her books. She has in fact stated that her Native American readership is her "first audience," the audience she hopes she can invite to "read, laugh, [and] cry" (Coltelli 24).

Erdrich's fiction calls for both laughter and tears, for although she is essentially a comic writer, one who repeatedly affirms a human will to survive, she does not overlook a bleaker vision of human existence. In fact, many of her characters either do not survive or pay a steep price as the cost of survival. Survival, in Erdrich's vision, is closely associated with humor, and thus in several published interviews she defines "survival humor" as an ironic perspective that enables people to endure what they "have to live with." Humor, she suggests, offers a form of redemption, a means of realizing a "life worth living" (Moyers 144) even when, or perhaps especially when, the conditions of existence seem overwhelming. Erdrich sees "survival humor" as essential to Native Americans' response to their overwhelming experience of cultural catastrophe and therefore endows most of her Native American characters with a wry attitude that is expressive of survival humor.

Erdrich, for whom it is important that the "most serious" and threatening occurrences be leavened with "jokes" (Moyers 144), counters the tragic episodes depicted in her work with instances of humor. Because the tragic and the comic are often closely linked together, her uses of humor often take on the aspect of the grotesque, as reviewer Geoffrey Stokes suggests when he describes *The Beet Queen* as a "grimly funny" (Stokes 61) book. Like other features of her style, however, Erdrich's uses of humor serve a variety of purposes. Her humor, for example, frequently offers a political statement, as it does when she describes in *Love Medicine* Nector Kashpaw's encounter with a white woman who pays a fee to paint him as a noble, naked Indian brave, or as it does in *Tracks*, when Fleur Pillager watches her forest collapse around the men from the lumber company.

She also uses humor to depict human foibles, as is the case in *The Beet Queen* when Mary Adare, out of misplaced righteous indignation, imprisons an innocent school teacher in her toy box. Sometimes humor is redemptive, as it is in *The Antelope Wife* when Rozin's unexpected appearance, naked, before a crowd of party guests serves to restore her husband's lost sense of humor. Often, of course, her humor expresses the wry or ironic bemusement of those who are the survivors of calamity, and in her depiction of *Tracks*'s Old Nanapush as a tricksterlike joker and tease, Erdrich emphasizes this feature of her comic vision. Occasionally, too, her use of comedy seems playful, and in *Tales of Burning Love* she presents an extraordinarily funny scene in which three women who have all been married to the same man attend what they believe is his funeral. As readers suspect, Jack Mauser is of course very much alive.

While the complexity of Erdrich's fiction admittedly makes demands upon her readers, it also offers rich reward. As a writer who continually experiments with the form of the novel, Erdrich challenges the boundaries of genre, and, in so doing, invites readers of fiction to enlarge their reading strategies and to participate in the act of using literary form to make meaning in new ways. Erdrich's novels, written from a multicultural perspective, offer readers an opportunity to arrive at new understandings of meaning encoded in different cultures, and to appreciate significant differences in assumption that underlie Native American and Euro-American cultural traditions. Through the art of her storytelling, she affords readers occasion to listen to a variety of distinctive voices and to recognize the ways in which many individual stories are all part of life in a community.

ERDRICH'S OJIBWA TRADITION

Although a familiarity with Ojibwa tradition, custom, and belief is by no means required to appreciate Erdrich's fiction, readers might nevertheless find a few brief observations useful.[3] Some critics, in fact, have conducted extensive research into Ojibwa legends or cultural practices to which Erdrich makes reference in her novels, and in doing so they have contributed both fascinating background information and interestingly contextualized readings of her fiction to a growing body of scholarship that addresses her work. In an article entitled "The Metamorphoses of an Ojibwa *Manido*," Victoria Brehm, for example, provides a wealth of information about a *manido* known as Micipijiu (Misshepeshu in Erdrich's novel *Tracks*). The manitou, as Erdrich spells it, is an eternal spirit who has existed among the Ojibwa since the time of the creation of the world. And Kristan Sarvé-Gorham, in an article that examines Erdrich's use of the motif of the Ojibwa's sacred twins, offers fascinating insights into the *Midéwewin*, the secret Medicine Society of the Ojibwa.

It is in *Love Medicine* that Erdrich first introduces the Ojibwa word *windigo*, a term that thereafter reappears in other novels of hers. In *Love Medicine*, the meaning of *windigo*—"deranged"—is quite clear in the contexts in which it is used. Nevertheless, in Ojibwa tradition, the word—used either as a noun or as an adjective—denotes a special kind of madness, a form of craziness that, as Erdrich later shows in *The Antelope Wife*, arises from an all-consuming hunger. In Ojibwa tradition there are many legends featuring the figure of the *windigo*, and in his book, *The Manitous*, Ojibwa scholar Basil Johnston provides the following summary of accounts of this figure:

> *Weendigo* (Weendigook or Weendigoes): A giant cannibal (or cannibals). These manitous came into being in winter and stalked villagers and beset wanderers. Ever hungry, they craved human flesh, which is the only substance that could sustain them. The irony is that having eaten human flesh, the Weendigoes grew in size, so their hunger and craving remained in proportion to their size; thus they were eternally starving. They could kill only the foolish and the improvident. (Johnston 247)

Another scholar, Victor Barnouw, offers a slightly different account when he states that the only way someone can combat a *windigo* is by becoming a *windigo*, by assuming a giant size and turning into ice. In either case, the *windigo* is a gigantic, northern, frosty, hungry spirit who in *The Antelope Wife* metaphorically represents the grieving Rozin's fear that she will be devoured.

Many of Erdrich's critics have been interested in her novels' uses of Ojibwa myth, and much of the focus of this interest has been directed toward her representations of the figure of the trickster. *Trickster*, a term whose origins lie in nineteenth-century anthropology, denotes an archetypal figure who frequently emerges in polytheistic cultures. Known primarily as boundary-crossers, or, in some cases, boundary creators, tricksters are, as Lewis Hyde describes them, "the lords of in-between" or the spirits of "the doorway . . . and of the crossroad" (Hyde 6). Often lusty, usually mischievous, sometimes shape-shifters, the tricksters of different cultures play various roles within a communal collection of stories or myths, but even when they serve as culture heroes, they are figures whose place in society is close to its margins, close to the site where change occurs. Hyde summarizes well the characteristics of this archetype when he observes that "trickster is the mythic embodiment of ambiguity and ambivalence, doubleness and duplicity, contradiction, and paradox" (Hyde 7).

In Ojibwa tradition the trickster is Nanabozho,[4] a mythic figure about whom literally hundreds of stories are told. Nanabozho, whose name means "trembling tail," is also sometimes called the White Rabbit. In some accounts Nanabozho is portrayed as a manitou, and in others he is depicted as an ordinary man, but in most stories he appears "to be neither a human being nor a god, but something of both." In other words, he seems "to fall into Lévi-Strauss's category of mediators between men and gods" (Barnouw 51), and in so doing clearly plays the trickster's role of messenger or crosser of boundaries.

In some cultures the trickster is a creator, and this is indeed the case with Nanabozho, who makes the earth from grains of sand the earth-diver brings him. He is also a shape-shifter (in the creation myth he assumes the form of a beaver, a tree stump, a snake, and an old woman) and thus possesses the flexibility characteristic of the trickster. In some tales Nanabozho is presented as a culture hero, a savior of his people; for example, when he tricks the Great Gambler at his own game, he saves the spirit of his people from the threat of the *windigo*. He is also a wanderer, and, in fact, sets out on a quest (as Erdrich's Lipsha does) to search for his parents. He is a teacher and a healer, and often pauses in his wanderings to instruct his people in the medicinal uses of plants. In many stories, however, another side of Nanabozho is revealed, for, like other tricksters, he is also sometimes foolish, a buffoon and a blunderer. Occasionally he is even malicious, for, as Gerald Vizenor points out, "the trickster is capable of violence, deceptions, and cruelties: the realities of human imperfections" (Vizenor 4).

Erdrich's fiction makes reference to Nanabozho or the legends of his exploits in a number of ways. Old Nanapush, one of the narrators in *Tracks*, tells the listeners of his tales, for example, that he was himself named in honor of the trickster. A joker and a tease as well as a healer and a man who is both cunning and flexible, Nanapush indeed embodies the spirit of his name. Through Lulu, to whom he gives his name, the tradition of the trickster is passed along to members of the Pillager family. *Love Medicine*'s Gerry Nanapush, for instance, represents the trickster as culture hero, the figure at the margins of society (Gerry is a criminal) who crosses the boundaries of the law on behalf of his people. His son, Lipsha Morrissey, is the trickster in quest of his parents, the trickster as gambler, and also, of course, the trickster as buffoon and blunderer.

Erdrich's clear references to trickster tradition in both *Love Medicine* and *Tracks* invite readers to consider her other characters or episodes in light of the figure of the trickster. Indeed, Jeanne Rosier Smith argues that "a family of tricksters wanders through" (Smith 71) the pages of Erdrich's novels, always reinvigorating the community life depicted in the books through a tricksterlike ability to adapt and change. The transformative energy of the trickster is thus linked to Erdrich's recurring treatment of the theme of survival, for those characters who possess the trickster's flexibility are those whose very survival guarantees the preservation of cultural tradition.

Smith further suggests that Erdrich, like Maxine Hong Kingston and Toni Morrison, employs tricksterlike narrative strategies in her writing when she uses trickster characters as "rhetorical agents" who "infuse narrative structure with energy, humor, and polyvalence" (Smith 2). Erdrich's use of myth and folklore, including the tradition of the trickster, provides her means as "trickster author" (Smith 103) to cross cultural boundaries in her work and to thereby shape for her readers an experience of multiculturalism. As Smith also points out, the tradition of the elusive and quick-tongued trickster is moreover embedded in Erdrich's storytelling technique, for "tricksters are consummate storytellers," commanding the attention of "their listeners with their artful use of words" (Smith 22). Erdrich's storytelling, Smith observes, invites dialogue both among a novel's characters "and with the reader, thereby lending a sense of orality to the written text" (Smith 23).

ERDRICH'S CENTRAL THEMES

Erdrich's novels generally play out variations on a set of central themes, and, indeed, one of the most noticeable features of her fiction after *Love Medicine* is that she is able within different books to rework or to refashion a familiar theme in such a way that it appears to be treated anew. This is particularly true within the series of books that comprise the "North Dakota novels." While most critics or reviewers respond to these narratives as independent works, the interesting patterns of repetition and variation of theme among the five books seem to invite a different kind of criticism, one that regards the separate novels as all part of the design of a larger whole, a multivolume work similar to Marcel Proust's *Remembrance of Things Past*.

Erdrich's novels include several characters who are orphans; while some characters are orphaned through the death of their parents, many others are left orphans when their parents abandon them. Elaine Tuttle Hansen, one of the critics who does trace Erdrich's handling of a theme through several novels, is particularly interested in Erdrich's depictions of the figure of the "mother without child" (Hansen 15)—the mother who, like June Kashpaw, Adelaide Adare, Fleur Pillager, or Pauline Puyat, deserts a child or children for one reason or another. Hansen perceptively examines the variations Erdrich plays upon this theme through *Love Medicine, The Beet Queen, Tracks,* and *The Bingo Palace,* where Erdrich introduces Shawnee Ray Toose, a young, unmarried mother who has made the decision that she will not be a mother who abandons her child. Although Hansen was not able to include in her study a discussion of the last novel in the series, *Tales of Burning Love,* she would have found there another interesting variation on her theme, for the baby in that novel, far from being abandoned, has not one but two mothers to nurture him.

In his influential essay "Native American Novels: Homing In," William Bevis uses the term *homing* to contrast the plots of fiction by D'Arcy McNickle, N. Scott Momaday, Leslie Marmon Silko, and James Welch with those of canonical works by Euro-American writers, whose plots often feature accounts of leaving home.[5] An important difference, Bevis argues, between the "centrifugal" plot of leaving home and the "centripetal" (Bevis 16) plot of coming home lies in distinctions between Euro-American and Native American definitions of identity; whereas a Euro-American concept of selfhood emphasizes the freedom and opportunity of the individual who moves into the future by leaving the past behind, the Native American's sense of identity is "transpersonal and includes a society, a past, and a place." In other words, plots that depict the Native American experience of coming home emphasize a "tribal rather than an individual definition of 'being' " (Bevis 19).

For Louise Erdrich—whose characters' individual lives are always portrayed in the context of community—homecoming, the return to "a society, a past, and a place," is a central and oft-repeated theme. Beginning with *Love Medicine,* whose multiple narratives are structured around the idea that home is the site of identity and connection (and whose last word is in fact "home"), Erdrich plays out variations on the homecoming theme in all of her novels. Homecoming is not always a joyful occasion, as Lipsha Morrissey discovers when he comes home for a second time in *The Bingo Palace*, but it is the necessary occasion of characters' coming to terms with questions of who they are and where they belong. Even Karl Adare, *The Beet Queen*'s seemingly homeless wanderer, at last seeks out his connections with others, with his daughter and his old lover, when he at last returns to Argus. Erdrich occasionally reconfigures her definition of home, as she does in *Tales of Burning Love*, where characters find where they belong when they recognize the love they share with another, but in this novel, too, the idea of home is linked to a realization of identity.

Other themes of Erdrich's novels—her recurring representations, for example, of the redemptive power of love, forgiveness, or, certainly, humor—are often expressed in relation to another of her central concerns, that of survival. Throughout her novels Erdrich celebrates her characters' survival of loss or calamity—and the survival as well of the communities depicted in her fiction. Often survival depends upon a tricksterlike ability to adapt to changing circumstances, as it does, for example, in *The Beet Queen*, where the community of Argus must restructure its entire economy around the sugar beet in order to survive. In *Tracks*, the Native American characters depicted as tricksters not only survive the loss of their traditional economy, as well as the land upon which it is based, but they also survive the threat of the loss of their cultural heritage. Erdrich is, of course, particularly interested in portraying the survival of Ojibwa cultural tradition, and, indeed, her own work as novelist contributes to that purpose.

NOTES

1. For further discussion of Erdrich's use of multiple interpretive codes, see Catherine Rainwater's "Reading between Worlds: Narrativity in the Fiction of Louise Erdrich" or James Ruppert's "Celebrating Culture: *Love Medicine*."

2. In "Louise Erdrich's *Love Medicine*: Narrative Communities and the Short Story Sequence," Hertha D. Wong discusses examples of *Love Medicine*'s stories within stories. See pages 175–176.

3. The meanings of Ojibwa words Erdrich uses are generally made clear in their contexts, as indeed are many of her references to Ojibwa tradition. She occasionally offers brief explanation of other references, as for example when she mentions in *The Bingo Palace* the origin of Shawnee Ray's jingle dress.

4. There are many variant spellings of Nanabozho, including Nana'b'oozoo, Nanabush, and Wenebojo.

5. Bevis has in mind such novels as *Moby Dick, Portrait of a Lady, Huckleberry Finn, Sister Carrie*, and *The Great Gatsby*, books that relate the stories of characters who seek indentity or opportunity by venturing far from home.

3

Love Medicine
(1984, 1993)

Louise Erdrich's widely acclaimed first novel, *Love Medicine*, was origi-
nally published in 1984. Winner that year of the National Book Critics
Circle Award, *Love Medicine* also received, among other honors, the *Los
Angeles Times* Award for Best Novel of the Year, the Janet Kaufman
Award for Best First Novel, and the Virginia McCormack Scully Prize
for Best Book featuring Indians or Chicanos. Two years earlier, "The
World's Greatest Fishermen" (*Love Medicine*'s opening chapter) had been
awarded the Nelson Algren Prize for short fiction, and another chapter,
"Scales," had been printed in *The Best American Short Stories of 1983*. A
national best-seller, *Love Medicine* also rapidly made its way onto the
syllabus in many literature classrooms.

With *Love Medicine*'s publication, readers were introduced to the landscape and to the community of characters to which Erdrich would later
return in much of her other fiction. In fact, over the course of her five
North Dakota novels, Erdrich constructed a mythic world that has often
been aptly compared to William Faulkner's Yoknapatawpha County. A
comparison with Faulkner's work is appropriate in other ways as well,
for *Love Medicine* is interested in genealogies and in the legacies of generations, in people dispossessed of their land and in the subsequent destinies of their children. With what one reader characterizes as "protean"
(Gleason 51), or richly variegated humor, *Love Medicine* chronicles fifty
years in the lives of three generations of five related families. Readers'

enthusiastic reception of the book has reflected widespread recognition of both the power of its lyrical style and the amplitude of its subject matter.

In 1993 *Love Medicine* was reissued in a new and expanded edition. As well as particular changes in wording, the later version of the novel offers four entirely new chapters and an additional section within the chapter entitled "The Beads." Some of the changes in language are subtle, but others might interestingly express Louise Erdrich's response to certain interpretive observations registered by her readers. For example, some readers have described the sexual encounter in "Wild Geese" as a scene of rape. As Erdrich explains in a published interview, this reading was not one she had intended to evoke. Agreeing, however, that the first edition's presentation of the scene was perhaps somewhat ambiguous, Erdrich made changes to suggest that her male character's actions, while "wrong" (Chavkin and Chavkin 234), might nevertheless be construed in terms not quite so stark.

In preparing a new edition of a previously published literary text, Louise Erdrich joins company with W. B. Yeats, Henry James, Robert Graves, Gore Vidal, and John Fowles, who reissued *The Magus*. Like writers such as these, Erdrich does not regard the printed volume as a necessary expression of the writer's final word. Indeed, she describes publication as a useful means of providing the writer with a place for "temporary storage" (Chavkin and Chavkin 232). Published separately as independent short stories, versions of several of *Love Medicine*'s chapters have been placed, at one time or another, in "temporary storage."

Although the new version of *Love Medicine* necessarily alters certain patterns of organization readers discerned in the earlier edition, the significant effect of the additional chapters is that of strengthening this novel's links to *The Beet Queen, Tracks, The Bingo Palace,* and even *Tales of Burning Love,* all books that inhabit a shared fictional landscape. In fact, *Love Medicine*'s expanded edition appropriately marks a shift in the novel's position within a larger dimension of Erdrich's narrative art. The book once perceived as a "first novel" has been transformed in some respects into the third volume within an unfolding cycle of tales that Erdrich has aptly suggested is perhaps "one long, convoluted story" (Chavkin and Chavkin 235). Thus, readers who wish to start at the beginning of the "long story" might choose to read *Tracks* and *The Beet Queen* before turning to *Love Medicine* and *The Bingo Palace.* Erdrich's use of the word "convoluted" is also significant, however, for stories told in all the books circle back upon themselves in the recurring patterns of their telling and retelling. For example, the haunting first story of *Love*

Medicine is also the first story of *Tales of Burning Love*. There, twelve years after *Love Medicine*'s original appearance, readers are told once more of June Kashpaw's long walk home in what then becomes the twice-told tale that frames the plot in both these novels.

While *Love Medicine*'s most recent edition clearly enhances the novel's intertextual connections to the other works that comprise Erdrich's "long, convoluted story," the added sections do serve other, intratextual purposes as well. Some characters, particularly those of the Lamartine family, are more fully revealed in the novel's second version, and certain of the book's central themes and motifs are elaborated in new variations. In the section added to "The Beads," for instance, the novel's exploration of relations between daughters and mothers is afforded further development, and one of *Love Medicine*'s dominant images, that of a figure crossing water, is granted expression in the context of a woman's laboring to give birth.

Although there are many copies still in circulation, *Love Medicine*'s 1984 edition has now gone out of print. The second version must therefore be considered the authoritative text at present, and that is the one hereafter addressed in this discussion.

GENRE

In her interview with Allan and Nancy Feyl Chavkin, Louise Erdrich characterizes herself as someone who has "always been on the edge" (Chavkin and Chavkin 230). As it happens, this description of herself well expresses Erdrich's position *vis-à-vis* the genre in which she generally works. Clearly, *Love Medicine* and the other books do not take the shape of traditional, linear, protagonist-oriented narratives. Rather, Erdrich writes at the "edge" of the genre of the novel, drawing narrative strategies from the oral traditions of her Native American heritage to fabricate unconventional designs for her storytelling. Literary theorists have been greatly interested in studying the ways in which Erdrich's work challenges or extends traditional definitions of the novel. Focused primarily upon *Love Medicine*, this academic interest has generated thoughtful discussion about how Erdrich's fiction might be classified and how her distinctive narrative strategies work to reshape readers' experiences of the universe of fiction.

With the exception of *The Antelope Wife*, chapters or sections from all of Erdrich's novels have been published separately as short stories. As this feature of her writing indicates, individual chapters within the novels possess the patterns of coherence and the gestures of closure that are traditional characteristics of the short story. In her discussion of *Love Medicine*'s genre, Karen Castellucci Cox also uses the expression, "novels-in-stories" (Cox 151). Some theorists have therefore appropriately suggested that the books are best described as examples of the "short story sequence" or the "short story cycle," terms that have been advanced to accommodate the structure of James Joyce's *Dubliners*, William Faulkner's *Go Down, Moses*, Eudora Welty's *The Golden Apples*, and many other twentieth-century works of fiction.

While collections of stories have long been part of the West's literary history (as evidenced, for example, in the work of Homer, Ovid, or Chaucer), recent interest in the generic properties of integrated story collections dates from Forrest L. Ingram's 1971 study, *Representative Short Story Cycles of the Twentieth Century*. Arguing that those collections of short stories that can be identified as "story cycles" constitute a distinct literary genre, Ingram defines a cycle as "a set of stories linked to each other in such a way as to maintain a balance between the individuality of each of the stories and the necessities of the larger unit" (Ingram 15). In other words, the stories of a cycle are coherent narratives in and of themselves at the same time that they are essential parts of a larger narrative structure. If Ingram's identification of the cycle as a particular genre provides a useful means of characterizing a book like *Love Medicine*, it is interesting to further note that this concept of the cycle can be extended to account for a relationship among all of Erdrich's North Dakota novels. *Love Medicine, Tracks*, and the other books are in themselves coherent and singular fictions, but they are also all part of the narrative design of a larger fictional world.

All of Louise Erdrich's novels present the voices of multiple narrators who relate stories or versions of stories to readers. Her books therefore assume an episodic structure that is characterized by these shifting points of view. Narrative theorists such as Ingram offer insights into the question of how it is that the many stories of a work like *Love Medicine* can be perceived, as he says, to be "linked to each other" in ways that invite the reader to experience them as parts of a larger whole. In directing readers' attention to cyclic patterns similar to those within Erdrich's fiction, Ingram's theoretical language highlights the ways in which repeated themes and motifs serve to forge intertextual connections among the several stories that her different narrators recount. In *Love Medicine*, for instance, references to water or images of flowing water resonate throughout the separate stories, and repeated scenes of homecoming give shape to the book's overarching theme. Although *Love Medicine* speaks to readers in many different voices, recurring patterns within its characters' stories situate those voices in the world that they share.

Ingram's ground-breaking study of modern short story cycles encouraged further analysis of the genre it identifies and then proceeds to explore. More recently, Robert M. Luscher has proposed that Ingram's use of the term "short story cycle" be replaced with the rubric "short story sequence." In making this suggestion, Luscher slightly shifts Ingram's focus on the narrative effects of repeated patterns to emphasize the importance of the sequential arrangement of stories gathered together within a text. Comparing the effects of an arranged set of stories' overall narrative structure to the effects of a musical sequence, he explains that "the story sequence repeats and progressively develops themes and motifs over the course of the work; its unity derives from a perception of both the successive ordering and recurrent patterns, which together provide the continuity of the reading experience" (Luscher 149).

While both Ingram and Luscher offer terms that might well help readers understand the design of a work like *Love Medicine*, J. Gerald Kennedy reminds them of the ways in which Erdrich is writing at the "edge" of the novel. Positioning the story sequence within the context of tendencies in modernist and postmodernist fictions, Kennedy observes that "in its more experimental aspect, then, the novel has for about seventy-five years been veering toward the story sequence as a decentered mode of narrative representation" (Kennedy x). That many of those who now experiment with the form of the novel are women or ethnic writers is also a matter of interest to theorists, who suggest that these writers' new styles of storytelling give shape to new narrative structures. Like Gloria Naylor, Amy Tan, or Ana Castillo, Erdrich finds in the possibilities of the story collection a means of enlarging the horizons of the novel.

When *Love Medicine* is categorized as a "novel-in-stories," an important question immediately arises: Why did Erdrich choose this special mode of narration? In what ways are the narrative effects of the story cycle or sequence different from those of a more traditional novel? Erdrich herself provides one answer when she explains that her technique "reflects a traditional Chippewa motif in storytelling" wherein an account of one incident "leads to another incident that leads to another" (Jones 4) in an unfolding cycle of tales. Erdrich's familiarity with two different narrative traditions positions her to see how the patterns of oral storytelling might be represented in the form of a written story collection.

Susan Garland Mann's *The Short Story Cycle* offers further insights into Erdrich's choice of narrative technique. Mann's descriptions of differences in form between the traditional novel and the story cycle account for many readers' questions about *Love Medicine*'s characters and plot. Although some readers have identified one or another of the book's characters as its protagonist (often Lipsha, sometimes the haunting presence of the absent June), *Love Medicine*'s many stories are not the centered story of the traditional protagonist. As Mann notes, "there is much less emphasis on a protagonist in the short story cycle than is generally the case in other fiction" (Mann xii). Rather than presenting a main character's story, *Love Medicine* offers a community of storytelling voices. "If we insist," Hertha D. Wong declares, "on isolating a protagonist in *Love Medicine*, it would most likely be the community itself" (Wong, "Louise," 173).

If *Love Medicine* resists the novelistic impulse to focus upon a central character's story, it follows that its plot will not trace a trajectory typical of the traditional novel. Once again, Mann observes that "there is considerably less emphasis in unified short story collections on plot or chronology, at least as these terms are usually defined" (Mann xii). Indeed, readers often find it difficult to provide for *Love Medicine* the kind of plot summary that can succinctly represent all that happens within the book. Like that of the picaresque novel, *Love Medicine*'s plot is distinctly episodic. This plot, however, differs from that of the picaresque in that it neither features a protagonist nor depends upon a linear chronology. As Cox explains: "where more conventional narratives emulate 'real time' experience in moving forward toward a conclusion, the fragmentary story cycle progresses erratically and nondirectionally, looping forward and backward, often omitting causal links between physical and psychological events" (Cox 151). Although *Love Medicine* does not follow a continuous action to its climactic resolution, plot functions in each of its separate episodes to progressively give shape to one of the recurring patterns embedded in the text. Through recognition of this pattern, readers can locate in the book's erratic sequence of events the unifying action that is clearly brought to closure in the novel's final scene.

In their interesting discussions of *Love Medicine*'s genre, both Wong and Cox focus on ways the book's unconventional narrative strategies function to enlarge readers' experiences of fiction. Wong, for instance, suggests that when readers' "expectations" of encountering "an autonomous protagonist, a dominant narrative voice, and a consistently chronological linear narrative" (Wong, "Louise," 173) are not realized in the book, they are then able to see its structure as one that represents a communal, "rather than a hierarchical, organization of society and literature" (Wong, "Louise," 173). And Cox, who is also interested in the design of narratives that "plot new fictions of community" (Cox 151), ultimately demonstrates how an understanding of *Love Medicine*'s intricate structure will "guide the reader to read anew" (Cox 170). Addressing ways readers can negotiate the gaps that lie between the cycle's stories or account for the occurrence of fantastic events, Cox notes that readers "must learn to withhold expectations in order to assimilate the jarring elements" (Cox 152) that are implicit features of Erdrich's "novel-in-stories."

PLOT

Love Medicine is plotted around journeys, encounters, and the occasions of departure and return that chart its several characters' efforts to find where it is they might belong. The novel's central setting, an Ojibwa reservation that borders the mythical town of Argus, North Dakota, serves as the locus of the characters' succession of comings and goings. In their quests to identify a place that is home, *Love Medicine*'s characters must traverse the difficult terrain of a cultural landscape that has been imprinted with the heritages of both Native American and non-Native tradition. They must therefore confront questions of identity, for, as Erdrich observes in a published interview, as well as being an American citizen, the Native American is also "a member of another nation" (Bruchac 77). *Love Medicine*'s plotting dramatizes how the experience of their "dual citizenship" (Bruchac 77) is often implicated in characters' desires and in their courses of action.

Love Medicine's opening chapter actually presents two scenes of return. In the first section of "The World's Greatest Fishermen," a third-person narrative voice recounts the story of June Kashpaw's final journey home. June has earlier traveled across the state to Williston in hopes of discovering that which "could be different" (3) in the course of her life. On the day before Easter Sunday in 1981 she is waiting for her bus and "killing time" (1) when she encounters a man who perhaps "could be different" from others she has known. When this vague hope is not realized, and when her bus is no longer there, June sets out on foot toward home. In the epiphanic language that makes clear where June finally belongs, readers are told that "the snow fell deeper that Easter than it had in forty years, but June walked over it like water and came home" (7).

June Kashpaw's death in the Easter snowstorm occasions the family reunion depicted in the remaining sections of *Love Medicine*'s first chap-

FAMILY CONNECTIONS IN *LOVE MEDICINE*

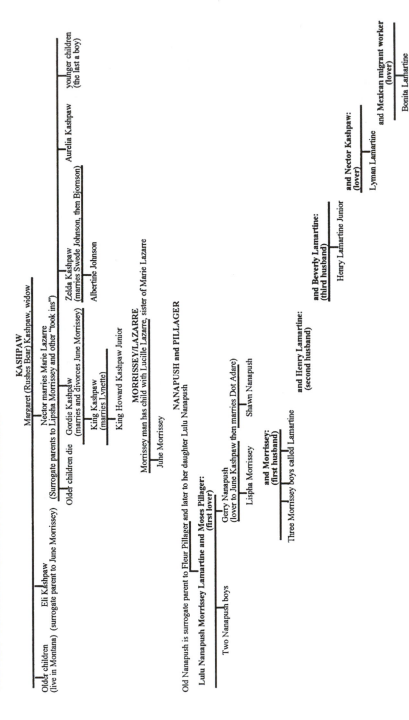

ter. Through the first-person voice of June's niece, Albertine Johnson, readers learn more about June and become acquainted with several members of her family. Like Albertine, who is a nursing student living in Fargo, June's son King has tried to make a life in a world that is "far from home" (7). But unlike Albertine, who can with satisfaction "see the earth lifting" (11) when she returns to the reservation, King feels keenly that he does not belong. When he is in the city, King sports a cap that proclaims him the "World's Greatest Fisherman." But when he is on the reservation and in the presence of his Uncle Eli, who has always lived off the land, he knows that his boast is empty bravado. The measure of King's estrangement from traditions represented by life on the reservation is taken at the close of the chapter. In a scene of terrible violence expressive of his grief and sense of isolation, King attempts to drown his wife after he has viciously smashed all the freshly baked pies prepared by the women. For him, the location of "home" is deeply problematic—as can readily be seen when his wife remarks, "You always get so crazy when you're home [the reservation]. . . . We'll go back to the Cities, go home" (42).

In "Saint Marie," *Love Medicine*'s second chapter, readers are told of a journey that was undertaken in 1934. In her own voice, Marie Lazarre (who will later be Marie Kashpaw, Albertine's grandmother) tells of going up the hill that overlooks the reservation to seek a cloistered life among the "black robe women" (43) who live in the convent. Marie has much to prove to those who "never thought they'd have a girl from this reservation as a saint they'd have to kneel to" (43) and therefore engages in a passionate battle of wills with her sadomasochistic mentor, the fierce Sister Leopolda. Through a grotesquely comical turn of events, Marie does realize the ambition that drew her to the convent, but she also comes to understand that this site of black and twisted love is not where she belongs. It is in the third chapter, "Wild Geese," that her journey of return from a hard-won but empty sainthood brings her directly to the path of the young Nector Kashpaw.

Nector, who has earlier been sent away to school and has also traveled through the wheat belt, adventuring all the way to Kansas, relates the story of his encounter with Marie. In Kansas Nector had discovered that the "greater world," as he puts it, "was only interested in my doom" (124). Having therefore recently returned to a life on the reservation, he has lately had in mind a different kind of quest. In fact, he has already been "saving for the French-style wedding band" (63) that he plans to buy for Lulu Nanapush, the only girl he wants. Nevertheless, it so happens that one incident indeed "leads to another incident that leads to another," and when Nector at last takes Marie's wounded hand in his, he must admit to himself that "I don't want her, but I want her, and I cannot let go" (67).

Nector's journey toward a rendezvous with Lulu is thus abruptly interrupted. However, although the wild geese he carries with him are, as Lipsha Morrissey will much later assert, a symbol of the fidelity of those who mate for life, the symbolism turns out to be ironic. Not unlike King, for whom home is neither on the reservation nor in the city, Nector comes to live his life suspended between the attractions of these two women, Lulu and his wife, Marie. In "The Plunge of the Brave," *Love Medicine*'s seventh chapter, he finally makes the decision to leave Marie for Lulu. Nevertheless, in the next chapter, "Flesh and Blood," Marie relates the story of his coming home again. In an account that echoes the circumstances of their very first encounter, Marie tells of visiting Leopolda in the convent on the day when Nector departs and then eventually returns. When he does finally come home, this time it is Marie who holds out her hand for him.

As these examples suggest, the characters' accounts of their comings and goings give shape to a subtle network of connections that becomes increasingly apparent as the reader moves through the text. Both Wong and Cox describe this network as "web-like" (Cox 150) to emphasize the circularity that is inherent in its patterns. Lulu's own story is of course another strand within the web, and therefore readers hear in chapter four, "The Island," about the journey that she undertakes after she has been left behind by Nector. In one of *Love Medicine*'s many instances of the story within a story, readers also learn that much earlier Lulu had also been left behind by her mother—and then, like Nector, sent away to school off the reservation.

In time, Lulu Lamartine makes herself a home where she knows she belongs, on the reservation. "Lulu's Boys," the sixth chapter, depicts the family life she shares with her children, the eight brothers who are the sons of several different fathers. Lulu's family life is sharply contrasted with that of Bev Lamartine, her childless brother-in-law who is visiting the reservation. Bev, who now lives in the Twin Cities, has for many years envisioned for himself a home with a son. Believing that he is the father of one of Lulu's boys, he in fact plans to "claim Henry Junior and take him home" (109) to his wife. It is not long, however, before he recognizes that his plans will have to be revised. On the one hand, it is very clear that the brothers are a "pack," bound together by the "simple,

unquestioning belongingness" (118) of their family life, on the other
hand, it is also the case that Bev cannot resist the power of Lulu's ability
to enchant him once again, and it therefore comically comes to pass that
he becomes a bigamist.

In chapters that detail characters' movements during the 1970s, *Love
Medicine*'s cycle of stories continues to circle back toward its beginning,
the day of June Kashpaw's walk in the snow. By now, members of a
younger generation have begun to venture forth, and readers thus learn
about the time Albertine ran away from home and the time Henry Lamartine Junior and Lyman Lamartine (two of Lulu's eight sons) drove
their red convertible to Alaska on a whim. These stories too are connected to one another, for when she journeys to Fargo in the ninth chapter, "A Bridge," Albertine spends the night with a shell-shocked Henry
Junior, just returned from Vietnam. The chance meeting in the city is for
both of them a makeshift means of trying to bridge their distance from
home.

In the tenth chapter, "The Red Convertible," Lyman reveals that
Henry Junior was in fact never able to find his way "home" after the
years in Vietnam. The glorious adventure recounted at the beginning of
the chapter marks for both brothers the last carefree summer of their
youth, for it is right after the journey to Alaska that Henry joins the
Marines. At the end of the chapter, when Henry's boots have "filled with
water," he has in effect "bought out" (181) with his life all Lyman's
interest in the car they have shared. Lyman therefore sinks that red convertible before he leaves the river to head homeward with the lie that
he will offer to his mother.

In "Scales," the last chapter whose date precedes June's Easter death,
Albertine tells of her friendship with Dot Adare and her husband Gerry
Nanapush, who is yet another of Lulu's sons. Dot is pregnant, and while
she and Albertine work at the truck scales and await the birth of the
child, they attempt to keep secret the fact of Gerry's lurking presence.
An enormous man who believes "in justice, not laws" (202), Gerry is
hiding from the police. Like his mother, he is someone who knows
exactly where he belongs. Yet it is Gerry's ironic lot that he can never
"go back to a place where he was known and belonged." As he will later
tell Lipsha Morrissey, " 'I won't ever really have what you'd call a
home'" (362).

With "Crown of Thorns" *Love Medicine* closes a circle that has brought
readers back to the scenes of homecoming depicted in chapter one. After
her death, June's former husband, Gordie Kashpaw, begins to drink him-

self to death. It is his journey into memory that finally brings him to oblivion in the fourteenth chapter, "Resurrection." Gordie's hands make him drink, for it is in his hands that he remembers the lines and curves of June's youthful body and, too, it is in the hands that he remembers the force of blows that he dealt her. The hands strike out once again when June returns to him in the form of a deer and Gordie frantically bludgeons her to death.

In the novel's title chapter Lipsha Morrissey tells of Nector's death by choking upon the "love medicine" Marie has served to him. Lipsha and Marie had hoped that the dish they had prepared would cause Nector to forget his enduring interest in Lulu, but, in a wonderfully ironic turn, it actually comes to pass that after Nector's death both Lipsha and Marie discover Lulu for themselves. In "The Good Tears" Lulu describes how Marie comes to her assistance after her operation and how the two women mourn Nector. And, in "The Tomahawk Factory," Lyman offers an account of the women's newly discovered roles in the political life of the reservation. In fact, it is much to his chagrin that Lyman must learn the hard way—when the factory explodes—that those two grandmothers, Lulu and Marie, are forces to be reckoned with.

Although neither Henry Junior nor Gordie has been able to find a path that might lead beyond despair, Lyman's experience is ultimately different from theirs. After Henry's death, Lyman sinks to a deep "place" from which he cannot move for nearly a year. Then, unexpectedly, it is an IRS form that jolts him from his stupor. "Uncle Sam taketh away [Henry's life] and Uncle Sam giveth" (299), Lyman has reason to wryly observe. His ambivalence about government notwithstanding, he finds himself joining it when he takes a position with the Bureau of Indian Affairs.

In addition to accounts of reconciliation and scenes that portray characters' responses to the losses they have suffered, *Love Medicine*'s closing chapters present several revelations. Indeed, it is in these final chapters that the many strands that configure the novel's web of connections are woven together. After the startlingly public revelation that it was Nector who indeed was his father, Lyman finds himself drawn to Marie, the figure who now becomes for him the image of a second mother. And, when Lulu reveals to the "little orphant" (342) Lipsha that she is his grandmother, and that his parents were June Kashpaw and Gerry Nanapush, Lipsha understands that it is time to shrug off his studied innocence and undertake a quest. He knows he must, as he says, "get down to the bottom of my heritage" (342).

It is in the long and eventful final chapter, "Crossing the Water," that Lipsha Morrissey carries out his self-appointed quest. *Love Medicine*'s last story is artfully designed to bring to closure the novel's episodic unfolding of its characters' adventures and encounters. The chapter's strong sense of closure is realized, in part, in the reader's recognition of a symbolic significance in Lipsha's own adventure. Tellingly, it is only in Lipsha's case that the search for identity, for knowledge of the place where he belongs, is undertaken with fully self-conscious intention. In the daily living of their lives the novel's other characters have made their journeys and looked to find some source of love or happiness or meaning, but when Lipsha purposefully sets forth, his quest becomes the emblem of all the characters' pursuits.

Closure is also signaled in the chapter's title and in its final scene. After he has won from King the car that is their mother's legacy, and after he has used "June's car" (357) to carry his father to Canada and freedom, Lipsha heads back to the place where he has now determined he belongs. When he comes to the river that marks the boundary of the reservation, he pauses on the bridge. There he thinks about June, and he finally forgives her for deserting him. In the novel's last sentence, when Lipsha crosses the water and makes his way toward home, readers are reminded of all those who crossed before him and of those, like Henry Junior, who could find no way to cross. Lipsha's coming home thus completes the cycle of returns that began with his mother's walk across the snow.

CHARACTERS

Love Medicine features some twenty characters, many of whom reappear in Erdrich's other novels. Six characters tell stories in their own voices, and in so doing reveal much about themselves and their relationships with others. Other episodes are narrated in a third-person voice that emphasizes particular characters' points of view. While the six first-person narrators all play important roles within the book, other characters, particularly June Kashpaw and Gerry Nanapush, are also central figures.

After *Love Medicine*'s brief account of June Kashpaw's final hours, readers see her only in the stories other characters relate about her. For this reason—because her own story cannot be fully told—June remains mysterious, her ghostly presence haunting readers just as their memories of June haunt her family members. As Elaine Tuttle Hansen points out, June is an example of the "mother without child" (Hansen 121), the mother who for one reason or another has abandoned a child. Although there is no direct account of her desertion of Lipsha, in "The Beads," a chapter narrated by Marie, readers learn that June herself was a child without a mother. When June Morrissey was nine, she was discovered alone in the bush, living "like a deer" (87). Although Marie tried to replace the mother who had died, June could no longer "trust" (92) the figure of the mother and chose instead to live with Eli Kashpaw, a man accustomed to life in the bush. Perhaps June's early experiences hint at why she was looking for a life that "could be different" from the one she had known, but what could have made a difference remains as mysterious as June.

Although, like June, both Marie and Lulu have been separated from their own mothers, these two women, in their quite different ways, come to embody the novel's figuration of the mother. As mother, "Saint Marie" not only nurtures and protects children of her own, but she also provides a home for "took-ins" (253) like Lipsha who have no family of their own. As his wife, Marie has ambitions for Nector, and it is therefore she who encourages him to become a leader in tribal affairs. After Nector's death, Marie becomes politically active herself, thus assuming the Native American grandmother's role of preserver of tradition.

When Nector leaves Marie for Lulu, he puts a note of farewell underneath the sugar jar. Hearing the dogs signaling her husband's return, Marie refolds the note and purposefully places it beneath a can of salt. Although she decides that she will not bring up the matter of the letter, she hopes that Nector will sometimes look at her and wonder, "salt or sugar?" (165). The trope of the two cannisters is altogether apt: Marie is indeed the salt in Nector's life, and Lulu is the sugar. Because Nector is "greedy" (125) and can "never have enough of both" (126), he cannot make the choice between sugar and salt.

Several critics have discussed Erdrich's use of the figure of the trickster in developing certain of her characters, particularly Gerry Nanapush. Interestingly, Jeanne Rosier Smith suggests that *Love Medicine* is in fact inhabited by "a family of tricksters" (Smith 71), all modeled on Nanabozho, the Ojibwa's legendary trickster. While Lulu is clearly one example of the "good mothers" (Hansen 131) depicted in the novel, Smith sees her as "Erdrich's feminist revisioning of the trickster, sharing Nanabozho's physical flexibility, artful gambling, and sexual prowess"

(Smith 79–80). Indeed, Lulu's sexual adventures are themselves the stuff of legends, and she is the adept crimper of cards who teaches Lipsha the system he uses to win June's car from King. Tricksterlike in her ability to transcend the boundaries of her body, she is able to open herself to the world and to "all that lived in its rainy arms" (276).

In *Love Medicine*, the act of crossing water is imbued with significance. June walks across the snow as if it were water, and Lipsha drives across the water to return to his home. Lulu also crosses water when she makes her way by boat to the island that is the home of Moses Pillager, the first of her lovers (and the father of Gerry Nanapush). Marie is yet another character who is described as crossing water—this time in a metaphoric sense. In the second section of "The Beads," when Marie is experiencing a long and difficult labor, she speaks a word from the old language to help her find a rhythm. The word, "Babaumawaebigowin" (102), is one that is spoken in a boat. When one of her midwives also speaks the word, Marie understands that she must let her "body be driven by the waves, like a boat to shore" (103), and when she has finally crossed the water, her last child is born.

Nector is a character who describes himself as someone who is swept along and buffeted by the currents of a river. The river imagery occurs to him after a woman in Kansas has painted him leaping naked from a cliff to certain death in a river below. *Plunge of the Brave*, as the painting is called, reinforces Nector's suspicion that the "greater world" is interested only in the "doom" of the Indian, and he therefore vows to himself that he will "survive the raging water" (124). Surprised when the current that was carrying him to Lulu branches off to take him to Marie, Nector nonetheless continues with the river's flow. Soon enough, time is the river, and Nector is caught in "a swirl that carried me so swift that I could not look to either side" (127). Only when he is in his dotage does it appear that Nector's raging river has finally carried him to a place where the water is deep. Near the end of the novel Lipsha envisions him as placidly fishing for "big thoughts" (234) from the middle of a lake.

Lyman is clearly Nector's son, taking up where his father left off in the building of the tomahawk factory. (Although Nector did not know it at the time, he nearly killed this son when he set fire to Lulu's house.) After his brother's death, Lyman's happy-go-lucky days are over, and he begins to draw in earnest upon his Kashpaw talent for politicking and making money. When the tomahawk factory turns into a disaster, Lyman pulls himself together and concocts a bold new plan. He will, he decides, first open a bingo parlor, and then, when the time is right, a

"Chippewa casino" (327). Lyman sees a future for the reservation, and the future that he sees is "based on greed and luck" (328).

Albertine Johnson, Gerry Nanapush, and Lipsha Morrissey are the three other characters in whose portrayals Smith locates references to the trickster Nanabozho. While Albertine does not actively play the role of trickster, Smith points out that she does experience a vision that is remarkably similar to one attributed to Nanabozho in Ojibwa legend. In the novel's first chapter, Albertine and Lipsha lie in a wheat field and watch the northern lights. To Albertine, the "pulsing" patterns in the sky seem as "rhythmical as breathing" (37), and she experiences the same sense of "oneness with the rhythm of the Universe" (Benton-Benai 57) that the famous trickster is said to have felt. Memories of June merge with her vision, and Albertine imagines her aunt dancing in the sky. Smith remarks the appropriateness of this image of June when she notes that "in Chippewa myth the joyful dancing of the dead in the afterworld creates the northern lights" (Smith 75).

Gerry Nanapush, whose surname makes reference to the great Ojibwa trickster, enacts in Erdrich's novel Nanabozho's traditional role of hero to his people. Gerry's rise to fame as the "hero whose face appeared on the six-o'clock news" (118) begins quite simply with a barroom scuffle provoked when a cowboy insults Gerry's people. Gerry is arrested and then sent to jail, but because a prison does not exist that can "hold the son of Moses Pillager" (285), the Ojibwa's wily hero escapes each time he is recaptured. Certainly it is not without great price that Gerry plays out the trickster's role of culture hero, for in living the life of a fugitive, he has had to relinquish all hopes of ever going home.

Lipsha is the other character Smith includes in her discussion of Love Medicine's "family" of tricksters, and she describes, in particular, the way "Erdrich comically recasts the Nanabozho origin myth in the story of Lipsha's search for his parents" (Smith 79). As Smith explains, both Nanabozho and Lipsha learn from a grandmother the identity of their parents. Like Nanabozho's mother, who was swept away by a powerful wind, Lipsha's mother too is claimed by a storm. Both Nanabozho and Lipsha set out on a journey, and for both of them the success of the quest depends upon the use of trickery in gambling. In her analysis of Erdrich's uses of Ojibwa myth, Smith shows how elements of Nanabozho's trickster tradition are represented in a variety of characters. Nanabozho, of course, is himself a shape-shifter, and it therefore seems fitting that his characteristics are embodied in several different figures.

Trickster like in his gambling skills, Lipsha, the "little cabbage" (Coltelli 21), also possesses the shaman's healing touch. The power of the touch is Lipsha's inheritance through the Pillager line, through Fleur Pillager, the medicine woman who is his great grandmother; through her cousin Moses, the grandfather whose true name only Lulu knows; and through Lulu herself, the "jabwa witch" (332) who has the power to enchant. It is of course because Lipsha has the touch that Marie approaches him about a love medicine for Nector, and it is because Lipsha knows that he cannot use the touch in Nector's case that he agrees to seek some other remedy. Lipsha well understands that a love medicine is not something "for the layman to handle" (241), but he decides to risk the danger to help "Grandpa and Grandma Kashpaw get back some happiness within the tail ends of their lives" (237). After Nector's death Lipsha's touch deserts him for a while, but then, when he takes up Nector's lowly task of prying dandelions from the earth, his power is restored.

THEMES

In his study of the intricacies of Erdrich's uses of comedy, Kenneth Lincoln observes that "in *Love Medicine* the dandelion's iconic humor—weedy, whip-singing, willowy, unwanted—blooms as a naturalized image of (Native) American resilience" (Lincoln 241). The dandelions are "thick as thieves" (*LM* 257) when Lipsha goes to dig them, and it is in their "buried roots" and in their leaves "full of bitter mother's milk" (258) and in the earth itself that he finds the means by which his touch can be restored. When Albertine first learns that her aunt has died, she leaves her cramped apartment to find a place where she can turn her thoughts to June. The spot she comes to choose is a patch of green grass where spring's first dandelions have already begun to bloom. In these scenes, where the dandelion—resilient, ubiquitous, "indestructible" (258), as Lipsha would say—is whimsically emblematic of the will to survive, Erdrich expresses one of her novel's most important themes.

In readily apparent ways, all of Erdrich's novels offer stories of survival. Telling such stories, as Erdrich explains, is especially important for Native American writers, for "in the light of enormous loss, they must tell the stories of contemporary survivors while protecting and celebrating the cores of cultures left in the wake of the catastrophe" (Erdrich, "Where," 23). *Love Medicine*'s survivors find renewal in the land, and it is for this reason that Albertine seeks out a patch of unpaved ground in the middle of the city and Lipsha digs in the earth to recover the power he has lost. In her portrayals of Albertine's, Lipsha's, and other characters' connections to the land, Erdrich gives voice to yet another of the novel's themes.

For old-timers like Eli, Moses, and Fleur, who embody the "core" of a tradition and its culture, connection to the land is an essential component of identity. All of these characters are creatures of the land, and when Fleur twice loses possession of her land, she twice finds a way to get it back again. For Lulu, June, Albertine, Lipsha, and other characters, the land is the site of the place where they belong, the place where home, family, community, and memory significantly define a relation to the world. In the novel's many scenes of homecoming, these characters find occasion to renew their connections to the land. The experience of renewal is not, of course, a possibility for someone like King, and in Erdrich's portrayal of this character, readers are shown the great cost of the loss of a connection to home, family, and land.

In playing out her themes of loss and survival over the passage of fifty years' time, Erdrich is able to illustrate how the conditions of survival change from one generation to another. Rushes Bear, Old Nanapush, Eli, Fleur, and Moses are all survivors of the time of epidemics and of the time when government and business made claims upon their lands. Lulu, Nector, and Marie have survived the efforts of institutions—religious and government schools, for example—to dispossess them of their cultural inheritance. As their stories reveal, these characters are also survivors of hard times and of the years of grueling poverty that have been part of their experiences of reservation life. Near the end of their days, when their children are all grown, both Lulu and Marie willingly assume the survivor's responsibility of "protecting and celebrating" the community's traditions.

New challenges arise for members of *Love Medicine*'s younger generation, but in their different ways Gerry, Albertine, Lipsha, and Lyman all possess the will to survive. Gerry's political activism is part of his generation's effort to preserve and to improve the status of Native American peoples. As Lulu says of her son, "inspiring the Indian people, that was his life" (288). In Albertine, who is, as her mother Zelda proudly boasts, "an *Indian*" born and raised, and in Lipsha, who has both sought and claimed his "heritage," traditional values are preserved. Lyman's plan to build a casino on the reservation offers the promise of a new economy for his people, and he also sees in this gesture an ingenious way of preserving one particular Native American tradition: Games of chance, as Lyman well knows, are an "old-time thing" (326) on the reservation.

Love Medicine's survivors are connected to their land, but Erdrich's novel is primarily interested in their connections to one another. It is through their stories that characters account for their relationships with others, and it is her use of a narrative strategy that relies on this device through which Erdrich subtly shapes her novel's vision of community. In the individual tales, readers learn of characters' loves and hatreds and of their desires and regrets. When the stories they have told are then retold or elaborated by others, the web of connections that defines the world as a community is gradually unfolded, and readers can see that each single story takes the shape of a pattern within the book's overall design. Thus "all the grieving and drinking and lusting and dying, the loving and torturing and birthing and joking, the working and musing and wising-up" (Grantham 16) detailed in the separate stories together reflect the experience of life in *Love Medicine*'s community.

ALTERNATIVE PERSPECTIVE: READER-RESPONSE

Reader-response theorists are interested in questioning how it is that readers arrive at the meanings they discover in a text. Assuming that readers are active participants in the process of interpreting a text, adherents of this critical approach reject the idea that a work of literary art is an autonomous object that contains its own meaning—and thus interprets itself. In other words, the reader-response theorist does not regard reading as a passive activity wherein the reader simply absorbs the meaning presented by a text. Rather, the act of reading is seen as a creative process wherein a reader interacts with a text in the production of meaning. Although reader-response theorists do not all agree in their assessments of the nature of the relationship between texts and readers, all are interested in exploring the role the reader plays in the act of interpretation.

Love Medicine is a particularly interesting novel to consider in the light of reader-response criticism for several reasons. One of these reasons, simply enough, is that since its publication readers and critics have interpreted the book in a remarkable variety of ways. As Wong notes, for *Love Medicine* there is "no monolithic readership. Some reviewers and students have seen the characters overall as poverty-stricken, alcohol-addicted Indians who are 'durable,' but desperate and ultimately 'doomed.' " Other readers, Wong goes on to say, have described the novel's characters as "complex and resilient humans" (Wong, "Louise," 185) who ultimately manage to survive despite the problems they encounter. Some critics have read June's death as an instance of spiritual defeat, while many others have interpreted it as an account of this character's spiritual transcendence. These examples are but a few of many that suggest that *Love Medicine* is a text with which readers interact in markedly different ways.

Love Medicine is also interesting in the challenges it poses for its readers. The British writer Angela Carter asserts that "reading is just as creative an activity as writing" (Carter 69), and this observation seems particularly apt in respect to Erdrich's novel, which demands from its readers creative activity to an exceptional degree. As reviewer Geoffrey Stokes describes it, in *Love Medicine* "Erdrich constantly thrusts responsibility on the reader, saying, as poets effectively do, 'Here it is. Here it *all* is. I've done my best, now it's *your* turn.' " And in an interview with Stokes, Erdrich herself says about her first novel, " 'I'm not sure that the structure really *had* to be that complicated' " (Stokes 59). In interpreting the novel, readers must account for obvious gaps in many of the stories and also for the variations that exist among characters' different versions of a story. Because it is only readers who are finally privy to all the novel's stories, the task falls to them of apprehending a context in which all the accounts can be seen to fit together. As critic John Purdy succinctly describes the reader's position, "in any storytelling event, the audience has a role to play" (Purdy 91).

Yet another interesting question about the novel's readership concerns the matter of its intended audience. While Erdrich has stated in an interview that "my first audience is American Indians" (Coltelli 25), her novel has in fact commanded the attention of both Indian and non-Indian readers. Erdrich herself lives within the spheres of two different cultures, and, in its themes and symbols as well as in its structure, *Love Medicine* obviously draws upon both Native American and Euro-American cultural traditions. Because two distinct cultural codes are in fact inscribed in the novel, reader-response theorists have been interested in studying how interpretations of it by Native and non-Native readers might be different, and how readers from these two groups might learn to see the novel through each other's eyes.[1]

Characterizing *Love Medicine* as a "mediational text" (Ruppert 132) in which the "conceptual frameworks" of both Native and non-Native traditions are encoded, James Ruppert argues that the novel is artfully designed to invite interpretation "through the paths of understanding unique to each culture" (Ruppert 131). He then goes on to demonstrate how several passages in the novel might be differently interpreted by Erdrich's two different audiences. When Gordie Kashpaw, for example, fears that June has returned in the form of a deer, non-Native readers are likely to conclude that Gordie is suffering from alcohol-induced delirium and feelings of guilt. The text, on the other hand, specifies that in speaking June's name, Gordie has violated a prohibition observed among the Ojibwa, and thus readers familiar with that tradition will recognize that Gordie has actually summoned June from the spirit world. When Henry Lamartine Junior jumps into the river, his suicidal act makes sense to non-Native readers familiar with the effects of post-traumatic syndrome. Ruppert, however, points out that from the Native perspective, Henry's drowning might well be seen as a result of "the fact that his actions [in Vietnam] are out of harmony with the Chippewa sense of war, death, honor, and right thinking" (Ruppert 139). Henry's death, in other words, might be understood from a psychological or sociological perspective, or it might be understood in terms of the communal and mythic traditions of his people. In these examples and others, Ruppert shows how Erdrich's mediational text offers the non-Native reader exposure to the values of Native tradition. For "the implied Native reader," the same text illustrates "that new perspectives and new languages can sustain cores of culture" (Ruppert 133).

Focusing on questions about *Love Medicine*'s reception, reader-response theory acknowledges the different cultural experiences that inform readers' understanding of the world depicted in the book. It examines the reader's role in interpreting that world and demonstrates how the text itself invites multiple interpretations.

NOTE

1. Essays written by Barbara L. Pittman, Catherine Rainwater, and James Ruppert offer cross-cultural readings of *Love Medicine*.

4

The Beet Queen
(1986)

In her second novel Louise Erdrich transports her readers to Argus, North Dakota, a small town that lies near the borders of the reservation she earlier depicted in *Love Medicine*. Like the first novel, the second book explores several characters' connections to one another through a series of stories they tell about their lives; like those in *Love Medicine*, these stories speak of characters' efforts to survive hard times and to confront the confusions of identity that inevitably mark the experiences of people who are separated from their families. In *The Beet Queen*, however, characters' relationships are much more tenuous than those portrayed in *Love Medicine*, and most of these characters feel no strong connection to the land or to a cultural tradition that might help define for them the conditions of belonging. Their lives, in other words, are not deeply rooted in either the earth or the community, and thus it is one of the novel's ironies that it is finally a shallow root, the sugar beet, that promises to secure the future of the town.

The Beet Queen's action begins in 1932, during the early years of the Depression, and ends in 1972 when the town has realized its citizens' efforts to establish a new economic base. At the end of the novel Argus's success in its endeavor is celebrated in a carnival—a festival dedicated to honoring the beet. In the scene of carnival comically depicted in the novel's closing pages readers are reminded of a similar event described near the beginning of the novel, for it is in 1932 at the "Orphans' Picnic, a bazaar held to benefit the homeless children of Saint Jerome's" (10) that three of the book's characters are suddenly made orphans themselves. *The Beet Queen* is thus framed by its scenes of carnival, occasions when its world is turned topsy-turvy. As the narrative theorist Mikhail Bakhtin suggests, the carnival can be read as the site of exuberant grotesquerie and violent disorder. Anything, it seems, can happen at the carnival, and anyone can be crowned "queen" for a day.

As in *Love Medicine*, characters' lives in *The Beet Queen* span three generations, and readers are shown how each generation must respond to the circumstances of the changing times. The novel is arranged in four parts, each of which offers chapters that unfold the action in chronological order over the course of passing decades. *The Beet Queen*'s linear narrative structure is therefore not as complex as the narrative design of Erdrich's first novel. In the second book, however, the writer does add one obvious embellishment: Throughout the novel sections narrated in the third person are interspersed with the characters' first-person accounts. The voice of an omniscient narrator thus fills gaps in the stories, providing, as reviewer Dorothy Wickenden points out, "scenes [that] are sketched with a detachment the characters lack" (Wickenden 46) in their own reporting of events.

The Beet Queen's episodic plot first unfolds accounts of the complete dissolution of a family, and then traces the courses of lives that are ineluctably shaped or changed in the aftermath of that calamity. The stories told in the first half of the book therefore recount characters' various efforts to find means to survive the abrupt upheaval in their lives. In the second half of the novel, when Dot Adare claims her place at the center of their concerns, characters begin to see that they must construct for themselves a redefined understanding of what constitutes a family. The task is not an easy one, for Dot is a difficult child and those who love her are all jealous of their roles in her life, but in the end, as Catherine Rainwater asserts, *The Beet Queen* emphatically "insists that many alternative kinds of ties, not biological, link people" (Rainwater 418) in ways that are often surprising.

In her discussion of narrativity in Erdrich's fiction, Rainwater points out that the novels characteristically depict the lives of "culturally and socially displaced characters whose marginal status is simultaneously an advantage and a disadvantage, a source of both power and powerlessness" (Rainwater 405). It is in portraying both her characters' idiosyncratic strengths and the powerlessness that attends their marginal positions that Erdrich is able to successfully blend the comic with the

tragic in the novel's vision. Although *The Beet Queen* affirms the strength
of a human will to move beyond adversity, its comic perspective is
darker, more surreal, and finally less celebratory than the comic vision
Love Medicine earlier offered. Reviewer Russell Banks describes Erdrich's
second book as "a Dickensian story, an angry comedy" in which characters' endeavors to find meaning in their lives are played out in the
context of the powerful "economic and social forces" (Banks 460) of
which they are all victims.

PLOT

In a brief prologue entitled "The Branch," readers catch a first glimpse
of Karl and Mary Adare, a brother and sister who serve as two of the
six first-person narrators in the novel. Karl, fourteen, and Mary, eleven,
have traveled to Argus by rail in a boxcar. Readers learn that the children
intend to search for relatives who run a butcher shop in the town, but
before they can reach their destination events conspire to separate them.
Transfixed by the splendor of a small tree in bloom, Karl pauses while
Mary "trudge[s] solidly forward" (2). When a large dog attacks him, Karl
seizes a branch and runs back to the train. Mary, meanwhile, trudges on
to discover the shop where she will spend the rest of her days.

Mary, in the novel's first chapter, tells readers why she and her brother
journey to Argus in the cold spring of 1932. Her tale is one of children
abandoned, for when Adelaide Adare can find no way to support Karl,
Mary, and the baby boy she refuses to name, she decides one day to
simply fly away. It is, of course, a carnival that provides Adelaide the
occasion to take to the air; her children's last vision of their mother is
that of Adelaide, her "long red crinkly hair" (12) floating behind her,
vanishing into the sky with The Great Omar, "Aeronaught Extraordi-
naire" (11). When their infant brother also disappears, carried from the
carnival by a grieving father whose own baby has recently died, Karl
and Mary leave Minneapolis to search for Kozka's Meats, the business
owned by their Aunt Fritzie and her husband Pete.

As the prologue makes clear, the Adare family is completely dispersed
before Fritzie and Pete can offer their assistance. They can, however,
provide a home for Mary, and this possibility is one to which she is
determined to cling. In fact, Mary plans, as she readily admits, to make
herself "essential" to the Kozkas, to become "so depended upon that
they could never send me off" (19). Indeed, the desire for permanence

that is the young Mary's response to abandonment comes to shape the course of her life. "Throughout the remainder of the novel," as Louis Owens observes, "Mary will be consistently described as heavy, immovable" (Owens 207), and when the Kozkas eventually decide to retire, it is the stolid and dependable Mary whom they will choose to oversee their butcher shop.

While Fritzie and Pete warmly welcome their strangely orphaned niece, Mary's presence in their home disrupts the life of her cousin Sita, the Kozkas' only child. Sita, another of the novel's first-person narrators, tells the story of her displacement, of her bitterness at having to share with Mary her room and possessions and of her anger when Mary steals the attentions of her friend Celestine James, a character who also narrates sections of the novel. Unlike Mary, who is content with her surroundings, the beautiful Sita longs for a life filled with glamour and romance— the very kind of life that she supposes her stylish Aunt Adelaide is living. As soon as she is old enough to flee Argus and the butcher shop, Sita determinedly pursues the world of her dreams. The life of which she dreams, however, proves time and again to be but an airy illusion, and Sita's frustration with a world that is not at all to her liking eventually drives her mad.

Although Mary does not share Sita's aspirations to become someone who is noticed and admired, she does enjoy, while she is still a child at school, a moment in the limelight. As it happens, Mary is the unwitting cause of a miracle in Saint Catherine's schoolyard. When she lands on her face beneath a frosty slide, the bloody impression she leaves in the ice is seen by the nuns and the priest as a manifestation of "Christ's Dying Passion" (40). (Mary herself sees the face of her brother Karl in the ice, and her friend Celestine can see nothing at all.) Mary's miracle occasions another carnival scene, for the face is cordoned off and people drive from miles away to visit the site and to adorn the surrounding fence with flowers, rosaries, and ribbons. Sister Leopolda, always interested in miracles, takes the photographs that will later appear in catechism textbooks.

The Sister Leopolda who records the miracle (and later flogs herself at the site of the impression in the ice) is a character who also appeared in Erdrich's first novel. Interestingly, Mary's brother Karl encounters another of *Love Medicine*'s characters in the figure of Fleur Pillager, a medicine woman who saves his life. When Karl hops back on the boxcar, he meets there a tramp with whom he experiences the first of his many sexual adventures. After this encounter he leaps from the speeding train and shatters his ankles when he hits the ground. It is Fleur who finds him lying by the railroad tracks, and it is she who skillfully shapes splints from the branch Karl has carried with him. While his bones are mending, Karl travels with Fleur as she peddles her wares throughout the countryside. This early adventure presages the course Karl's life will later take, for he ends up becoming a traveling salesman himself.

Whereas Mary settles in Argus once and for all, Karl, who is always on the move, wanders in and out of the lives of *The Beet Queen*'s other characters. He first meets Wallace Pfef, yet another of the novel's narrators, at a convention in Minneapolis in 1952. The sexual encounter that takes place in Karl's hotel room proves enlightening to Wallace, who finds that he must acknowledge to himself his own homosexuality. Wallace is a leading citizen in Argus, and he keeps a picture of his "poor dead sweetheart" (159) hanging on the wall. Wallace does not actually know the woman in the photograph, for he purchased the picture at an auction he once attended, but its presence in his living room answers the unspoken questions of the people of Argus, and he is thus able to keep his sexual identity a secret—from all but himself and his sometime lover. Although Wallace tries hard to suppress all thoughts of Karl, he is never able to break free of his fascination with his only lover.

Louis Owens sees Karl as a tricksterlike presence in the novel, a figure who is "an eternal wanderer, a lover of both men and women, a sexual shapeshifter alternately identified with both Christ and Satan" (Owens 207). Shortly after his dalliance with Wallace Pfef, Karl meets and seduces Celestine James, Mary's oldest friend. Celestine, who is a mixed-blood Ojibwa (and related to *Love Medicine*'s Kashpaw family), tells of her brief affair with Karl and of her subsequent pregnancy. Although Celestine knows that she cannot continue to live with Karl—he has already driven her half-brother Russell Kashpaw from their home, endangered her longtime friendship with Mary, and interfered with her own ability to dream—she agrees to a marriage of convenience, a mere formality. While this arrangement leaves Karl homeless once again, he is nevertheless a man who can at long last make claim to family connections.

In a scene that alludes to fairy tale tradition, Wallacette Darlene Adare enters the world during a blinding snowstorm. Wallace Pfef tells how Celestine attempts to drive to the hospital but soon finds herself lodged in a snowbank. When she sees a distant porch light "barely visible through the waves of snow" (169), she manages to make her way to Wallace's house and there gives birth to the child. Because Wallace boils the water, fetches the sheets, and generally serves the role of midwife, Celestine chooses to name her daughter in his honor. Wallace is "blinded by happiness" (172) at his unlikely good fortune and, with Mary, stands as godparent to the child. As it happens, Mary also stakes her claim to the naming of the baby, for it is she who provides the pointedly mono-syllabic nickname, Dot. In this fashion an outline of a set of "family" connections begins to take its shape around the life of Dot Adare.

The Beet Queen's surreal effect is in part achieved in its suggestive references to fairy tale scenarios. The birth-in-the-snowstorm scene is by no means the only instance where such a reference occurs. Another ex-ample can be found in the book's early account of events at the Orphans' Picnic, where the kidnapping of Adelaide's youngest child is distinctly reminiscent of numerous folk stories about the figures of the foundling or the changeling. And Adelaide herself, clearly a damsel in distress, is rescued and swept away by The Great Omar, her own version of the knight in shining armor. Yet further instances include the occasion when Sita is forced to play the role of the abducted bride and when Wallace takes it upon himself to enact the part of fairy godmother to Dot's Cin-derella. Karl, of course, is quite ironically cast in the role of Prince Charming.

The (fractured) fairy tale allusions can be seen as elements of Erdrich's use of the discourse of carnival,[1] and the sections of the novel that are narrated in the third-person also serve this purpose. Every chapter ex-cept the last one, narrated by Dot, closes with a scene presented in the lyrical style first introduced in the novel's prologue, the brief passage entitled "The Branch." Several of these scenes include the word "Night" in their titles, and indeed all of these sections offer readers glimpses of characters' solitary experiences of moments of insight or despair—ex-periences that take place during the dark nights of the soul. It is in "Karl's Night," for example, that readers see the image of a boy whose heart has been "ripped open" (26) making his leap of desperation into the darkness beyond the moving train. In "Wallace's Night" the man who is determined to think about "anything but Karl" (108) is sitting alone in Lover's Lane when he suddenly conceives his marvelous plan to bring the sugar beet to Argus.

In other interludes—aptly described by Geoffrey Stokes as "third-person fugues" (Stokes 59)—readers learn something of the lives of char-acters who are peripheral to the novel's central action. In "Rescue," for example, the fate of Adelaide's youngest child is at last disclosed. Cath-erine Miller, a young woman whose own son has died, sees in the foundling carried home by her husband a chance to find deliverance from the "blind agony" she has suffered with her loss. In her joy and thankfulness she names her baby Jude, after the patron saint of "lost causes, lost hopes, and last-ditch resorts" (45). In a later fugue, when Karl once again visits the site of the Orphans' Picnic, he actually meets Jude Miller, by then a young seminarian, and he quickly recognizes in this long-lost brother Adelaide's own distinctive facial features and her "dark red and springy" (80) hair. (When Jude looks closely at Karl, however, what he sees standing there is "the devil" [82] taunting him.)

It is in "Celestine's Night," another of the third-person passages, that readers are offered the delicate image that Erdrich herself describes as "the emblem" (Tompkins 15) of her book. Late one night, near dawn, when Celestine is drowsily nursing her sleeping daughter, she notices, "in the fine moonlit floss of her baby's hair, a tiny white spider making its nest." As Celestine looks on in utter fascination, she sees that an almost invisible web is slowly being formed; the web is assuredly "a complicated house" (176), and Celestine realizes that she cannot bring herself to destroy this fragile construction. Occurring near the middle of the book—at the very end of Part Two, in fact—the image invites readers to consider how the "invisible strings" (176) that link people's lives to the welfare of a child form the complicated houses in which children dwell. In the second half of the novel, when the plot turns its focus to the life of Dot Adare, readers witness the construction of the web that is built around this child.

From the moment of her birth Dot Adare presents herself as a force to be reckoned with. When he first holds the newborn child, Wallace observes that already she looks "formidable," her face set with "stubborn purpose" (171–172). Dot indeed fulfills the expectations suggested by these early indications of her nature, and in Part Three of *The Beet Queen*, Mary, Celestine, and Wallace all recount stories of the bizarre misadventures of her tempestuous childhood. In these accounts all three of the speakers characterize their relationships to Dot, but their stories also tellingly reveal the ways in which their interests in the child all too often leave them at odds with one another. As readers therefore see, the task of constructing the web of family connections that encircles Dot is one that is by no means easily achieved.

Unlike the several characters who are orphans in the novel, Dot is surrounded by loving adults. Celestine is both a good and conscientious mother, but, as Elaine Tuttle Hansen points out, "she has to compete with two other childless adults . . . who also want to parent Dot" (Hansen 137). While she often sympathizes with the positions of her child's surrogate parents, occasionally Celestine is unable to control her desire to undermine her rivals. It is, for example, an impulse of this sort that inspires her to write the name "Mary Adare" on the jello salad filled with nuts and bolts that she brings to a Christmas party held at Dot's school.

For her part, Mary recognizes a soul mate in the figure of her niece. Like Mary, Dot is "pale, broad, and solid" (181), and Mary also sees herself "in Dot's one-track mind" and in her "doubled fists" (182). Mary is in fact convinced that she enjoys a "mental connection" (180) with this child and therefore strongly believes that "if anyone, Celestine should have named her after me" (179). Resentful of her "sideline role" (182) as mere aunt to a child who so closely resembles her, Mary bides her time and waits for any opportunity she can find to champion the interests of her beloved Dot. After one such occasion, when she has stuffed Dot's teacher into a toy box, Mary is called to answer to the law. This scene is among the most comical in the novel, for Mary's act of righteous indignation is the result of a foolish mistake. When Officer Lovchik finally understands that his investigation centers on a confusion about the nature of Mrs. Shumway's "naughty box," he agrees to try to get the assault charges dropped.

"Uncle" Wallace believes that both Celestine and Mary are too possessive in their love of Dot, and he can sometimes see in the child her relatives' worst qualities: "Mary's stubborn, abrupt ways, Sita's vanity, Celestine's occasional cruelties, Karl's lack of responsibility" (233). Nevertheless he too loves Dot Adare, for she is the most admirably fearless person he has ever met. As one of her loyal guardians, he sees his role as that of helping this difficult child to succeed in her endeavors. He therefore plans for her a special birthday party (which turns into a spectacular disaster) and later presents her with the twenty-pound shot that makes it possible for her to join the track team. Dot's teen years, however, are particularly trying ones, for she is "either lit up by her imaginary future, or depressed, a dark lump" (303), filled with despair over her many disappointments.

Wallace is therefore determined to concoct a bold new plan. In particular he desires to make one of Dot's many wild fantasies come true. He will, as he vows, play the storybook role of the godmother who possesses the magical power to grant one wish. Because the sugar beet is now "king" (304) in Argus, it seems particularly fitting that he should organize a festival that closes with the crowning of a queen. And Dot, he knows, is the person who will indeed be crowned that queen, for Wallace decides that he will rig the election.

In Part Four of *The Beet Queen* the movement of the plot sweeps readers toward the moment when Dot will be crowned. In one way or another, dead or alive, most of the book's characters are present for this occasion. Jude Miller, for example, whose mother has finally told him of his past, makes his way to Argus, like his siblings before him, to search for Kozka's Meats. Although the young priest does not know anyone in the crowd, he joins the people gathered in the grandstands. Russell Kashpaw is also present and rides in the parade. The community's most-decorated war hero has earlier had a stroke and therefore sits in his wheelchair on top his float, and during the course of the parade eerily suffers a near-death experience. Of course Mary and Celestine also join the crowd, and they bring with them the corpse of Sita, who has just died while in their care. Even Karl comes from afar to see his daughter crowned, and thus the stage is set for Dot's day of triumph.

Dot herself is the narrator of the last chapter in the book, and she first tells of her ride on the queen's royal float—where she uses the "windshield-wiper wave" (331) appropriate to the occasion. Dot is well aware that the dress she is wearing, a garment purchased by her Aunt Mary, is hideously unfashionable; it seems to her to resemble the skin that a dinosaur has shed. It is not, however, until she hears someone in the crowd mention that her election was rigged that her embarrassment suddenly turns into fury. Dot quickly decides upon a plan for revenge, and she finds her inspiration in the old story of her Grandmother Adelaide. Knowing that her Uncle Wallace has hired a pilot to write her name in the sky, she leaps aboard the plane and flies far from the fairgrounds and her coronation.

Whereas Adelaide's flight signaled separation, Dot's is finally a gesture of return, an occasion for homecoming. She is, after all, the one who has drawn all the members of her family together, and when the plane at last heads back toward the deserted grandstand, her single thought is that of home. Celestine is waiting for her daughter, and when she approaches her mother, Dot immediately sees "in her eyes . . . the force of her love" (337). Later, alone in her bed, Dot listens to the wind and then smells the refreshing rain that promises to end the long drought in Argus.

CHARACTERS

Like *Love Medicine, The Beet Queen* presents no heroine or hero but rather a chorus composed of several different characters. Readers naturally become best acquainted with those characters who narrate their own stories, but the novel's third-person fugues offer intriguing glimpses of the figures who remain in the background. One of these figures is Adelaide Adare, who, like June Kashpaw, never tells her own story. In "Aerial View of Argus" and "The Birdorama" readers briefly see Adelaide through Omar's point of view. Although she seldom talks "about her children or her life before him" (60), Omar comes to realize that Adelaide has never forgotten those she left behind. From time to time she suffers terrible fits of pent-up rage; although Omar does not know the cause of her frustration, readers are left to assume that her dramatic flight did not fully resolve the problems in her life.

In its refusal to sentimentalize life in small-town America, *The Beet Queen* depicts characters whose weaknesses and failures are fully in view. As reviewer Nan Nowick observes, "one of the interesting features of this work is that although several of the characters are compelling, few are attractive" (Nowick 71–72). Although the central characters often show themselves to be both selfish and foolish, for each of them there exists some passage in the book that palpably invites the sympathy or understanding of the reader. In several instances these passages can be found in the third-person interludes, where characters either confront their own demons or suddenly recognize some pattern in their lives.

The young Karl is depicted as a frail and delicate child, one who often faints in times of duress. The boy's fainting spells can be understood to be a form of emotional escape, a kind of flight from a reality that seems threatening to the child. This early pattern of flight obviously persists throughout the course of Karl's life, and in this respect he resembles his mother. After Adelaide has flown away Karl seeks some explanation of her action, and in the scenario he envisions, readers can see another effort to evade a harsh reality. When Karl tells himself that his mother did not leave him but was in fact kidnapped by Omar, he is able to escape the pain of confronting her desertion.

Karl's leap from the boxcar and his later leap from the bed in the hotel room are failed attempts to fly, to somehow soar free of his circumstances. As Catherine Rainwater points out, this wandering figure who falls over the precipice sometimes seems to resemble the image of the

Fool in the Tarot deck. Indeed the likeness is especially conspicuous early in the novel when Karl springs from the boxcar, a branch in his hand and a dog at his heels. Traveling about as a carefree con man, Karl survives near the edge of society, free of any obligations to family or community. As he puts it himself, "all my life, I traveled light" (316). Certainly Karl's state of perpetual flight ensures that he carries with him no emotional baggage. Near the end of the novel the eternal wanderer pauses to take stock of the life he has lived. Suddenly seeing himself as part of an overwhelmingly "senseless landscape," Karl acknowledges to himself that "I give nothing, take nothing, mean nothing, hold nothing" (318).

Mary's response to her mother's desertion is very different from Karl's. She experiences no desire for flight, but rather is determined to never move again. Mary accepts Adelaide's behavior as an act of abandonment, and the scenario she imagines is accordingly different from Karl's. In her version of the story, the plane flies on and on until Omar sees that he is running out of fuel. The aeronaut does not love Adelaide and wants to save his life, so naturally he decides to hurl her from the plane. Mary sees her mother falling and falling, and when she knows that she can never love her again, she is ready to allow her to "hit the earth" (16) at last. Mary's stubborn refusal to be willing to forgive is deeply rooted in her nature and is only overcome in her relationship to Dot. Certainly she never forgives Sita for her arrogant ways or Wallace for bringing the sugar beet to Argus. When Adelaide eventually mails a postcard to Fritzie, Mary responds with a note announcing, "all three of your children starved dead" (58).

While Mary is most noticeably stubborn and completely settled in her ways, she is also strangely attracted to the realm of the bizarre, to theories about killer robots or the world of the afterlife. Perhaps because her own life never changes much, indeed is thoroughly predictable, she is fascinated by fortune telling and employs Tarot cards, a Ouija board, yarrow sticks, and egg yolks to peer into the future. As time passes by, various interests of this sort increasingly become a passion with Mary, and in her later years she even sports a turban. In "Mary's Night" readers are told that this aging woman occasionally thinks about the miracle she caused and yearns to find some way to duplicate the "splendor" (142) of that day.

Like that of Karl, Sita's life is marked by a series of flights and, in her case, a continuing quest to find a safe haven. When she escapes from Argus, Sita does realize her initial goal of becoming a model in one of

Fargo's best department stores. However, her first disappointment comes at age thirty, when nothing more has happened to her and it is now too late for her to try her luck in Hollywood. The fastidious Sita has kept her slender figure, attended refresher courses at the local charm school, and worn a Band-Aid on her forehead to prevent the wrinkling of her skin, but all these efforts are to no avail when she must compete with the younger models. Sita therefore concludes that the time has come to seek refuge in matrimony. When it becomes clear that the married doctor who has been stringing her along does not plan to leave his wife, she reluctantly accepts the proposal of an old boyfriend from Argus.

Her marriage to the loutish Jimmy Bohl and subsequent return to Argus signal a step down for Sita, and she slips further down when this marriage fails. In an attempt to bolster her position, she tries to transform the fried-food restaurant she has acquired from Jimmy into Chez Sita, a four-star dining palace. An outbreak of food poisoning and a dearth of customers soon bring this venture to an end, and the increasingly neurasthenic Sita begins her slide into speechlessness and then insanity. For a time she finds refuge in her second marriage, but when this husband dies, Sita is left with only her drugs to protect her. It is on the day of the coronation of the beet queen that she decides to swallow all of the remaining pills, and so it happens that Celestine and Mary find her propped against a tree, her gaze blank and her lips characteristically "set in exasperation" (291).

"I need to belong" (160), Wallace Pfef admits, and to fill his empty life he joins the Eagles, Moose, Kiwanis, Elk, the Chamber of Commerce, the Optimists, the Knights of Columbus, the piano club, and every other board or organization Argus has to offer. Indeed, Wallace appears to be the character most committed to the welfare of the community, but readers perceive what Mary also sees when she observes that this social gadabout is in fact a deeply lonely man. (Of course Mary does not know that he is isolated from others, in part, because of the secret he must hide.) Wallace therefore uses his public persona to convince himself that he belongs in Argus, and when the birth of Dot Adare offers the promise of a more personal connection, he gladly seizes the opportunity to make himself a part of her life.

Erdrich interestingly hints at subtle dimensions of her characters when she makes reference to what they like to read. Mary, of course, is committed to the occult and likes to read about unusual occurrences and bizarre misfortunes. Wallace particularly enjoys times of bad weather because he is then afforded the chance to stay in bed with stories of "crime and espionage" (160). (He thus appears to be attracted to accounts of the secret lives of others.) Sita reads mysteries to soothe her frazzled nerves, and readers might suppose that she finds this genre satisfying because it traffics in a world where all problems have solutions. The sensible Celestine, surprisingly, likes to read romances, and when she is seduced by Karl, she measures her responses against those she has read about in novels. Her interest in this genre, as she points out herself, is partly explained by the fact that she has had no mother who could tell her about the experiences of love.

Celestine, the novel's good mother, and her fiery daughter Dot together exemplify both the joys and the frustrations of the relationship between a parent and a child. Celestine represents the figure that *The Beet Queen*'s several orphans have lost or never known, the guardian and nurturer whose presence is a given. As a loving mother, Celestine is often tempted to hover over Dot, to comfort and protect her, but she is also wise enough to understand that her daughter must have the room she needs to find her own direction. For her part, although she is often embarrassed by it, Dot needs her mother's love—a truth that is poignantly depicted in the scenes that follow the Christmas play debacle and the aborted coronation. As Dot reveals at the very end of that long and trying day, "I want to lean into her the way wheat leans into wind" (338).

THEMES

The Beet Queen opens with two scenes of disconnection: first the scene that portrays Karl's separation from Mary, and then the passage that depicts Adelaide's earlier desertion of her children. From this point on, the novel unfolds a continuing series of scenarios that examines the complicated means by which characters are either separated from one another or significantly linked to each other—sometimes in quite surprising ways. In the end, Erdrich's second book makes the strong argument that the meaning of people's lives lies in their connections, in the "invisible strings" (176) that shape a community's "complicated house" (176). Although the connections studied in the novel are frequently shown to be fragile, tenuous, or subtle, they always underlie the characters' conceptions of their own identities. Whereas isolation or disconnection results in the loss of identity (as in the instances of Sita or Karl), in *The Beet Queen* relationships create the conditions that make possible characters' affirmations of their selfhood.

Karl's long life of flight from connections with others brings him near the end of the novel to a clear recognition of his own loss of identity. When he sees himself as merely a part of the "senseless landscape," living a life that essentially means "nothing," he is finally able to recognize that he must claim a relationship to something beyond himself. The something that occurs to him is an abstraction, simply a sudden impression of a great "sweetness." When he then links his daughter "with that moment of sweetness," he knows that he must make the journey to Argus in time to see her crowned. Karl's connection to Dot is the slightest of threads, for he has only seen her once in all the years of her life, but this thread is strong enough to save him from despair. As he drives nonstop toward Argus, he begins "to link other people with that moment too," and thus he returns to a web of connections he thought he had "left behind forever" (318).

In *Love Medicine* Albertine Johnson felt a strong connection to June Kashpaw, the bad mother who was nevertheless the perfect figure of an aunt. Similarly, Sita is fascinated by her Aunt Adelaide and aspires to emulate her style. She never chews gum, for instance, because she once heard her aunt proclaim that "only tramps chewed gum" (29). The connection she feels to her aunt inspires her to steal from Mary a small box containing a few of Adelaide's possessions, and after she has redeemed the pawn ticket she finds in the box, she becomes the rightful owner of Adelaide's legacy, an elegant filigree necklace with rich garnet settings. It is only fair that she makes claim to Adelaide's treasure, for her father Pete gives Mary Sita's own legacy, the cow's diamond that is his butcher's luck. Sita's connection to her Aunt Adelaide is subtly expressed on the day of her death, for she is indeed wearing the garnet necklace when she is found.

Some of *The Beet Queen*'s characters feel that they are linked to the lives of people they have never met. Catherine Miller, for example, who has saved all the news clippings about the abduction at the Orphans' Picnic, honors her implicit bond with the Adare family when she finally mails a letter that explains what became of Jude. When Jude himself hears the story of his past, he too feels a link to people who are strangers, and that is why he finds himself peculiarly swept into the frenzy of the carnival in Argus. Readers might observe that although Jude is present at both the novel's opening and its closing scenes of carnival, in neither case is he at all aware of what is happening around him.

Yet another of the novel's delicate connections is surprisingly granted expression when Adelaide sends a sewing machine to her daughter Mary. Mary, of course, has long since disavowed any relationship to her mother and therefore chooses to present Sita with this gift. Mary's persistent refusal to forgive once again blocks any possibility that she might reestablish a link to her mother, but Adelaide's gesture nonetheless affirms her own feelings of a continuing connection to her daughter. Adelaide has worried from afar about Mary's welfare, and is convinced that if she could learn to sew she would always have a skill upon which she could depend.

The Beet Queen's theme of disconnection is repeatedly expressed in its recurring images of characters' flights and their falls. Adelaide and Dot both fly away, and Karl spends most of his life both flying and falling. Mary symbolically severs her connection to her mother with an act of imagination that graphically envisions Adelaide's plunge to the earth. Both Sita and Russell experience disconnection when they fall into speechlessness, and Sita's flight from harsh realities eventually leads to her fall into madness. Even Mary's fall, into the ice beneath the slide, represents a moment of disconnection from her otherwise most ordinary life.

The tiny spider's web obviously serves as *The Beet Queen*'s emblem of its characters' links to one another. Its "invisible strings" are the threads that connect people's lives. Erdrich explains that air is the element she associates with the dominant images in this novel, and indeed it is in respect to the element of air that characters' separations and certain of their expressions of connection are both depicted. On the one hand, characters pursue airy illusions or leap or fly off into the airy beyond; on the other hand, however, a thread of connection can suddenly and often unexpectedly appear, as it were, out of the very air. This is clearly what happens when Adelaide sends the sewing machine to Mary, when Mary sees her vision of the birth of Dot Adare, or when Karl experiences the moment of sweetness that finally draws him back to Argus.

ALTERNATIVE PERSPECTIVE: FREUDIAN LITERARY ANALYSIS

A figure who is irrepressibly elusive and irresponsible, the bisexual Karl Adare is among the most enigmatic of *The Beet Queen*'s many memorable characters. Critics have variously described him as a wanderer, a demon, or a trickster or have linked him with the figures of the confidence man or the archetypal fool. Flagrantly promiscuous and thus apparently needful of some form of human connection, Karl is nonetheless seemingly unable to sustain a close emotional attachment. *The Beet Queen* does present enough information about Karl's background to suggest that some explanation of his adult nature might be found in his formative experiences, and, indeed, a Freudian psychoanalytic reading of this puzzling character's behavior can offer some speculation along these lines.

Contemporary psychoanalytic literary criticism grows out of the work of Sigmund Freud (1856–1936), whose revolutionary studies of the workings of the human mind laid the foundation for the Western world's modern science of psychology. While numerous thinkers since his time have either taken issue with his theories or offered elaborations upon them, Freud must nonetheless be credited with establishing a vocabulary that describes a theoretical model of human psychology. Freud believed that for human beings to lead productive and satisfying lives as stable adults, they needed to experience certain phases of psychological development. In cases where this development might be arrested for one reason or another, people's passage into adult maturation would necessarily be blocked.

One possible reading of Karl's character that takes into account both his unstable adult identity (his bisexuality, for example) and his sometimes infantile behavior (his frenzied leaping up and down on the bed in the hotel room, for instance) suggests that he might indeed have suffered some form of arrested development. When Mary describes the Adares' family life prior to Adelaide's departure, she does offer clues as to the origin of the problems Karl experiences during his adulthood, and the scenario she presents closely corresponds with Freud's conception of the human experience he chose to call "the Oedipal drama." Freud of course believed that all infants strongly desire to claim for themselves complete possession of their mothers. Recognizing their fathers as rivals for their mothers' attention, young boys experience fantasies wherein these rivals are destroyed. Sooner or later, of course, boys arrive at the understanding that their fathers' powers are clearly superior to their own, and they then begin to fear the powerful figure who now represents the embodiment of authority.

Freud argued that normal psychological development requires that boys pass through and thus resolve their Oedipal crises. After the boy comes to fear his powerful father, he first learns to repress his desires for his mother and then to identify with his father's position. In this way he associates himself with the power and authority embodied in his father. When the boy has acknowledged his father's superiority, the Oedipus complex is destroyed, and the boy passes into manhood. If the Oedipal crisis is not resolved, the boy will continue to desire or experience a repressed desire to possess his mother (as some critics have argued is the case with Hamlet). Such a person, as Freud also believed, is likely as well to find it difficult to acknowledge the social institutions that represent sources of authority and power.

As a boy, Karl does not know his father, and, as readers can tell from Mary's description, he is thoroughly attached to his mother Adelaide—in fact, there apparently exists a great deal of sibling rivalry between the brother and the sister. There is, however, a father figure in the household, a Mr. Ober who visits two or three times a week, late in the evenings. Mr. Ober is clearly Adelaide's long-time lover, and Karl deeply resents this man's all too frequent intrusions. (Mary reveals that she enjoys these visits because she can see that they brighten her mother's life.) If Karl wishes, as indeed he seems to, that Mr. Ober could be expunged from his mother's life, then his wish is surely granted, for one day it so happens that this rival is smothered under bushels of wheat. It is Karl who first notices the report about Mr. Ober printed in the newspaper, and when he shows it to his mother, apparently he cannot conceal his deep satisfaction. " 'You're glad!' " she cries out, and then immediately comes forth with the revelation that " 'he was your father' " (7). In Freudian terms, the young Karl has clearly realized his deep-seated desire to overcome the power of his father, to eliminate this rival for his mother's love. In his mind, another rival appears when the baby boy is born several months later, and all his life he blames this brother for Adelaide's disappearance. It is, of course, for this reason that Karl is cruel to Jude Miller when he recognizes him many years later at the Orphans' Picnic.

With the death of his father, Karl has no opportunity to resolve his Oedipal crisis. He cannot acknowledge his father's superiority, for with the realization of his childish fantasies he has proved himself superior; he might even feel guilty that his wishes have come true and therefore blame himself for the wrongful usurpation of his father's power. Unable to identify with the authority vested in his father's position, Karl clings to his mother. " 'Take me!' " (13) he screams when she flies away, and when he later tells himself that Omar is a kidnapper and therefore no rival, he swears that one day he will kill the aeronaut and claim his mother back. As he imagines this scene, Adelaide rushes toward him, over Omar's dead body. Then, "she held me close," he says, "and when she kissed me her lips were lingering and warm" (53).

NOTE

1. As described by Mikhail Bakhtin (1895–1975), the language of the carnival is that of the common folk and is generally concerned with matters crucial to survival. Erdrich's references to fairy tales clearly draw upon folk tradition, and the interludes, focusing on moments of crisis, depict characters struggling to survive.

5

Tracks
(1988)

For each of her novels Louise Erdrich experiments anew with narrative technique. *Tracks*, the third book published in her North Dakota series, omits altogether the third-person point of view the writer employed in sections of both *Love Medicine* and *The Beet Queen*. In *Tracks* Erdrich moves away as well from her earlier use of several narrative voices and instead unfolds her plot through the alternating perspectives of only two first-person speakers. One of these speakers, Pauline Puyat, directly relates the story of her life, but the other narrator, Old Nanapush, addresses his stories to a specific unseen listener. In other words, for Nanapush's sections of the novel Erdrich makes use of the technique of the dramatic monologue, where readers understand that more than one character is present although only one voice is heard. Recognizing that Nanapush is talking to his granddaughter Lulu, readers are fully aware that his stories serve a special rhetorical purpose in respect to his audience. As the implied audience of both narrators' versions of events, readers are placed in the interesting position of listening to Pauline's account and eavesdropping upon the story Nanapush addresses to his fictive listener.

Presented in nine chapters, *Tracks* chronicles the lives of Ojibwa people living in North Dakota between the winter of 1912 and the spring of 1924. Each chapter is identified by year and by season, and the Ojibwa name of each season, or sun—*qeezis*—is printed first in the characters' native tongue and then in English translation. The dates serve as markers of the plot's linear progression, and the naming of the seasons reminds readers of the cyclical nature of traditional Ojibwa time. Because there are nine chapters, the speaking roles are obviously not evenly distributed, and, indeed, it is Old Nanapush who has both the first and the last words in the novel.

The third novel's chronological setting predates those of *Love Medicine* and *The Beet Queen*, and its central characters are among the older generation depicted in those books. Readers of the first two novels have been afforded glimpses of Fleur Pillager, Eli Kashpaw, Old Rushes Bear, and others, and are therefore well aware that all these characters are the survivors of earlier difficult times. In *Tracks*, her most overtly political novel, Erdrich directly portrays the historical circumstances of which these characters are survivors and thus invokes images of cultural catastrophe. Whereas Gerry Nanapush and *Love Medicine*'s traditional grandmothers are dedicated to protecting the core of culture that remains to them, characters in *Tracks* have lived closer to that core and must survive the experience of a people's "enormous loss" (Erdrich, "Where," 23).

Although Erdrich did not publish *Tracks* until 1988, she worked on versions of its manuscript for many years. In fact, she made the move from mainly writing poetry to writing fiction with the draft of *Tracks* she worked on during her years as a graduate student in the Johns Hopkins Writing Program. Ten years later, she returned to the manuscript, and, as she explains to Michael Schumacher, "compressed every bit of material I found worthwhile in those 300 pages of book into one story" (Schumacher 177). The resulting story was first published in *Esquire* with the title "Fleur," and later it became the second chapter of *Tracks* ("*Miskomini-qeezis*," "Raspberry Sun"). Whereas *Love Medicine* had been constructed from a collection of stories, "nothing," as Erdrich notes, in *Tracks* had "*started out* as a short story" (Schumacher 176).

Erdrich is a writer who conscientiously practices revision, and the first finished version of *Tracks* presented her with a complicated set of challenges. As she says, the manuscript was "tangled, problematic for me, difficult." She ended up making use of bits and pieces of it in various of her other works and thus fondly describes that early version as "the old junked car in the yard front, continually raided for parts" (Chavkin and Chavkin 239). In her valuable discussion of the ways *Tracks* engages "political and historical issues," Nancy J. Peterson observes that:

> writing such a novel did not come easily to Erdrich: she put
> the original . . . manuscript for *Tracks* aside for ten years, and

only after she had worked backward in time from *Love Med-icine* to *The Beet Queen* did she take it up again and begin to link it to her already completed novels about contemporary generations of Chippewa and immigrant settlers in North Da-kota. (Peterson 982)

If writing about contemporary survivors prepared Erdrich to focus on the historical circumstances that shaped their forebears' lives, she none-theless still faced the challenging task of finding a way to tell their story in a work of fiction. Understanding that "there's no way to speak about Indian history without it being a political statement. You can't describe a people's suffering without implying that somebody's at fault," Erdrich was interested in writing a historical narrative, but, as she put it, not a "polemical" (Schumacher 174) book. Peterson describes the difficulties inherent in Erdrich's desire to write a historical saga in the postmodern age, and, in her own way, so does Pauline early in the novel. Thinking about "old men" who inevitably tell themselves a story of what has happened, she reflects that "it comes up different every time, and has no ending, no beginning. They get the middle wrong too" (31). In *Tracks*, history is shown to be subjective; any version of a story necessarily re-flects the perspective of the storyteller.

In "History, Postmodernism, and Louise Erdrich's *Tracks*," Peterson describes how Erdrich finds means to write a novel that "enables readers to think through the issues and the stakes involved in the crisis of history surrounding Native Americans" (Peterson 984) by deciding to structure her narrative around the voices of its two speakers. Characters who are unsympathetic and often hostile to one another, Nanapush and Pauline respond in very different ways to the circumstances of their times, and, indeed, come to dedicate themselves to sharply contrasting political po-sitions. Peterson argues that Erdrich uses both of their perspectives to offer her readers an appropriately " 'indigenous' account" (Peterson 989) of events portrayed in *Tracks*.

HISTORICAL BACKGROUND

"Land," Old Nanapush tells Lulu, "is the only thing that lasts life to life" (33). *Tracks* is essentially a story about land—and the lives of the people connected to it—and thus earth is the element Erdrich associates with this novel. Although Nanapush makes frequent reference to a "storm of government papers" (1), he does not specifically name the various treaties or congressional acts that serve to dispossess certain of the novel's characters of their land—as, indeed, living Native American people were once dispossessed of theirs. It is therefore useful for readers to recognize that *Tracks* is set during the historical period when the Dawes Allotment Act of 1887 allowed tracts of arable land that had been communal reservation property to be allotted to individual tribal members. In *Tracks*, for instance, Margaret (Rushes Bear) Kashpaw has been granted an allotment on what was once Ojibwa reservation land, but all of her older children have had to move to Montana, the site of their allotments.

The Dawes Allotment Act was specifically designed to encourage Native Americans to abandon their traditional hunting and gathering practices in favor of finding ways to use their land for profitable enterprises. The United States government assumed that those Natives who began to use their land for farming, logging, or other money-making ventures would necessarily adopt the values of the dominant capitalist culture and would thus rapidly become assimilated into that social order. The connection between ownership of land and the loss of traditional ways of life is of crucial interest in *Tracks*, for the characters who resist assimilation, who in fact refuse complicity in the exploitation of their land, are left with insufficient means to pay the fees or taxes they are told that they owe.

The Dawes Act originally provided that Native owners of allotted land needed to pay no property taxes during an initial twenty-five-year trust period. *Tracks*'s opening scene, set in 1912, marks the end of that period of grace (and, in any case, subsequent congressional acts shortened the trust period for many Native people). As Nanapush reveals in the novel's opening chapter, the Ojibwa in particular had suffered harsh winters and devastating onslaughts of disease around the time when their land taxes were coming due. In their desperation, some landowners simply sold their allotments, often at prices well below their value. Others borrowed against their allotments to secure necessary provisions and then lost their land when they could not repay their loans. In *Tracks*, Fleur Pillager loses her allotments of valuable timber land when she cannot pay her taxes.

While *Tracks* never directly cites the Dawes Allotment Act, its plot graphically depicts that act's many consequences. Not only do characters like Fleur and Nanapush lose their family land, they are confronted with the spectacle of the imminent loss of their people's traditional values— values that are associated with the Ojibwas' connections to the land. Community life is also disrupted, especially when characters like the

Morrisseys take advantage of the act and profit "from acquiring allotments that many Old Chippewa" (63) are not able to keep. Thus members of the tribe are divided one against another, and even families and friends suffer divided loyalties: When the Kashpaws learn that the money they and Fleur and Nanapush have worked together to raise is not enough to cover all their taxes, Margaret and Nector use the entire sum to pay the fees on their own land. In the end, the loss of her land and the life it represents cause Fleur Pillager to give up her beloved daughter.

PLOT

In the first chapter of *Tracks* Old Nanapush immediately introduces readers to one of the novel's central characters when he describes how he rescued Fleur, "the last Pillager," from disease and starvation in the winter of 1912. Addressing his narrative to Lulu, Fleur's only child, Nanapush promises to speak of the "passing of times" that his listener "will never know." Readers recognize that Nanapush is intent on helping the daughter understand the complicated story he has to tell about "the one" that Lulu "will not call mother" (2). Indeed, Nanapush believes that if Lulu is to know why she was abandoned, she must hear the full story of her mother's struggles to survive.

Nanapush, who has himself lost his wife and children to consumption, discovers Fleur surrounded by the bodies of her parents and three siblings in the Pillagers' cabin near Lake Matchimanito. The Pillagers, members of the bear clan, are known to possess strong powers, and therefore Edgar Pukwan, a member of the tribal police who has accompanied Nanapush on his mission of mercy, refuses to enter their house. Nanapush carries Fleur home with him and nurses her back to health, and Pukwan mysteriously retires to his bed and starves himself to death. With the arrival of spring, seventeen-year-old Fleur returns to live alone on the Pillager land, and when the Agent comes to ask for the fee on her allotments, he disappears into the woods and is never seen again. The Agent, as Nanapush reports the local rumors, is said to have joined those who gamble with the ghosts.

Pauline Puyat begins to tell her story in the novel's second chapter, and she too opens her account with tales about Fleur's early life. Pauline has heard rumors that Fleur, who cannot swim, twice drowned in Lake Matchimanito before she was fifteen. In both instances those who hap-

FAMILY CONNECTIONS IN *TRACKS*

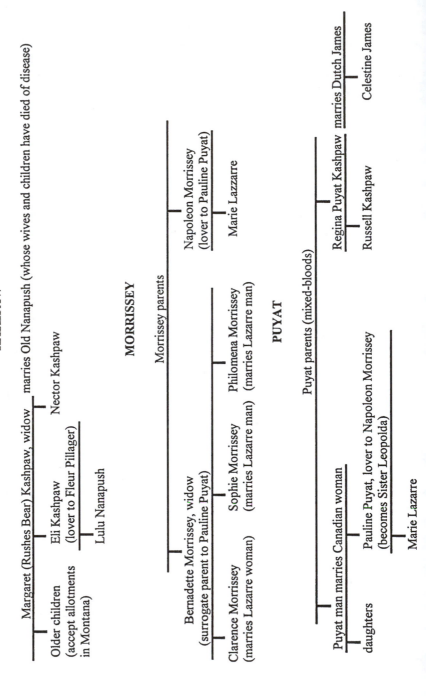

KASHPAW

Margaret (Rushes Bear) Kashpaw, widow   marries Old Nanapush (whose wives and children have died of disease)

Older children (accept allotments in Montana)

Eli Kashpaw (lover to Fleur Pillager)

Nector Kashpaw

Lulu Nanapush

MORRISSEY

Morrissey parents

Bernadette Morrissey, widow (surrogate parent to Pauline Puyat)

Sophie Morrissey (marries Lazarre man)

Philomena Morrissey (marries Lazarre man)

Napoleon Morrissey (lover to Pauline Puyat)

Clarence Morrissey (marries Lazarre woman)

Marie Lazzarre

PUYAT

Puyat parents (mixed-bloods)

Puyat man marries Canadian woman

Pauline Puyat, lover to Napoleon Morrissey (becomes Sister Leopolda)

Regina Puyat Kashpaw   marries Dutch James

daughters

Marie Lazarre

Russell Kashpaw

Celestine James

pened to find her soon thereafter died themselves (one by drowning in a bathtub), and thus many local people believe that Fleur belongs to Misshepeshu, the water monster of the lake. Although Pauline has heard stories about Fleur, it is in the summer of 1913 that she actually comes to know her, when the two young women both find jobs in Argus, where they work at Kozka's Meats, the butcher shop that is also featured in both *The Beet Queen* and *Tales of Burning Love*.

Pauline is a couple of years younger than Fleur, and she has traveled to Argus from the reservation with the hope of learning lace-making from the nuns in the convent. A mixed-blood who belongs to a clan "for which the name was lost," Pauline seeks to leave her Indian heritage behind by finding a new life in the "white town" (14). In her desire to make lace rather than to work with beads or with quills (arts she has repudiated, just as she has refused to speak the old language), Pauline clearly expresses her new cultural loyalties. As it happens, however, there is no position for her in the convent, and so Dutch James,[1] who is married to her Aunt Regina, arranges for her to sweep the floors in the butcher shop where he works and to care for Russell Kashpaw, her young cousin.

A "skinny big-nosed girl with staring eyes" (16), Pauline is well aware that she is of little interest to the people around her; because she is practically invisible to others, she readily assumes the role of observer, one who pays close attention to the activities of others. She naturally finds Fleur particularly fascinating, and her account reveals to readers the ambivalence she feels about this full-blood Ojibwa woman and her family's mysterious powers. On the one hand, Pauline admires Fleur's strength of will and purpose, but, on the other, she resents her impenetrable aloofness and is envious of her unfailing ability to command attention and respect.

Fleur, of course, has come to Argus to earn the taxes for her land. Her wages at the butcher shop are not sufficient to this end, so she begins to play at cards with Dutch, Tor, and Lily, the men who work for Pete. For weeks Fleur plays only for low stakes, winning exactly one dollar each night. Lily, with his fat dog on his lap, grows increasingly frustrated, for he cannot figure out how and why she cheats. Convinced that Fleur is unable to bluff, he waits until Fritzie and Pete are out of town and then arranges the game where he will raise the stakes at last and then defeat the impudent woman. When all the money is in the pot, and the tricksterlike Fleur has won the hand, her opponents grow surly over the insult to their manhood. Fortified by the whiskey they have stolen from Pete, all three exact their revenge by pursuing and raping Fleur.

It is Pauline, the invisible observer, who recounts these events, and she admits that she does not directly see the assault, but instead hears Fleur cry out in the old language, repeating "over and over" (26) her name and Russell's. She reports that young Russell tries to intervene when the men give chase to Fleur, and acknowledges that she too should then have tried to save her, although it is perhaps doubtful that she could have been of help. These details are important insofar as they reveal Pauline's own response to what she thinks has happened. Indeed, she is later haunted by dreams of the attack and of its aftermath, for it is she who serves as the instrument of a terrible retribution. When, on the day following the card game, a tornado descends on Argus, Pauline locks Dutch, Tor, and Lily (with his dog) in the meat locker where they have sought out shelter. Several days pass before Fritzie and Pete find the remains frozen in their locker; the only survivor is Dutch James, who must later undergo a series of disfiguring amputations.

Fleur Pillager never acknowledges being raped or even speaks about what occurred in Argus. In Chapter Three, after both young women have returned to Ojibwa land, Nanapush questions Fleur and mentions that Pauline has had stories to tell. When Fleur's response is simply, "Uncle, the Puyat lies" (38), readers can see, as Laura E. Tanner observes, that "it is, then, only in Pauline's imagination that the act of violation remains present in the novel" (Tanner 117). While many critics have read Pauline's "persecution of Fleur" as action that "personifies the historical destruction of Native American culture" (Shaddock 109), Tanner argues that not only does Pauline seek to overcome the powerlessness she experiences as a member of a racial minority, but also that which is the experience of a woman—particularly a woman victimized by violent acts of men. Tanner notes that Pauline internalizes what she imagines Fleur has suffered, and thus becomes a "surrogate" for her, a "character who exposes the consequences of a rape" (Tanner 147).

Tanner's analysis of Pauline's character and behavior adds a significant psychological dimension to a reading of her actions. While Pauline feels guilty that she did not rescue Fleur, she also suffers, in her act of imagination, the terror and humiliation that mark the experience of being raped. These mixed feelings exacerbate her earlier ambivalence toward Fleur, whose powers she increasingly regards as threatening to her own image of selfhood. Determined to exorcise her vision of herself as victim, Pauline makes claim to the power of the dominant white society to assimilate the Ojibwa people and also to the power of the male to define a woman as vulnerable. As Tanner describes it, Pauline "defines herself according to what she is not—white, Pillager, male" (Tanner 125), and in so doing comes to believe that she must match the force of her will against that of Fleur.

Nanapush describes how Eli Kashpaw and Fleur come to be lovers, despite the efforts of Eli's mother, Margaret, to keep them apart. Margaret, of course, listens to Pauline's stories and therefore does not know whether the child Fleur is carrying has been fathered by Misshepeshu, or by Dutch, Tor, or Lily, or perhaps by her son. (When Lulu is born, even Pauline comments that she has the "Kashpaws' unmistakable nose" [70]; her green eyes, however, seem to Pauline to blaze like those of the monster in the lake.) Acting as her surrogate father, Nanapush himself gives Lulu her name. Margaret, it turns out, cannot stay away from her baby granddaughter, and thus she and Nector spend most of their time with Nanapush, Eli, and Fleur. Even though she senses that she is unwelcome, Pauline visits often and observes that these families have joined together to form "a kind of clan" (70).

After leaving Argus, Pauline lives with—and works for—the Morrisseys: Bernadette, her three children, and her brother Napoleon, who has a "weakness for drink" (64). The Morrisseys are prosperous farmers, having acquired several allotments of reservation land from their unfortunate neighbors. Pauline particularly finds comfort in accompanying the widow Bernadette when she attends to the dying and the dead, and for a time these dark ministrations afford her relief from the nightmares of Argus. Pauline knows that she possesses a "scavenger's heart," and therefore takes satisfaction in making "death welcome" (69).

She once again begins to dream, however, after she has observed in Eli and Fleur the obvious signs of their passion. First she tries to warm herself "at the fire between them," but then she readily admits that "jealousy" is "such a small step to take from that" (75). Armed with a love medicine she has acquired from Fleur's cousin Moses Pillager, Pauline carefully engineers a sexual encounter between Eli and the fourteen-year-old Sophie Morrissey, Bernadette's nubile daughter. Pauline desires Eli for herself, but because she understands that she cannot attract him, she schemes to find a substitute. In arranging the scene of seduction, which she witnesses from her hiding place in the brush, Pauline makes her first attempt to overpower Fleur.

Events that follow the encounter between Eli and Sophie afford Pauline occasion to witness a "private miracle" (94). On the day following the seduction, Sophie makes her way to Fleur's cabin at Matchimanito and kneels there in the yard. Pauline, of course, perceives that Fleur has used her power to lure the hapless girl straight to her door. Sophie is seemingly paralyzed and rooted to the ground, for when Napoleon and her brother Clarence both attempt to move her, they find she cannot budge. Confused, the two agree to seek the help of the priest, and when they rouse him in the middle of the night, Clarence impulsively seizes the statue of the Blessed Virgin from the nave of the church. It is only after Clarence has positioned the statue directly in front of his sister that she is able to move again, and it is Pauline's belief that only she and Sophie have witnessed the miracle of the Virgin's tears.

For months Pauline broods on the mystery of the tears, wondering if the Virgin was moved by pity for Sophie. Finally, after she has engaged in repeated sexual encounters with Napoleon, she arrives at the understanding that it was not pity, but rather sympathy that caused the Virgin to weep. Indeed, she envisions the Immaculate Conception as an experience of brutal violation:

> In God's spiritual embrace She experienced a loss more ruthless than we can imagine. She wept, pinned full-weight to the earth, known in the brain and known in the flesh and planted like dirt. She did not want him, or was . . . frightened at the touch of His great hand upon Her mind. (95)

As Pauline begins to see in Christian tradition the source of a power to master both the spirit and the flesh, she grows ever more determined to make her claim to that power. Not one to practice Christian humility, she in fact becomes militant, increasingly ferocious, and arrogant in her espousal of her beliefs.

Bereft and disgusted by his act of betrayal, Eli turns to Nanapush to seek his suggestions about how to win Fleur back. He explains that he was "witched" (98), but Nanapush knows that Fleur will never choose to accept that excuse. Nanapush tells how Eli is at last successful with Fleur when he follows the advice that he give her cause to pity him, and then he relates the story of how the Morrisseys exact their revenge upon Eli's family. The tale of the bald women begins with Eli and Sophie, but, as Nanapush knows well, it also has to do with the politics that divide the Ojibwa people. Because the Morrisseys and Lazarres support the idea of cash settlements for land while the Pillagers and Kashpaws remain firmly opposed, there is bad blood between these factions. After Clarence

Morrissey and Boy Lazarre shave Margaret's head (her hair has never been cut before), Fleur too shaves herself bald in a gesture of loyalty to her mother-in-law.

Nanapush, Fleur, and the Kashpaws must answer the insult to Margaret, and thus, as Nanapush sees it, Clarence and Boy are three times cursed. Fleur snips locks of the culprits' hair and prepares a bad medicine. An experienced hunter and trapper, Nanapush determines that he will snare his prey, and so he and Nector devise carefully hidden traps. After Clarence has indeed stepped into his noose, Nanapush enjoys the satisfaction of watching his helpless foe balance precariously on the edge of the pit below. Taking pity, he decides not to strangle his victim, but he is pleased when the Morrissey emerges from his ordeal marked by the twisted mouth, a permanent reminder that it was he who caused the "Pillager baldness" (123). Boy Lazarre, whom Margaret bit when she was abducted, soon dies of his infection. When all the scores are settled, the appreciative Margaret begins to see Old Nanapush in an entirely new light, and so it comes to pass that the two elders become lovers themselves.

In Chapter Six, the season of the "Wood Louse Sun," Pauline tells the stories of two different births. Her first account describes the birth of Marie, her own daughter by Napoleon. By the time she knows that she is going to have a child, Pauline has already "betrothed" (131) herself to God. She therefore attempts to induce an abortion, but Bernadette intervenes and vows that she will raise the child herself. Named for the Virgin, Marie is born on Armistice Day—and after the delivery Pauline at long last enters the same convent where she had once aspired to learn lace-making from the nuns she now seeks to join.

Pauline begins her new life by erasing the old: She tells of a vision in which the Lord reveals that she was never a Puyat but is indeed "wholly white," an orphan whose parents both died in a state of grace. In further revelations she learns that she must forget Marie completely and dedicate herself to searching out and destroying the "devil in the land" (137). It is her search for the devil that draws her time and again to the cabin near Matchimanito, for she sees Fleur as the "hinge" (139) between the Ojibwa people and the monster in the lake. Convinced that the power of the old spirits, the Manitous, is steadily weakening among people she now thinks of as "them" instead of "us" (138), she vows that she, not Fleur, will open a door for the Ojibwa.

It is during one of her many visits to Matchimanito that Pauline witnesses the premature birth of Fleur's second child. When she first approaches the door, Pauline's offensive odor immediately drives Nanapush away (refusing to bathe is one of the means by which the ambitious novice mortifies her flesh). Left alone with Pauline, Fleur and Lulu kindly bathe her and then scrub clean her filthy clothes. It is after these exertions that Fleur begins to hemorrhage, and therefore requests her visitor's assistance. Although Pauline, by her own testimony, has calmly ministered to the sick on many previous occasions, she proves to be unable to help Fleur. Clumsy and inept, she drops the boiling water and cannot find the special herbs that are required to stop the bleeding. When Lulu is dispatched to fetch Margaret, Pauline notices that the child is wearing the thin shoes that Eli has given her, but she says nothing as Lulu heads off into the snow.

While Pauline offers up her prayers, Fleur tries desperately to save the infant who has been born "too soon" (155). Certain that Fleur and the baby are both dying, Pauline is surprised when Fleur suddenly gets up and walks barefoot out the door. Pauline follows, just as she had in Argus, and finds herself on an unfamiliar road. The road, filled with "other Indians" (159), leads westward, past large herds of buffalo, to the land of the dead. Fleur has come there to gamble with the ghosts for the life of her child, and those with whom she plays are Dutch, Tor, and Lily, with his dog on his lap. Lily understands, now, that his opponent can bluff, and he wins the first round and claims the newborn child. Fleur is only jolted from her stupor when Lily proposes yet another round, and this time his stake is a lock of Lulu's hair and one of the shoes she wore in the snow. Although Lily has good cards, it is the determined mother, with the queens in her hand, who wins the second round.

In Chapter Seven Nanapush describes how he warms Lulu's feet in the hollows under his arms, lulls her from her pain with his ceaseless songs and stories, and refuses to permit the white doctor to perform amputations. After Lulu has recovered, the families once again gather together in Fleur's cabin, for they must find ways to survive the harsh winter and also to raise the land taxes that will come due in the spring. Desperate to save her family and her land, Fleur tries to call upon the powers bequeathed to the Pillagers, but her failure to rescue her youngest child has left her greatly weakened. Thus, the families survive the bad winter of 1918 only by accepting their share of the government's rations. There is still a chance, however, that they can save the Pillager and Kashpaw allotments by selling cranberry bark, quill boxes, fish powder, and animal pelts. When the families have finally managed to scrape together the exact amount they need, Nector carries the sum to the Agent's office.

In the last chapter narrated by Pauline, readers learn of her final effort to destroy Misshepeshu before taking her vows. After one last visit to Matchimanito, she knows that she will have no further interest in the Ojibwa, the "lost tribe of Israel" (196). Using an old and leaky boat, she makes her way to the middle of the lake and then calls out to Nanapush, who is fishing on the shore. When the spring winds come up and chunks of ice threaten to capsize her boat, a large crowd gathers near the lake. Bernadette is present, and also the young child named Marie. Both the priest and Nanapush attempt a rescue with a flimsy canoe, but neither is successful, and thus, when night falls, Pauline is left on the lake to wait for her "tempter" (200).

After many hours Pauline's boat is drawn to the shore, and by then she is ready, "strong as a young man" (201). She grapples with the figure she finds on the beach and at last succeeds in strangling her foe with the rosary she carries. When the early light of dawn reveals that the enemy with whom she struggled fiercely was in truth Napoleon, she feels no "guilt" or "fault," for she realizes that she could never have known what form the "devil would assume" (203). After she hides the body in the brush, she returns to the convent to begin her new life as Sister Leopolda.

In the last chapter of *Tracks* Nanapush tells Lulu how the families that had once joined together as "a kind of clan" have come to be separated. Hoping that Lulu will at last forgive her mother and reconsider her decision to marry a Morrissey, Nanapush describes how he and Fleur finally learn that the tax money was not enough to cover the Pillager land (because the payment was late, the Kashpaws had to pay fines on their fees). When she first hears of the betrayal, Fleur gathers stones into her pockets and walks into the lake. Eli drags her from the water and for a time she lies "drowned and gray"[2] (212) beside Matchimanito. Then the earth begins to tremble and Nanapush senses the presence of what lives in the water. Fleur fixes Eli with the power of her gaze and pronounces her curse upon his younger brother, and when she then smiles her wolfish Pillager grin, Eli is quickly driven away.

The surveyors who are measuring what was once Fleur's timber land eventually find Napoleon's body, and Fleur is blamed for his death. Because Lulu earlier found the corpse and built a secret playhouse around it, she assumes, when she is sent away to school, that she is being punished "for playing near a dead man in the woods" (218). This is not the case, however, for Fleur is greatly worried about her daughter's safety and believes that she must wait until Lulu is far away before she draws upon her powers to enact her revenge. Her day of reckoning arrives when the loggers reach the stand of oaks that surrounds the Pillager cabin. The morning is bright, clear, and still when the loggers gather in the clearing, but Nanapush, who has come to visit Fleur, senses the coming of a change in the weather. As the wind begins to build, he warns the men to move away, but the warning is not heeded, and Fleur looks on in amusement as the forest around her crashes to the ground.

CHARACTERS

Namesake of the Ojibwa trickster Nanabozho, Old Nanapush is, as Pauline observes, the "smooth-tongued artificer" (196) who practices his tricks of survival through the art of telling stories. The last surviving member of his family, he indeed made himself well during the days of the sickness by out-talking death (who finally became "discouraged" and then "traveled on" [46]). Through the power of his stories Nanapush also soothes and heals his granddaughter Lulu, the frostbitten child—just as it is his expressed desire, through his narratives in *Tracks*, to soothe and heal the young woman who is listening to his tales. For readers of the novel, who are listeners as well, Nanapush's voice "tracks" the events of a particular historical period through his use of an oral, storytelling tradition.

The embodiment of a storytelling voice, Nanapush distrusts the "chicken-scratch" (225) of government papers not out of ignorance (for with his early Jesuit training he is fluent in reading, writing, and speaking English), but because his long experience has shown him that the wind itself "is steadier" than the history of "government promises" (33) spelled out in endless treaties. In fact, understanding that his name loses some of its power whenever it is "written and stored in a government file" (32), it is his common practice to withhold his signature. Nevertheless, the role of traditional trickster requires that he use his knowledge and cunning to adapt to his circumstances, and he does exactly that when, in the last pages of the novel, he tells of becoming a tribal bureaucrat so that he can make his own use of government papers to bring Lulu home again.

Nanapush is one of the several surrogate parents within Erdrich's depictions of Native kinship systems. He serves as mentor to Eli, passing along to him a hunter's knowledge of the woods and also counseling him on matters of the heart. For both Fleur and then her daughter Lulu he is the spiritual father who provides care and nurture, a family connection, and continuing support. His support of the Pillager women proves later to serve as a model for Eli, who, as readers learn in *Love Medicine*, eventually becomes June Morrissey's guardian and spiritual father.

Much to Pauline's discomfort, the tricksterlike Nanapush is a joker and a tease, a character who fully gives expression to what Erdrich has on more than one occasion described as Native American people's "survival humor—the humor that enables you to live with what you have to live with" (Moyers 144). While critics have debated and variously described Pauline's function in the novel,[3] there is no doubt that this earnestly obsessive and humorless young woman is a character who is portrayed as lacking an ability to ever draw upon laughter's saving grace. In this respect Pauline/Sister Leopolda is a rarity among the many characters who people Erdrich's books, and readers might consider that this figure's fanaticism is perhaps somehow symptomatic of her humorless perspective.

Pauline's story is that of a young woman who is determined to re-fashion her identity and thereby empower herself. Ironically, however, as she unfolds her account, she gradually reveals the ways in which she makes herself a victim of her own fears as well as her desires. An outsider, a figure at the margins of other people's lives, Pauline fears the lonely life of the invisible observer. Yet she counters that fear by becoming a busybody, an unwanted presence whose active interference in people's lives works more and more to estrange her from the community around her. Later, to counter her fear of being seen by others as ordinary, she engages in the grotesque acts of masochism that leave her severely disfigured. In these instances she also makes herself the victim of her willful pride and monstrous ambitions, for her many acts of self-mutilation clearly do not serve her as expressions of contrition or gestures of humility, as she often claims, but are rather occasions for her to prove to herself that she has power to wield.

While Pauline appropriates her power from the paternalistic traditions of the dominant society and its religion, Fleur is depicted as possessing the "raw power" (7) emblematic of her culture's traditional animism. Her name itself makes reference to the vegetable world around her, and she possesses knowledge of the medicinal properties of the plants and herbs she collects. She knows the ways of animals and is said to draw upon the power of the bear when she goes out to hunt. The woods and the land contain the powerful spirits of her ancestors, and the Manitou in the lake is reported to lend her his power. Even the smooth stones from Matchimanito, the spirit rocks that she always carries with her, are for her a source of strength. Fleur is the medicine woman whose power is derived from her connection to the earth and the forces of nature.

Like June Kashpaw and Adelaide Adare, Fleur does not herself tell the story of her separation from her child, but Nanapush assures Lulu that in sending her off to school during times of dangerous uncertainty, "she saved you from worse" (210). Fleur's way of life is centered in her connection to the land, and when the land is gone, the purpose of her life is changed. After the trees have fallen, Fleur gathers her lake stones, her roots and herbs, and her family's grave markers into a cart that she can pull herself and then sets forth on her solitary way with Nanapush's blessing. Readers of *The Beet Queen* encounter Fleur and her cart when she stops to heal Karl Adare, and in *Love Medicine* and *The Bingo Palace* readers are told that every time she loses the Pillager land, she manages to once again reclaim it.

THEMES

In both its characters and themes *Tracks* is closely linked to *Love Medicine*, the first novel Erdrich published. In fact, in *Love Medicine*'s enlarged edition, Erdrich adds accounts of Rushes Bear, Lulu, and Moses Pillager that serve to strengthen the connections between the two novels *Love Medicine*'s theme of forgiveness, expressed in Lipsha's decision to embrace the memory of the mother who deserted him, is reiterated in Nanapush's efforts to persuade Lulu to forgive her mother Fleur. The theme of homecoming, prominent in *Love Medicine*'s opening and closing chapters, also serves to bring closure to *Tracks*, for on the last page of the book Nanapush describes Lulu's joyful return to her home on the reservation in a scene that echoes Lipsha's crossing of the water.

Like others of Erdrich's novels, *Tracks* is also interested in depicting its characters' survival. Although Nanapush often speaks in elegaic tones of the losses his people suffer, he is enduring and adaptable, ready in his old age to serve as mentor to the young and ready even to marry again. His great gift, the art of storytelling, is itself the legacy that the survivor bequeathes to all those who come later. Although both Fleur and Pauline suffer personal misfortunes in choices they make, they too, albeit in their quite different ways, find means to survive. In the end, it is through the bloodlines of these two powerful women that the preservation of cultural traditions is later assured, for their daughters, Lulu and Marie, are the matriarchal figures who in *Love Medicine* become guardians of their culture. Thus Pauline's words are prophetic when she reflects that "power travels in the bloodlines" (31), and Nanapush's observation is indeed appropriate when he declares Fleur to be "the funnel of our history" (178).

Questions about power are also important in *Tracks*, a novel that portrays a time when the power of government papers threatens a Native people's traditional way of life. In Nanapush's view, to sign the government's documents is to acquiesce to their power and thereby to diminish the power of the tradition represented in an individual's name. Finally, of course, the power of the papers proves to be overwhelming, and Nanapush must at last resort to the use of that power to bring Lulu home. Although he is successful in this endeavor, he nonetheless rues the day when the Ojibwa were forced to become a people "of file cabinets and triplicates . . . a tribe of pressed trees" (225).

Both of the narrators in *Tracks* find occasion to meditate on the nature of power, for both have a special interest in Fleur and the power she possesses. Like that of her cousin Moses, Fleur's shamanistic power "travels in the bloodlines" of the Pillager family, and among the Ojibwa people she is known to be a powerful medicine woman. However, as Kristan Sarvé-Gorham points out, "her powers are limited to the traditional Anishinabe world. She can save neither her land nor her people from the encroachment of Anglo landgrabbers and their commercial values." As traditional medicine woman, "she represents the old Indian world of animism, community, and affinity with nature" (Sarvé-Gorham 177), and that world, as Nanapush knows and admits, is rapidly being overpowered by the weight of government papers.

"Power dies" (177), Nanapush observes, and this is a lesson that Lipsha Morrissey also learns when he loses his touch. After Fleur's failure to defeat the gambling ghosts with whom she plays for her infant's life, she is both weakened and disheartened, and the world suddenly seems to her to be a "dangerous" (186) place for Lulu; she therefore begins to draw upon her power not as her art or discipline, but as a desperate measure. As Nanapush describes it, she loses her power when she comes to rely upon it, when her "obstinate pride" (178) leads her to believe that she owns her "own strength" (177). When her land and family are lost and she no longer knows the desperate need to rely upon the possession of power, it is restored to her.

Pauline carefully watches Fleur, making herself a student of the use of power because she desires to acquire its possession. She first feels empowerment when she helps a young girl suffering from the lung sickness find relief in death. The secret knowledge that she has the ability to make "death welcome" whets an appetite for power that she soon attempts to satisfy by bewitching Eli and Sophie. In exercising power on this occasion, Pauline draws upon Ojibwa tradition by making use of a love medicine. Later, when she determines that she will find the source of her own strength in Christian tradition, she seeks to overcome the power of Ojibwa tradition by battling Misshepeshu, its representative and Fleur's helper spirit. Interestingly, when the battle is over, she does not assume that in killing Napoleon she also destroyed the Manitou, for she claims merely to have "tamed" it and then "chained" (204) it to the bottom of Matchimanito.

ALTERNATIVE PERSPECTIVE: MULTICULTURAL CRITICISM

During the historical period depicted in *Tracks*, the United States government supported policies that encouraged the assimilation of all ethnic groups within its borders into the dominant society. In recent decades, however, this "melting pot" conception of national identity has been replaced with an understanding that American society is indeed pluralistic, composed of citizens with a rich variety of cultural backgrounds. The acceptance of pluralism has brought with it newfound appreciation of the nation's minority cultures and has led to the development of multicultural studies, a branch of inquiry that supports understanding and exploration of minority groups' cultural traditions. Theorists and critics interested in a multicultural approach to literature focus on the work produced by minority and postcolonial writers—those writers who, like Louise Erdrich, give voice to the experiences of peoples whose stories were rarely heard during the era of Western empire-building.

In literary studies, the introduction of a multicultural perspective has had the effect of opening the canon to the contributions of writers whose work represents the cultural traditions of minority peoples. Students in the United States, for example, are now frequently assigned texts written by African American, Asian American, Hispanic American, and Native American writers. The general public, too, has welcomed the voices of minority writers, many of whose works have appeared on lists of best-sellers. While the recent work of minority writers within the United States has unquestionably enriched the tradition of American literature, multiculturalism is also a global interest, and thus American minority writers have joined postcolonial writers from Africa, Asia, India, Latin America, and many other places in attracting the attention of an international reading audience. Louise Erdrich's novels, for example, have been translated into several different languages, and the work of an African American writer, Toni Morrison, has been recognized with the Nobel Prize for Literature, the world's most prestigious literary honor.

Set during a time when a colonizing power attempts to use its jurisdiction and economic strength to eradicate cultural diversity, *Tracks* portrays both the material suffering and the painful questioning of identity that are the tragic experiences of those who are colonized. In this respect the book is itself a postcolonial novel, a work that tells another version of the familiar story of America's "progress" and westward expansion. Insofar as *Tracks* also affords its readers insight into its Native characters' way of life and demonstrates how people confronted by pressures to assimilate are nonetheless able to ensure the survival of their cultural identity, it addresses multiculturalism's interest in the perspectives and experiences of people who are minority members of a diverse national population.

Advocates of multiculturalism advance three strong arguments in support of their perspective, and *Tracks* speaks to each of these concerns. The first argument, which offers a critique of the monocultural aims of the outmoded theory of the "melting pot," points out that any definition of American society that envisions its citizenry as sharing one language, one cultural tradition, or one central ideology presents far too limited a description of a society that has in fact been shaped by a continuing history of people's immigrations. In other words, a monoculturalist position by no means realistically accounts for the experiences of large numbers of American citizens, certainly including the indigenous population that Erdrich depicts. Like Julia Alvarez, Maxine Hong Kingston, Toni Morrison, and many other contemporary writers, Erdrich reminds readers that Americans are not a homogeneous people; in fact, as the kinship system in *Tracks* suggests, Americans might well think of themselves as an extended family of many different peoples who have joined together to form "a kind of clan."

Erdrich dramatizes multiculturalism's second important argument in her characterization of Pauline, the figure who is dissatisfied with her station in life. Pauline desires to reject her identity as a woman and

Native American because she perceives that the colonizing culture regards these social categories as inferior in status and power. As multiculturalists suggest, this kind of dissatisfaction with identity can be ameliorated when a society values the position of women and recognizes and respects the cultural traditions of its ethnic minorities. Pauline, however, who has learned to see "through the eyes of the world outside" (14) her own cultural tradition, internalizes that outside world's perception of her status and therefore comes to believe that she "must dissolve" (141) her identity to acquire the power she longs to possess.

Multiculturalism's third argument rests upon its political aims of supporting and promoting cooperation among ethnic groups through their mutual understanding of one another's cultural identities. In "Poetry," Marianne Moore wisely observes that "the same thing may be said for all of us"—we cannot respect, admire, or even always see that which is not understood. In the absence of understanding, it is not uncommon for people to associate members of other ethnic groups with stereotypical images that are vague, misleading, or unfair. Multiculturalists' goal of combating the use of stereotypes by encouraging people to learn more about each other's values and beliefs seems especially important today, when the world is increasingly becoming a global community. While efforts to enhance multicultural education can lead to greater acceptance of people's differences, it is also true that there is much of value to be gained from an understanding of other people's perspectives. The views of a minority culture, for example, can provide members of a dominant tradition an angle of vision that makes possible social critique.

In "Reading between Worlds: Narrativity in the Fiction of Louise Erdrich," Catherine Rainwater illustrates how the writer juxtaposes in her novels the conflicting cultural codes of Euro-American and Ojibwa tradition. As "a citizen of both nations" (Moyers 144), Erdrich calls upon her own multicultural experience to shape for her readers a textual experience that places them, Rainwater asserts, between these two worlds. From such a position readers are invited to consider the differences in perspective that underlie the religious beliefs, the conceptions of time, the definitions of family, and the constructions of identity that are embedded within these two cultural traditions. Viewing two societies from a place between them, readers find an angle of vision that affords a new perception of each culture in relation to the other.

NOTES

1. Dutch is the father of *The Beet Queen*'s Celestine James and the step-father of Celestine's half-brother Russell Kashpaw (Argus's most-decorated war hero).

2. As Nanapush observes, this is Fleur's third drowning in the lake. Although a few critics have read Fleur's walk into the water as an act of despair, most agree that the medicine woman enters the lake to reaffirm her connection to Misshepeshu, the Manitou who lends her his strength.

3. The most common reading describes Pauline as representing the plight of colonized people who come to internalize the perspectives of those who have oppressed them. Daniel Cornell argues that Pauline asserts herself as a means of resisting the disempowering gender role assigned to her by Nanapush and others. Laura E. Tanner focuses upon Pauline's terrible fear of violation (a result of Fleur's rape) and suggests that her discomfort with her own body reflects her inability to come to terms with her identity as a mixed-blood woman. Kristan Sarvé-Gorham sees Pauline as Fleur's mythic twin and describes the competition that exists between the two powerful medicine women.

6

The Bingo Palace
(1994)

As Old Nanapush remarks, his stories are "all attached," and once he begins to relate them, "there is no end to telling because they're hooked from one side to the other, mouth to tail" (*Tracks* 46). Readers of *The Bingo Palace*, the fourth of Erdrich's North Dakota novels, find that her stories are hooked "mouth to tail" as well, for there is yet more to be told of characters who earlier appeared in *Love Medicine* and *Tracks*. Set once again mainly on the reservation, the action of *The Bingo Palace* takes place later than that of *Love Medicine* or *The Beet Queen*; however, unlike the plots of the earlier novels, this plot unfolds within the passage of a single year.

While many of its characters are familiar to readers of the earlier books, *The Bingo Palace* nonetheless presents innovations in the mode of its telling. As noted previously, Erdrich continues to explore the possibilities of narrative technique, and in each of her novels she draws upon different kinds of strategies. Ten of the book's twenty-seven chapters are narrated in a first-person singular voice by Lipsha Morrissey, one of the novel's central characters. Interestingly, four of the chapters, including the first and the last, are presented in a first-person plural voice that represents the collective perspective of the reservation's community. In part the voice of memory and in part that of the ever-watchful observer, the choral "we" often seems to also express the viewpoint of the reader.

The remaining chapters are third-person accounts that focus on the point of view of seven additional characters.

On the last page of *Tracks*, Nanapush describes the joyful reunion that occurs when he and Rushes Bear Kashpaw welcome Lulu home from her years of exile in the government boarding school. In *Love Medicine*, Lulu nevertheless reports that on that same occasion it is only Nanapush who greets and embraces her while Rushes Bear stands by, remote and disapproving. This is but one example of the many instances within Erdrich's fiction wherein a story is told and then retold in another version, and in *The Bingo Palace* readers indeed find further occasions to revisit the accounts of events that other novels offer. For example, the tale of June Kashpaw's desertion of the baby Lipsha is recounted once again, and this time Lipsha is told a story that is significantly different in its details from the version he chose to accept in *Love Medicine*'s closing pages. In the telling and retelling of a cycle of tales, Erdrich's work suggests that a story has no final version: As *The Bingo Palace*'s choral voice finally observes, there is always "more to be told, more than we know" (274).

There is, within the world of Erdrich's continuing saga, "more to be told" because life on the reservation has changed since the time Lipsha crossed the water in *Love Medicine*'s final scene. Just as the sugar beet transformed *The Beet Queen*'s town of Argus, the presence of the bingo palace on reservation land signals the beginnings of a time of change—a time of "something bigger, something we don't know the name of yet" (15). For the Ojibwa, this means that the conditions of their survival are also undergoing change, for with the possibility of a new economic base comes the threat of the loss of the traditional values represented in the people's connection to their land.

Gambling, of course, is itself an ancient Ojibwa tradition and might prove to be the means by which the culture ensures its own continuing survival. However, Lyman Lamartine plans to build an immense resort and casino on Fleur Pillager's land near the shores of Matchimanito. As the skunk reminds Lipsha during his vision quest, Fleur's land, this ancestral Pillager land, the land that is emblematic of the Ojibwa's traditional culture, most certainly "ain't real estate" (200). Because it is not clear whether the introduction of casinos to the reservation can improve its people's lot and because it is not known how this new economy of land might affect Ojibwa culture, *The Bingo Palace* does not attempt to resolve provocative questions that it raises. Indeed, among Erdrich's novels this book is notable in that it ends not with epiphanic closure, but with ambiguity—with "our certainty or our suspicion that there is more to be told . . . more than can be caught in the sieve of our thinking" (274).

A story about love, luck, land, and the legacies of earlier generations, *The Bingo Palace* recalls many of the interests of the first three novels, but it introduces new themes as well. For example, the time of change it depicts calls for a renewal of its characters' connections to the Ojibwa's spiritual world, and thus its plot incorporates the motif of the vision quest. In a traditional naming ceremony, Albertine Johnson, who is studying Western medicine, is given the name Four Soul, a name that is said to have belonged to a traditional Ojibwa healer. Because Zelda Kashpaw Bjornson, Lyman Lamartine, and Lipsha Morrissey are all haunted by images or memories from the past, they must open themselves to the revelations of visions that might show them ways to exorcise old ghosts. In Lipsha's case, the ghost in question takes the form of a material presence, for twice within the book he encounters June Kashpaw herself.

PLOT

The novel's choral voice opens *The Bingo Palace* with an account of Lulu Lamartine's visit to the local post office. There she appropriates the wanted poster that bears the likeness of her son Gerry Nanapush, the famous criminal, and makes a copy to send to Fargo, North Dakota, where her grandson Lipsha is wasting his time and talents. That Lulu still possesses the power of the Pillagers is made apparent to readers when the narrative voice remarks the "witch gaze" (2) that she turns upon Postmaster Twin Horse. Her association with Misshepeshu, "the great horned cat, the underwater lion" (Brehm 677), is also suggested in the imagery that presents her as basking and purring. The community knows that something is afoot with Lulu, and thus it senses in the atmosphere the "drift of chance and possibility" (3). Entitled "The Message," the introductory chapter prepares the reader for Lipsha's second return to the reservation.

Lipsha's homecoming in *Love Medicine* was charged with the promise of renewal, but readers learn that since that time he has begun to drift aimlessly about and has ended up in Fargo, where he shovels the sugar produced by North Dakota's beets; indeed, the disgusted community is disappointed with the "son of that wanted poster" (7), and although the people suspect that Fleur Pillager, now a very old woman, waits to pass her legendary powers to her great grandson, they cannot approve her choice. When Lipsha suddenly appears at the winter powwow held on the reservation, it is clear to the community that there is "no place the boy could fit" (9). As the transgressor of boundaries, however, the trickster figure is positioned at the margins of society, and if Lipsha is to inherit Fleur's shamanistic power, it is, as Victoria Brehm notes, therefore not surprising that "he appears the least likely person to do so" (Brehm 696).

In *Love Medicine* Lipsha wondered if he would ever possess the "staying power" (*LM* 234) he observed in Marie Kashpaw's love for Nector. *The Bingo Palace* puts Lipsha's question to the test, for at the powwow he falls in love with Shawnee Ray Toose, the jingle dancer who is the reservation's own Miss Little Shell. As Lipsha describes her, Shawnee Ray is the "best of our past, our present, our hope of a future" (13), and, indeed, this beautiful young woman expresses her many talents "in both traditional and new ways" (Hansen 147). Using her skill with beads, quills, leather, and fabric, Shawnee Ray draws upon Ojibwa tradition to fashion the patterns of clothing she designs herself. A prize-winning traditional dancer, she plans to use her prize money to further pursue her study of art, and then, she hopes, she will eventually be ready to open her own boutique.

"Love is a stony road" (*LM* 242) *Love Medicine*'s young and inexperienced Lipsha once wisely observed, and *The Bingo Palace* proves his words to be prophetic. Indeed, Lipsha finds the path of love filled with obstacles. An unmarried mother, Shawnee Ray is more or less engaged to marry Lyman Lamartine, the father of her child and the brother of Lipsha's father. Devoted to her young son Redford, she respects Lyman's claims as parent and understands that the reservation's most successful businessman can offer a secure future to her and her child. Nevertheless, she reluctantly finds herself drawn to Lipsha, the undependable medicine boy whose future is uncertain. Thus Lipsha is entangled in the sort of love triangle he has read about in the drama of the "old-time Greeks" (17). In those Greek plays, as Lipsha knows, either he or Lyman would probably have to die, but luckily for them both, these kinds of twists of plot are cause for Indians to laugh. The rivalry also provides readers occasion to laugh, for when Lipsha and his uncle Lyman finally come to blows, their brawl takes the hilarious form of a food-fight in the Dairy Queen.

Lipsha's pursuit of Shawnee Ray is further complicated by the machinations of his Aunt Zelda, the community's resident do-gooder. When

Shawnee Ray decided that she would keep her baby, it was Zelda who stepped forward to provide a home for the young woman and her child. Zelda's generosity is accompanied by her proprietary interest in her beneficiary's future, and she is firm in her belief that Shawnee Ray's best interests lie with Lyman. She therefore schemes to encourage these two to set a firm date for the wedding that they have been repeatedly postponing. Like the plots of Erdrich's other novels, this one presents many interwoven threads, and thus readers perceive that when Zelda supports the prosperous Lyman's suit over that of the love-besotted Lipsha, she is in fact reaffirming a choice she made herself many years before.

In a story that she tells to Lipsha, readers learn that as a young woman Zelda was courted by Xavier Albert Toose, a man who seemed destined to follow his people's traditions and to live out his life in an "old-time cabin" (47). Although Zelda and Xavier were smitten with one another, Zelda stubbornly refused her young suitor's marriage proposals because she wanted to wait for a white man who would offer her a two-storied house and a life in the city. Zelda's tale is one of unrealized possibilities, for she in fact never became a "two-story woman" (47), and she chose to deny herself the love of a man who proved his devotion one Saint Lucy's Night. Following the old custom, Xavier proposed marriage four times to Zelda. Her refusals in the spring, summer, and autumn meant that his winter proposal would be the last one. On the longest night of the year, Xavier waited in the snow outside her bedroom window for Zelda's final response. The hand that he had placed over his heart froze during his long night of vigil, and that is how he came to lose the fingers of that hand.

Zelda tells her story to Lipsha after he has loosened her tongue with the gin slipped into her tonic water. Once she begins to speak of the past there is no stopping Zelda, and so it happens that she eventually turns her storytelling to her recollections of her listener's own early history. In *Love Medicine* Lipsha had at first not wanted to know his mother's identity because he had heard rumors that she had put him in a gunnysack and thrown him in the marsh. Lulu, however, assured him that those rumors were merely a joke when she finally told him the unhappy story of June and her lover Gerry. Zelda's account, though, confirms the truth of the rumors, for she reveals to Lipsha that she was the one who dragged the gunnysack from the slough. What has always puzzled Zelda, as she further reveals, is how it occurred that Lipsha, who was a long time in the water, was indeed able to escape the fate of being drowned.

Zelda's story presents Lipsha with yet another problem to confront, for although he would like to believe that her account has been "embroidered," has been "beadworked . . . with a colorful stitch," his dreams carry him from the "firm ground" (52) of his earlier knowledge to a place of murky waters. When the frightening dreams awaken him in the middle of the night, he returns to the bar, and there, reflected in the mirror, he sees his mother June. Startled and afraid, Lipsha nonetheless recognizes that "if I see a ghost, possibilities will open" (54). He therefore speaks with June and discovers that she has come to reclaim her legacy, the car that her son King had bought with her insurance money. In return for the car June offers her son a new legacy, a packet of bingo tickets. After the ghost has vanished, Lipsha rushes outside and looks up to the frozen stars and the "ancient light glitter" (55) of aurora borealis. When a single star suddenly shoots across the sky, he is filled with a strong conviction that his luck is finally changing.

"Luck" appears in the titles of nine of the novel's chapters, and like *The Beet Queen*'s "Night" chapters, this series of chapters in *The Bingo Palace* affords readers glimpses of its characters' solitary experiences. "June's Luck" follows the chapter recounting her appearance as a ghost, and there readers find an important clue to the mystery of her treatment of Lipsha. The chapter is a flashback, one that depicts June's life before her mother died, and in it readers are told that one night when Lucille Lazarre lay in a drunken stupor, her surly boyfriend raped her young daughter. Bound with ropes, June could not escape, so she tried to make herself smaller and smaller until she felt herself becoming a "flung star moving, speeding through the blackness" (60). Just before she passed out, June promised herself that no one would ever hold her again. Thus, in "June's Luck," readers gain new understanding of the woman described by the chorus as "much loved and very troubled" (5).

Just as he had in *Love Medicine*, Lipsha decides to embark upon a quest: as he sees it, his ultimate goal is to win the love of Shawnee Ray, but he is convinced that to do that he must prove himself to be successful. He therefore tries his luck at bingo, hoping to win the fancy van that Lyman offers as a prize. When his desire for the van becomes an obsession, he lands upon a plan to raise more money for bingo tickets; he will, he decides, charge a fee whenever he is summoned to use the power of his healing touch. The touch, though, is like Fleur's land and not to be sold, and therefore once again Lipsha loses his touch. In the end, June's tickets are in fact the source of his luck, and with them he wins the van and extra money as well.

The Bingo Palace is interested in money, luck, and the measure of what it is that cannot be sold. Although Lipsha tries to sell his touch, he refuses to sell his Grandfather Nector's legacy, the pipe that Marie passes on to him. It is Lyman, Nector's son, who wants to buy his father's pipe from the nephew who now owns it, but Shawnee Ray is the only price Lipsha will consider, and she, too, is not to be sold. In "Lipsha's Luck," the new owner of the pipe watches in trepidation as the "first non-Indian" to ever handle it allows its eagle feather to drag across the floor. What Lipsha fears is that after this unwitting desecration, the "sky would crash to earth" (35).

Whereas the dominant imagery in Erdrich's earlier novels invokes the elements of water, air, and earth, *The Bingo Palace*'s central images are associated with fire: the fiery shooting star that serves as an emblem of June, the endless matches that Xavier lights to signal his burning love on Saint Lucy's Night, and the pipe that represents the relation between heaven and earth. Indeed, by tradition it connects the earth with the heavens, for, as Zelda remembers near the end of her vision, the pipe is "the fire between that burn[s] in everything alive" (245). The pipe belongs between the sky and the earth below, and that is why Lipsha wonders, on the occasion when its feathers are allowed to touch the ground, if a crashing of the heavens will suddenly extinguish life's fire.

Although Lipsha will not sell the pipe, he lends it to Lyman, who carries it with him when he travels to Reno, Nevada, to attend the Indian Gaming Conference. In "Lyman's Luck," readers see another side of the smooth and polished businessman who plans to make big money on other people's hopes of beating the odds. In Reno, Lyman is himself seduced by the possibilities of the blackjack table, and before he must finally admit that his own luck will not hold against the odds, he loses the money advanced to him by the Bureau of Indian Affairs as well as the cash he receives when he pawns Lipsha's pipe. Although Lyman's trip to Reno provides him occasion to consider questions about the gambling business from the perspective of a loser, the lesson of this solitary experience is seemingly lost on him. Back on the reservation he soon concocts a new scheme to cover his losses. He does redeem Lipsha's pipe (and has it reblessed), but readers now know that as far as Lyman is concerned, his father's pipe *is* for sale.

Lipsha and Lyman disagree about what is for sale and also about the purpose and the value of money. For Lipsha, money is the "insulation" (95) that keeps hunger and other needs away, but for Lyman its value lies not in what it keeps away but in what it gets: power, prestige, more money and more power. Lyman attempts to teach Lipsha the meaning of money and finally persuades him to place his bingo winnings in a joint bank account. Through this ploy Lyman eventually reclaims the money his bingo palace loses to June's lucky tickets, and when Lipsha learns that his "sucker's fortune" (231) has completely disappeared, he in fact feels little sense of loss, for, as he says, "everybody knows bingo money is not based on solid ground" (221).

Neither Lipsha's van nor his bingo winnings proves useful in his pursuit of Shawnee Ray, and when he passionately avows his love for her, she tells him sadly that he has "the medicine" but not "the love" (112). Lipsha therefore decides that he will procure a love medicine to enchant the woman of his dreams, and so his quest next leads him to his great grandmother, Fleur Pillager, the medicine woman known as Mindemoya (Old Lady). Fleur is not pleased to hear that Lipsha is a Morrissey, and when he wonders if the Pillagers would want to claim him back, she answers, "Why not? There's none of us left" (133). When Lipsha asks for a love medicine, Fleur ignores the request and instead begins to speak to him in a strangely rasping voice; as she does so, it appears to her listener that she has assumed the form of the bear.

"Fleur's Luck," the chapter that follows Lipsha's visit to Matchimanito, is narrated by the novel's chorus. This chapter, too, is presented as a flashback, and in it readers learn how Fleur reclaimed her land the "fourth and last time" (139) she returned to the reservation. In characteristic fashion Fleur wins her land in a game of cards, but the way in which she draws the Agent into joining the game deepens the mystery that surrounds this enigmatic figure. As the chorus describes it, Fleur appears on the reservation dressed completely in white; she wears a hat with a veil, white gloves, and glimmering high heels. She drives a sparkling white Pierce-Arrow and is accompanied by a young white boy. As the community looks on, she and Nanapush sit down to play at cards, and when the mysterious boy sits down as well, Agent Tatro can no longer resist his desire to also join the game.

Because he appreciates that Shawnee Ray is deeply concerned with traditional culture, Lipsha next decides to try to approach her through that interest. When Lyman mentions that he is planning to go to the woods on a vision quest, Lipsha agrees to accompany him. Xavier Toose instructs the young men in the building of a sweat lodge, and after the two have been purified, each goes off to await a vision. In his narrative, appropriately entitled "Getting Nowhere Fast," Lipsha describes the hunger, loneliness, and boredom he experiences during his days alone in the wild. In his mind, he rereads *Moby Dick*, Nector Kashpaw's favorite novel; he also listens to Jimi Hendrix's recordings and rewatches all the *Godfather* movies. While he is interested to discover that he is "hooked up" to his brain (and therefore does not really need his Walkman), this insight nevertheless does not seem to him to qualify as a "major vision" (198).

While Lipsha's "spiritual journey" (194) comes abruptly to an end when he wakes to find a skunk nestled in his sleeping bag, his accomplished uncle's quest proves to be an unqualified success. (Lipsha leaves the woods carrying with him an overpowering odor and the notion that the skunk might have muttered, "This ain't real estate" [200].) Lyman, however, prepares himself for his vision when he starts to dance. For the first time ever he does not dance for money, although, as always, he dances in the memory of his older brother. Since Henry's death, Lyman has tried to keep his brother's spirit alive by wearing his dancing clothes each time he performs. When his vision begins, he hears Henry's voice tell him to "put those old dance clothes to rest." Later, after he dances the story of Henry Junior's drowning in the river, his brother's voice assures him that his spirit is calm. Lyman has long been haunted by the "drowned ghost" (204) from his past, and his vision suggests that he is finally at peace with the shadow of his brother.

Smarting from his failure to receive a "proper vision" (216), Lipsha retreats to his bed. When he wakes in the middle of the night, he is visited by all the memories from his past. He recalls his youth and his childhood and the time he was a baby, and then he also remembers what he now realizes he has spent his "whole life trying to forget." He thinks of lying on the muddy bottom of the slough and he remembers the crushing weight of the water. With his new understanding, he recognizes that his mother did to him what "was done to her" (217), for it was her own hurt, he believes, that she passed on to others. He now knows, too, the answer to Zelda's question about why he did not drown: There was something present in the water that rocked and cradled him. When Lipsha envisions a figure with horns and fins and a "lion-jawed" (218) face, readers recognize that it was Misshepeshu, the spirit helper of the Pillagers, who preserved the baby's life.

Lipsha recounts his memories in a chapter called "A Little Vision," and, indeed, after he takes stock of his life, he does receive a revelation. He thinks about the skunk and hears again the nagging refrain, "This ain't real estate." He then sees a vision of Lyman's pleasure palace, dome-shaped and surrounded by a parking lot that will cover the ground where Fleur's cabin stands. He wonders if she, the "poker sharp" medicine woman, will cast her lot with Lyman in the hope that traditional culture will thereby stay alive. Finally, however, he cannot but fear that the "bingo life" might well lead the Ojibwa in the "wrong direction," for his own experience tells him that the "money life has got no substance" (221).

After Lipsha receives his "little vision," the action of *The Bingo Palace* takes a surprising turn. In "Gerry's Luck," readers find that the famous criminal once again escapes the long arm of the law. Working with tribal leaders, Lulu has used the Indian Religious Freedom Act to arrange for her son's transfer to a maximum security prison that is close to his "medicine advisors" (224). When the small plane that is transporting the prisoner goes down near Fargo in a snowstorm, Gerry Nanapush survives the crash unhurt. Bound and manacled, he nonetheless manages to make his way to Fargo, and from there he calls his son. In a reprise of the role he played in *Love Medicine*, Lipsha is once again called upon to rescue his father.

Although *The Bingo Palace*'s love story has appeared to be Lipsha's, in "Zelda's Luck" readers are returned to the tale that Zelda told about Xavier Toose, the first man she had loved in the days of her youth. Zelda, too, experiences a vision, one that occurs after she suffers a heart attack. As she prepares to die, she thinks back over the events of her life and discovers, to her dismay, that she is "sorrier for the things she had not done" (242) than she is for those she had. Suddenly she sees the face of her father Nector, bearing the expression he had worn thirty years before when she had led him away from Lulu's burning house. Realizing suddenly that she had been afraid of the flaming passion in his eyes, she understands how it happened that she denied her own passion. She knows, now, that she has always loved Xavier Toose, and when she is certain that it is not yet her time to die, she finally goes to meet her lover.

Although it appears that Lipsha does possess "staying power" in his love for Shawnee Ray, it is also increasingly apparent to readers that his passion for her is associated with his great longing for his mother. Lipsha, for example, understands that the strong emotions his beloved inspires are "mixed up with the love" (154) that Shawnee feels for her son. In fact, he admires her for watching out for her boy by keeping her distance from a bad risk like himself. When he envisions the young woman rocking her child, he knows that there is no way he "can imagine June Morrissey doing that to me" (165), and so he wishes that he could somehow be Shawnee Ray's son. On the vision quest, he emerges from the "womb" (193) that is the sweat lodge with feelings of sorrow; when he is asked what is troubling him, his answer is simply, "I miss my mother" (194). As *The Bingo Palace* draws to a close, readers are therefore aware that before Lipsha's love story can finally be told, he will have to once again confront the ghost from his past. Shawnee Ray plans to go off to college, and Albertine, who sympathizes with Lipsha's feelings and hopes, nonetheless recommends that he let her go and that he wait, as she says, "until you get your own self together" (216).

Thus the young man's future is still uncertain when he goes off to meet his father. In Fargo, the rescue attempt does not proceed smoothly, and the fugitives end up stealing a car they find idling in a parking lot. As they drive away, a man frantically chases the car and then hurls himself upon its trunk. Gerry manages to shake the man loose, and it is only later, when a baby wails from the backseat, that Gerry and Lipsha understand what they have done. Gerry is desperate and will not turn back, so the men and their hostage continue heading north, driving through a snowstorm that soon becomes a blizzard. For a time they are able to follow a snowplow that clears the highway before them, but when the unexpected happens, when June's car suddenly appears, Gerry veers off the road in pursuit of a ghost who still haunts his dreams. When June stops in a field, Gerry slows down, and the car then gets lodged in a snowdrift. Lipsha wants to ask his father to remain with him, but Gerry is gone before he can speak, and he is therefore once again abandoned by his parents.

In the last chapter he narrates, "I'm a Mad Dog Biting Myself for Sympathy," Lipsha determines that the child left in his charge will be someone "who was never left behind." He therefore swaddles the baby in blankets and zips him inside his jacket. He understands, now, that he must accept his lot, and that, like the mad dog biting itself, he will only harm himself when he indulges in self-pity. He does not fear the snow, for his parents have already taught him what it means to be cold; he realizes that their absence, something he has always carried inside himself, has turned out to be nothing but a "piece of thin ice" (259). After the gasoline runs out and the car's heater stops, Lipsha slips into sleep with the baby he will not desert cradled beneath his coat.

In the novel's final chapters the chorus speaks again. Readers learn that Gerry's mother deceives and delays the federal agents who come to her door. Frustrated, the officers finally arrest Lulu for her possession of stolen government property in the form of the wanted poster they find in her home. As the people watch one of their elders being led away in chains, they know that the scene Lulu has staged will doubtless be replayed on the six o'clock news. The voice of the chorus also speaks of Fleur, who after the blizzard embarks on her final journey. Mindemoya's thoughts are of the boy who is lost in the snow, and although she is annoyed, she is determined that she will walk the road of death in Lipsha's place. Fleur is never seen again, but there are those who still hear the "chuffing" (274) sound that is the laugh of the bear, and many who believe that she "still walks" (273) the old Pillager land.

CHARACTERS

The Bingo Palace's cast of characters is large and includes several figures who play small albeit significant roles in the novel's plot. June Kashpaw is one of these characters, and in the chapter that portrays the terrors of her childhood, readers gain some insight into how she came to be, in the words of Marie, "damaged" (27), a child "you could not repair" (28). A woman "much loved," as the choral voice declares, it nevertheless appears that the love of Marie, Eli, Gerry, Albertine, and others could not assuage the sorrow or pain that left June "very troubled" while she was alive. In *The Bingo Palace* it furthermore appears that Lipsha's great love for his ghostly mother cannot soothe her restless spirit. Indeed, her appearance as a ghost in need of transportation signals that her wandering spirit has not yet come to rest, as the plot of *Love Medicine* had earlier suggested. While June's mysterious presence in the novel serves, as Elaine Tuttle Hansen points out, to reverse "the movement toward reconciliation and reunion" (Hansen 151) realized in *Love Medicine* and the other novels, Lipsha nevertheless once again does forgive his mother. In *Love Medicine* he forgave June for deserting him, and in *The Bingo Palace* he understands and forgives the mother who did to him what "was done to her."

As she also did in *Love Medicine*, Albertine Johnson plays a small but noteworthy role in *The Bingo Palace*. This character is still the watchful and perceptive observer, the person who can read and understand the characters and motives of the people around her. When she sees an image of Gerry Nanapush's face on the television screen, she immediately recognizes that the once defiant and resilient hero of the people has been reduced to the figure of a desperate and ravaged man. And it is Albertine who knows, long before her mother is forced by circumstances to admit it, that Zelda never did get over her repressed love for Xavier Toose. Albertine also realizes that Shawnee Ray feels trapped in the clutches of her mother's goodness and that this young woman, who has ambitions of her own, is not yet ready to choose between Lyman and Lipsha. Suspecting that Shawnee's choice will finally be Lipsha, Albertine wisely advises him to wait patiently until the woman that he loves is ready to accept him.

While they are at the center of *The Bingo Palace*'s tale of true love, Zelda and Xavier are two more of the novel's secondary characters. The good daughter who brought her father home after he had left her mother in *Love Medicine*, the aging Zelda is still trying to be good, to do the right thing. Until the moment of startling insight precipitated by her heart attack, she never doubts that she has the best interests of others in mind; her crisis, however, prompts her to reconsider her own habit of goodness, and that is when she realizes that she has been wrong. If Lipsha must indeed wait for Shawnee Ray, so too has her uncle waited for his beloved. A "ceremony man" (47), a man who practices the old traditions, Xavier has lived a full life following his interests, but when Zelda at last approaches him, after nearly thirty years have passed, he is still waiting and ready to welcome her.

Like *Love Medicine*'s Lulu and Marie and *The Beet Queen*'s Celestine, Shawnee Ray represents the figure of the good and loving mother—and is therefore, in Lipsha's eyes, everything that June Kashpaw was not. Shawnee accepted the responsibilities of her motherhood when she decided to keep her baby, and thus she did not follow the course of her two sisters, who are both bedeviled by their drinking problems. Although she is clearly burdened by her sense of obligation to Zelda, Lyman, and Lipsha, all of whom make their claims upon her, Shawnee Ray is nonetheless an independent young woman, one who is determined to pursue her own interests as she finds a way to make a life for herself and her child. In the last pages of the novel, in a scene that depicts her as a college student, readers discover that it is indeed Lipsha she misses. Maybe, she thinks, she will "buy two rings" (268) with the money that Lipsha has lent her.

Lyman and Lipsha, the rivals for Shawnee Ray's affection, offer readers a study in contrasts. The inheritor of Nector Kashpaw's role as tribal leader, Lyman is the consummate politician and, as Lipsha must acknowledge, the "reservation's biggest cheese" (15). An accomplished traditional dancer and a man committed to the preservation of his people's culture, Lyman indeed shares many of Shawnee Ray's own consuming passions. Like Zelda, however, Lyman is calculating, and he has his own plans for Shawnee Ray and Redford: He can imagine Shawnee as his assistant, helping him to manage his many business concerns, and he sees for Redford a fine future as a capital investor. Lyman, obviously, views the world in respect to his interest in money—he is a father who would rather play store than play trucks with his son. The secret of his success (and the reason he did not drown when he jumped in the river after Henry) is that Lyman is a man who has never, "not in any part of himself, ever given up" (149).

If Lyman is a man of reason, cool and methodical, Lipsha is a person who is governed by his passions. Although he does not realize it, the emotional outbursts in which he expresses his feelings for Shawnee Ray contribute to her growing sense of being pressured by the people around her. Whereas Lyman is always affable, Lipsha can be prickly, and indeed lands himself in a spot of trouble when he mouths off to the boys from Montana: It is only because Russell Kashpaw takes mercy on him that he escapes the ignominy of sporting a tatoo of Montana on his rump. Impetuous and often irresponsible, Lipsha is nonetheless a thoroughly good-hearted young man, a person whom even Zelda thinks of as "sweet" (49). Try as he might, he cannot hate his rival, Lyman, and at the end of the novel, when he takes the child into his arms, he refuses to do to someone else what was done to him.

THEMES

Louise Erdrich's first three novels all close with a scene of joyful home-coming: *Love Medicine*'s Lipsha crosses the water to return to the reservation, *The Beet Queen*'s Dot comes home to Celestine after reenacting her Grandmother Adelaide's flight, and *Tracks*'s Lulu is welcomed home by the surrogate father who rescues her. In contrast to these scenes from the earlier novels, *The Bingo Palace*'s homecoming occurs in the opening pages of the book and does not celebrate an occasion of reunion. In her fourth novel, Erdrich revises her treatment of her familiar homecoming theme, showing that the experience of return can bring disappointment and disillusion as well as the joy of reunion.

While Lipsha does not exactly elect to come home (in truth his grand-mother summons him), the novel's plot makes clear the design of necessity that occasions his return. When the novel opens, Lipsha apparently assumes that the understanding of June's desertion that he acquired in *Love Medicine* has provided him "firm ground" on which he can stand; however, the course of his life seems to belie this assumption, as the choral voice reveals when it tells how he has squandered his opportunities and "let his chances slip." Lipsha, the community believes, needs to "ground himself" (7), to stop his complaining, and, as he himself eventually describes it, to overcome the mad dog's urge to bite itself for sympathy. To "ground himself," Lipsha must learn to accept the fact of his parents' abandonment of him, and to do that he must suffer the disillusionments that await him when he comes home again. In other words, before he can open himself to the possibilities in his future, it is necessary that he return to the place that holds the secrets of his past.

As hinted in its repeated references to gaming, *The Bingo Palace* is interested in chance and design and in the ways in which destiny and possibility can be seen as intertwined.[1] The novel's characters are both lucky and unlucky, and it is often hard to distinguish their bad luck from the good. For example, it is by chance or bad luck that Shawnee Ray gets pregnant before she is married, but it is nevertheless this occurrence that opens up for her the joys of being Redmond's mother— and it is also likely that it is this stroke of fate that has shaped for her a life quite different from the lives her sisters lead. For Zelda, it is the chance occurrence of the heart attack that opens the possibility that she might review her life in the light of a changed perspective. It therefore turns out to be her good fortune that a moment of bad luck transforms her understanding. While Lulu, of course, is acting by design, the chance arrival of her summons opens the possibility that Lipsha's life can also be changed. His homecoming brings disillusionment, when he finally confronts what he has spent his life "trying to forget," but the knowledge that he gains provides an opportunity for him to finally come to terms with the troubles of his past.

Like other Erdrich novels, *The Bingo Palace* celebrates the survival of Ojibwa culture. Set in the 1990s, this book shows, in many of its scenes, how contemporary Native Americans practice and thereby preserve the traditions that are their legacy. Following the lead of Lulu and Marie, members of the novel's younger generation accept the responsibility of serving as guardians of their culture. Albertine, for example, is fascinated by her people's history, and after her naming ceremony she spends hours poring over the diaries, church records, and other documents that might include some reference to Four Soul, whose namesake she is. Albertine receives her name as a grown woman, but readers learn that Redford, the young child, has also had a naming ceremony.

The novel opens with a scene that depicts a powwow, and in it readers are afforded a vision of the community gathered together to watch the "whirling bright dancers" (9) and to listen to the songs and drums. At various points within her narrative, Erdrich describes the dancers' traditional clothes and offers an account of the origin of the jingle dress that Shawnee wears when she dances. Readers also learn about the significance of Nector's pipe and are even told something of its history. (Lipsha reveals that it was this very pipe that was used to start the "ten-summer sundance" [39].) In these details and many others, *The Bingo Palace* demonstrates the ways in which Ojibwa tradition plays a significant role in the life of its community of characters.

ALTERNATIVE PERSPECTIVE: PSYCHOANALYTIC CRITICISM

Although the idea of the unconscious mind did not originate with Sigmund Freud, his theories concerning the nature and workings of *das Unbewusste* ("the unknown") are at the heart of his significant contributions to the science of Western psychology. Believing that human beings' mental processes are mainly unconscious and that people's actions are frequently motivated by forces of which they are completely unaware, Freud looked to the unconscious in his search for an understanding of the problems that troubled his patients' conscious lives. Although many of Freud's theories have been contested or revised in recent years, his conception of the human psyche as essentially dual in nature—as consisting of both the conscious and the unconscious—has been generally accepted in the Western world. Indeed, so widespread is the assumption of this model of the mind that much of the vocabulary Freud introduced to describe it has become commonplace: words such as "repression," "sublimation," "projection," and many others are all familiar terms.

In *The Bingo Palace* readers are told that Albertine Johnson cannot "escape the iron shadow of her mother's repressed history" (23). A reference to the fact that Albertine's first name comes not from her father, but rather from a suitor her mother had rejected, Erdrich's language clearly invites the reader to consider the unconscious motivations that have shaped Zelda's "history" of repression. Albertine has never liked her name, but she understands very well the hidden reason why her mother selected it. In her choice of name, Zelda reveals what is buried in her unconscious mind. This is but one example of many in which Erdrich draws upon Freud's model of the dual nature of the psyche to characterize her fictional figures. In other words, Erdrich's conception of character is often expressed in psychoanalytic terms.

Erdrich's depiction of Zelda serves well to illustrate this point. Zelda is a person who must exercise control. When Lipsha sees her at the pow-wow, he reminds himself that she is one of the reasons coming home cannot be simple. He is certain, in fact, that she will somehow interfere in his affairs, for he remembers well her "deep instinct for running things" (14). (His suspicions are indeed confirmed when Zelda attempts to use him as the catalyst in her scheme to draw Lyman and Shawnee Ray together.) Zelda is obviously a character who is portrayed as a busybody, but Erdrich uses the account of her vision to explore the psychology that underlies her desire to manage others.

After her heart attack, Zelda sees the image of her father as he looked on the day he burned Lulu's house to the ground. When she envisions Nector's face and recalls the passion in his eyes, she experiences once again her anger at her father. She remembers that as a child she understood that it was his unbridled passion that had led to the betrayal of her mother and to the destruction of Lulu's house; in Nector she could clearly see the "effect of passion on a life" (243). To get even with her father, she decided at that time that she would never allow herself the extravagance of passion. Although she was later not consciously aware of it, readers recognize that it was clearly for this reason that she denied herself Xavier's love. Zelda learned as a child to control her desires and her emotions, and out of this impulse for control emerged her compulsion to arrange the lives of others. Through the experience of her vision, Zelda is able to bring to consciousness her repressed anger at her father and to finally admit to herself her passion for the man whose love she will not again refuse.

Lyman also experiences a vision when he makes his quest into the woods and hears the voice of his dead brother, Henry. Readers of *Love Medicine* know that Lyman responded to his brother's drowning with grief, anger, and despair, but *The Bingo Palace*'s account of his vision quest offers additional psychological insight into his feelings about the brother he has lost. While he is dancing in honor of the memory of his brother, Lyman admits that he once resented Henry for his superior dancing skills. When he acknowledges the ambivalence he felt toward the brother he both loved and resented, Lyman finds that he is ready at last to come to terms with Henry's ghost. Realizing that when he danced in Henry's shadow, he danced in a "friendly shade" (204) that indeed obscured the sun, but also protected him from its glare, all his resentment disappears. When Henry's voice instructs him to "put those old dance clothes to rest," Lyman finally understands that he no longer dances in Henry's shadow.

Whereas Zelda and Lyman become conscious of unresolved tensions from their pasts by experiencing a vision, a form of a dream, Lipsha's consciousness of his troubled past is awakened when he recovers his repressed memory of his mother's attempt to drown him. Freudian psychoanalytic theory posits that a man who is ready to marry seeks a woman who can replace the figure of his mother, and Lipsha clearly sees in Shawnee Ray the woman he desires as a substitute for June. His pursuit of Shawnee Ray is interrupted after he remembers what his mother did to him. Lipsha once more forgives the mother who has wronged him, but the subsequent unfolding of the novel's plot suggests that he will not be ready to replace June with Shawnee Ray until he fully accepts the cruel fact of his mother's desertion of him. Acceptance comes, of course, when Gerry and June's ghost abandon their son during the blizzard. Before he falls asleep in the cold, Lipsha acknowledges that he can no longer forget, deny, or explain away the absence of his parents.

In her survey of the scholarship that addresses Erdrich's work, Debra Burdick notes that "Erdrich's vivid characterizations" particularly "lend themselves to psychological interpretation, which has been done only to a limited extent" (Burdick 143). *The Bingo Palace* serves well to illustrate Burdick's point, for in that novel Erdrich not only uses psychoanalytic terms to portray her characters' natures, but she also presents scenes of dreams or visions wherein her characters recognize and confront impulses that arise from the unconscious.

NOTE

1. See Jeanne Rosier Smith's *Writing Tricksters* for an interesting discussion of chance and design in *The Bingo Palace*. Smith describes how Erdrich, as trickster author, plays with chance in the narrative structure of her novel.

7

Tales of Burning Love
(1996)

The last book, to date, in Louise Erdrich's series of related narratives, *Tales of Burning Love*, reintroduces several characters from the earlier novels and weaves a new design from stories those novels tell. Readers are alerted, on the last page of *The Bingo Palace*, that of its tale there remains "more to be told," and indeed the fifth book proves the truth of that prediction. Erdrich's readers, for example, learn the fate of Lipsha Morrissey when *Tales of Burning Love* offers a second account of the blizzard in which he and a helpless infant are stranded together. Surprisingly, though, the novel opens by telling once again the story of another blizzard, the one through which *Love Medicine*'s June Kashpaw walks in the first chapter of that book. With its tales of burning love and its scenes of bitter snow, the fifth novel accentuates the contrasting images of fire and ice.

Characters from all the previous novels are mentioned in this one, and there are interesting revelations about some of them. It turns out, for example, that Father Jude Miller, brother of *The Beet Queen*'s Karl and Mary Adare, has assumed a position at the convent in Argus, the town where Mary still runs the butcher shop she inherited from the Kozkas. Sister Leopolda, too, is still at the convent, and in *Tales of Burning Love* readers discover what finally becomes of her. Gerry Nanapush remains at large, having survived a plane crash in *The Bingo Palace*, and in the fifth novel he manages to visit Shawn, the daughter whose birth *Love*

Medicine describes. Lyman Lamartine still plans to build his Indian casino, and in *Tales of Burning Love* he thinks that he has finally found a way to do it.

The novel's main setting is Fargo, North Dakota, although several of its scenes are set in Argus and elsewhere. The action at the center of the plot takes place during 1994 and 1995, but *Tales of Burning Love* also features numerous flashbacks, including its account of June's last Easter Sunday in 1981. Although all Erdrich's books include stories within stories, like *The Arabian Nights* or *The Canterbury Tales*, the central plot of this novel frames the occasion of its characters relating stories to one another. When four of the five women who have been married to Jack Mauser find themselves marooned in the blizzard, the same storm in which Lipsha is marooned, they decide to keep one another awake by telling the stories of their lives (particularly their lives with Jack). The intricacies of the novel's plot demand numerous changes in scene and point of view, and thus the book is broken into four separate sections that contain, all told, forty-seven chapters. While this novel's return to *Love Medicine*'s opening scene might signal the completion of the North Dakota books, it might, of course, also be the case that there is yet "more to be told."

PLOT

Titled "Easter Snow," *Tales of Burning Love*'s first chapter transports readers back to Williston, North Dakota, in the spring of 1981. There a young oil worker named Jack Mauser is suffering from an excruciating toothache on Holy Saturday, when dentists are seemingly in short supply. Aspirin is no help, so Jack heads for the Rigger Bar with hopes of anesthetizing himself. Told in the third-person from Jack's point of view, this account of June's last day changes slightly the angle of focus readers find in *Love Medicine*'s opening scene. As in that book, however, Jack taps on the window, June enters the bar, and peels her blue egg. Conversation soon reveals that both characters are simply "killing time" (*LM* 1). Jack is waiting for his appointment with a dentist and June is waiting to catch the bus that will carry her back home. Because June looks to be Ojibwa, and Jack has Ojibwa family he does not wish to discuss, he does not tell her his name, but instead calls himself "Andy."

"Andy" and June make the rounds of the bars, and both end up missing their appointments. Jack is clearly touched by June, by her slightly crooked front tooth, by her wistful speculation that he might be "different" (7) from others, and by her deep appreciation when he buys her a meal. Late in the evening he suddenly decides that he should marry her, and when a "certified reverend" (8) is discovered in the bar, the ceremony is performed with rings from the pop-tops of beer cans. Thus June becomes the first of a series of women Jack will marry, and later that night, when they are sitting in his truck out in the countryside, he rejoices in the thought that she will be the one person with whom he can feel both "safe" and "whole" (9).

June stops drinking long before her new husband does, and in his effort to forget his aching tooth, Jack consumes too much. When he is unable to make love to his wife, his awkward embarrassment deepens to shame as the tears he cannot stop stream down his face. After a long silence, June leaves the truck,[1] and he waits for a few moments before he decides to go after her. In his headlights, he sees her striding forward eagerly and never looking back to see if he will follow. He wants to call out her name, but he does not know for certain whether it is "May," or "June," or some other month—and so, to his lasting regret, he allows her to walk into the storm. Thus it is Jack's fate that he will carry with him to all the other loves of his life the sorrowful memory of the woman whose name he failed to speak.

The novel's second chapter takes up the action after thirteen years have passed and Jack, who has sworn off drinking, is beginning a new life with his fifth wife, Dot Adare. Recognizing that since he let the first one go, he has been unable to "hold on to a woman" (13), Jack persuades himself that Dot, for whom he does not feel the "special madness" that he experienced with the others, is nonetheless a good choice for him, especially at a time when his construction business is failing and his life is generally in shambles. Dot, after all, is an excellent accountant, and Jack truly does admire her formidable energy and fierce disposition. She is, he believes, the very sort of woman "who would stick by him in his ruin" (14).

In "A Wedge of Shade," their decision to marry draws the Mausers from their home in Fargo back to the town of Argus, where both of them grew up. Dot wishes to first deliver the news of her remarriage to her mother and Aunt Mary and then introduce her new husband. To Celestine she confides that because she could never bring herself to sign her divorce papers, she is in fact married to Gerry as well as to Jack. In either case, it soon appears that Dot is fated to be the wife of a criminal, for no sooner does Jack make his appearance than Officer Lovchik arrives to arrest and handcuff him. Amazed at the sight of Lovchik leading yet another husband away, Celestine assumes that bigamy is the cause of the problem. When Dot then explains that unlike Gerry's offenses, Jack's are merely instances of white-collar crime, shrewd old Aunt Mary wonders if the boss has married his accountant so that she will be unable to testify against him.

Shortly after Jack arranges his bail, he returns to Argus to oversee a construction project. He decides, while he is there, that he will call upon his second wife, who is staying at the convent. Eleanor Mauser, who left her college teaching job after a student charged her with sexual harassment, is researching the saintly life of Sister Leopolda, who is the oldest and most mysterious of the nuns at Our Lady of the Wheat. Jack and Eleanor, readers learn, have remained in touch over the years and in fact meet from time to time, for although they could not live happily together while they were married, their fascination with one another has never quite burned out.

The former spouses rendezvous late at night in the convent's garden, and are therefore present when Leopolda comes to offer her prayers before the statue of the Blessed Virgin. As it happens, the statue is gone, for it is being replaced by a new one, and to hide himself Jack assumes the Virgin's position atop the pedestal. "End this torment" (53) is the 108-year-old petitioner's request of the Virgin, and when Jack hands Leopolda a bough of honeysuckle, the old nun's prayer is answered at last. Leopolda dies in peace, believing that she has witnessed yet another miracle. In the early morning hours, when a sudden thunderstorm appears, a bolt of lightning reduces the corpse to a cross-shaped scattering of ashes. Some at the convent believe that an assumption has occurred, and, indeed, Eleanor notices that the honeysuckle bushes continue to blossom in wildly rich profusion for several weeks after their normal blooming season ends.

Dot, it turns out, does not provide salvation for Jack, for by the end of the year he is facing both bankruptcy and yet another failing marriage. Realizing that it was a mistake to marry again, Dot acknowledges that she was tempted to do so only because she had, as she says, "been without my real husband for such a long time" (84). When Dot and her daughter Shawn move out of his house on New Year's Eve, Jack consoles himself with a bottle of scotch. Although he notices that a flaming spark is smoldering outside his fireplace, he chooses to ignore it, for he assumes that his automatic sprinkling system will douse the small blaze. Jack's house, however, was built by his own company, and it therefore follows that its construction was shoddy. The sprinkling system does not work, and as his house goes up in flames, he concludes that fate has offered him a rare opportunity: After prying loose a piece of his dental bridgework to leave in the ashes, Jack seizes the chance to walk away from his past. The novel's first section therefore ends with the official notice of Jack Mauser's death.

In "Part Two" of the novel, readers encounter Candice Pantamounty, D.D.S., and Marlis Cook—the third and the fourth of Jack's several wives. Candice, another native of Argus, is the prominent Fargo dentist who restored her husband's teeth, and Marlis, a blackjack dealer and aspiring musician, is the mother of John Jr., Jack's only child. Readers further learn that Candice, who is unable to bear a child of her own, has nevertheless longed to have a baby, and she therefore offered, when she heard that the fourth wife was pregnant and no longer with Jack, to adopt the child herself. Marlis, however, did not want to give up her baby because her own mother had given her up. So the two of them arranged a satisfactory compromise: These two women live together and share motherhood of Jack's son.

In the opening chapters of Part Two, Dot, Eleanor, and Candice all attend Jack's memorial service, held in Fargo at Schlick's Funeral Home, an establishment that is owned and run by Eleanor's own father. (A writer who is much admired for the twists of irony that inform her comic vision, Erdrich thoroughly enjoys describing in *Tales of Burning Love* the funeral of the man who is not dead.) While most of the mourners visit the funeral parlor simply hoping to discover how they can recover money they are owed, the wives, "who had once prided themselves on their separate escapes from Jack" (121), are nonetheless all sorry, for one reason or another, that he is gone. Among them, it is Eleanor who is most deeply grieved, for after Jack's spring visit to the convent, she comes to realize that "an awful and surprising thing was happening to her—she was falling in love with her own ex-husband" (64).

In part because she had always assumed that she would be buried beside Jack, Eleanor introduces the question of the disposal of his remains. She, of course, is certain that her ex-husband wanted to be buried, but Candice, who never cared for Eleanor, quickly disputes that claim. She in fact recalls that Jack insisted he wanted to be cremated, as it appears he has been, and she is furthermore quite sure that he wanted his ashes "to be thrown to the winds" (124). Dot, who is feeling guilty about abandoning Jack in his time of need, then enters the fray with her opinion that Jack would have wanted a large monument—an angel, she thinks. With no consensus in sight, the wives agree to go on to the B & B, the bar where Marlis works, to seek her opinion, carrying Jack's "remains" in a heart-shaped candy box. Dot, as it happens, has another reason for wishing to visit the bar, for Lyman Lamartine, who also attends the funeral, informs her that Gerry Nanapush is free and that she might be able to find him at the B & B.[2] At the bar, the question of what to do with Jack's "ashes" is resolved when the box is blown open by a sudden draft and the ashes are scattered over all the wives.

While others attend his funeral, Jack himself is hiding out in a garage his company owns. The question of what he should do next is abruptly answered when Hegelstead, "bank president and . . . the man to whom he owed everything" (181), finds his hiding place. Although the banker considers the option of having Jack locked up, he knows that he will never be able to recover his losses if his client does not earn the money to pay them. He therefore listens to the plan Jack proposes and eventually agrees that his desperate debtor should make one more attempt to bail himself out. Thus Jack will travel north, accept a contract to build Lyman Lamartine's casino, and, with this "mega-project" in hand, pay off all his loans. In accepting this solution to his problems, Jack knows that he will in effect make himself an "indentured servant" (183) to the ambitious Lyman, but he also recognizes that he has no other choice.

The last two chapters of Part Two set the stage for the novel's third section, entitled "The Tales of Burning Love." Dot, Eleanor, and Candice indeed spend the evening of the funeral playing blackjack at Marlis's table, and Dot does meet with her "real husband" Gerry when he appears disguised as an old woman. It is snowing heavily by the time the bar closes, and so the women all agree that Dot will drive them home in Jack's sturdy and dependable Explorer. A short distance down the road she picks up a hitchhiker who is completely swaddled in blankets, and this mysterious and silent figure crawls into the space that holds the spare tire and promptly falls asleep. All goes well until Dot drives into a snowdrift in an underpass beneath the railroad tracks. When the women realize they are stuck until they can be rescued, they recognize that they must not allow themselves to fall asleep in the cold. It is with this imperative in mind that they hit upon the plan of telling one another the stories of their lives with Jack, husband to them all.

The events of Part Three of the novel all take place during January 5 and the early morning hours of January 6—the night of the blizzard. Marooned in their car, Jack's former wives draw upon their tales of fiery passion to stave off the ice that threatens to engulf them. To avoid being asphyxiated, they must from time to time venture out into the storm to make sure the car's tailpipe is not clogged with snow. They accomplish this task by forming a human chain, holding tightly to one another so that one of their number will not be swept off by the wind. Thus, braced by their intermittent trips into the bone-chilling cold and warmed by the heat their various stories generate, the women manage their self-appointed goal of "surviving sleep" (267) through the long night of the blizzard.

The stories that the women tell—sometimes amusing, often poignant—on one hand relate the story of Jack's life during the passage of the thirteen years since he married June, and, on the other, they serve to characterize for readers the backgrounds and identities of the speakers themselves. The stories describe how each woman first encountered Jack and how each failed to find a way to make a life with him. Readers learn how Eleanor met Jack through her mother, who had saved him from freezing, as she had earlier saved Eleanor from burning when the family house caught fire. Candice describes how a dispute over the fate of a dog named Pepperboy first brought Jack and her together, and then how, much later on, the very same issue drove them apart.

Marlis then recounts how she and Jack tried to make a life as musicians traveling the circuit of motel piano bars, and how their interlude as wandering entertainers came to a sudden end when she announced that she was pregnant. To the horrified surprise but also the amusement of her listeners, she then goes on to tell of how she punished Jack when he refused to acknowledge the fact of her pregnancy. As the long night goes on and the talk turns to the birth of the baby, Candice and Marlis together tell the story of how they came to be lovers. Just before the break of dawn, the women realize that the tailpipe needs cleaning once again. This time, however, Marlis lets go of the hand she is holding, and Eleanor Mauser is blown off into the "white night" (363) of the storm.

Jack, meanwhile, decides to leave town on January 5, the day of his funeral. Before heading north, however, he stops at Candice's house to see his baby son. When the child's strong-willed nanny tries to call the police, a panicked Jack finds himself forced to restrain her. With the nanny tied up, he has no choice but to take his baby with him, and he therefore straps him into the backseat of Candice's extra car. Jack drives to the Amtrak station and leaves the sleeping baby behind while he runs in to quickly check the schedule. As readers of *The Bingo Palace* know, he emerges a moment later to discover that the car has been stolen. The desperate father gives chase, but the driver will not stop. Jack, however,

catches a glimpse of the driver and therefore realizes that it is Gerry
Nanapush who has abducted his son.

Part Four of the novel, entitled "Balancing Tricks," offers resolution
of the suspenseful action unfolded in Part Three. Eleanor, alone in the
storm, is tumbled and driven by the gusting winds until she suddenly
smacks into something very solid. For a moment she sees stars, and then
a dazzling bright light. Sensing a presence nearby, she approaches the
light and sees in its radiance the outline of a hooded figure. She supposes
that the figure must be that of the mysterious hitchhiker, who has seemingly followed her in an effort to save her, but when the figure speaks
with the voice of Leopolda, she wonders, "could it be?" (370). Eleanor
does not know whether she is witnessing a miracle or hallucinating while
she freezes in the snow, but when the apparition instructs her to cling
to a small branch, she sees before her the straight line of trees that leads
directly to Fargo's airport.

In "The Tale of the Unknown Passenger," readers find that Eleanor is
mistaken about the identity of the hitchhiker who snores peacefully in
the back of the snowbound car. After Marlis and Candice finally drift
off to sleep, Gerry Nanapush joins Dot in the front seat for the long
awaited reunion of husband and wife. When the team of snowmobilers
that Eleanor has summoned finally rescues the group, Gerry rides into
town and then jumps from the snowmobile and once more slips away.
Before he leaves Fargo for places unknown, he goes to Dot's apartment
to spend a joyful hour with the daughter whose childhood he has
missed. Shortly after he departs, federal agents come to question Shawn,
but, like her grandmother Lulu in *The Bingo Palace*, she grins the wolf
smile of the Pillagers as she deceives the men who relentlessly pursue
her father.

Because Jack knows that Gerry Nanapush has taken his son, he is able
to guess the car's likely destination; certain that the fugitive will head to
the north, Jack returns to his garage and fires up one of his company's
snowplows. The snow grows thicker as he travels up the interstate, and
the highway appears to be deserted, but after a time he spots the headlights of a car that is following in his wake. When, after many miles, the
headlights disappear, Jack wonders what has happened to the people in
the car. He thinks again of June, lost to another blizzard, and then he
circles back. When he comes to the place where the car left the road, he
sees two sets of tracks leading off into a field. With visions of June beck-
oning him on, Jack spends the night of the snowstorm searching for a
car that has been buried in the drifts. Finally, near morning, he stumbles
over the object of his search and at last rescues Lipsha and his son.

Tales of Burning Love closes with a final glimpse of its main characters' lives in the aftermath of the blizzard they have all survived. Dot recovers from the frostbite she has suffered and goes home to Argus. After years of running their butcher shop, Mary and Celestine are ready for a change, and Dot thinks that maybe she will help them transform their outmoded business into a modern convenience store. Where Gerry is she does not know, but she is ready to live with the hope that somehow, somewhere, they will find a way to "be together" (418) once again. Meanwhile, she tells herself, "I have to raise our Shawn, my part of the deal" (417).

In the hopes of salvaging his business and staying out of jail, Jack is indeed forced to go into partnership with Lyman. Since the night of the blizzard, when, "at last, he understood the shape of what other humans felt about their children," he has himself experienced a father's "protective love" (380) for his son and therefore visits John Jr. and the baby's mothers. Candice, in fact, replaces the bridge he removed on the night of the fire. Eleanor, whose inexplicable sighting of Leopolda has intensified her fascination with the nun, finds a small house at the edge of the reservation and resumes her investigation of the many mysteries of Leopolda's life. Lyman, as it happens, is also interested in her project, for if Eleanor can make a case for Leopolda's sainthood, there will be a good market for the postcards and statues he stands ready to produce.

In "A Last Chapter," readers learn that Eleanor welcomes Jack's visits to her secluded retreat. At peace with herself, she has come to conceive of her life as "an uncontrolled dance," and when she thinks of her lover, she understands that "what we ask for in love is no more than a momentary chance to get the steps right, to move in harmony until the music stops" (452). As for Jack, his return to Eleanor completes a circle in his life, for although Eleanor was not his first wife, she was his first love, and, like June, she was never forgotten. When Jack at last weeps for June, he is also weeping for himself, for through his love for Eleanor he has come to know how hard it is "to bear the pain of coming back to life" (452).

CHARACTERS

Another of the novels in which Erdrich's several characters' lives are intertwined with one another, *Tales of Burning Love* offers a series of connected stories rather than the single story of a central protagonist. At the heart of the book lies the tangled plot of Jack and his many loves, but the unraveling of that tale requires that each of the five main characters' stories be told. Like that of *Love Medicine*, the novel's plot is framed by the fragmented story of June, a character who remains an emblem of mystery and loss. When, in the second chapter, the setting shifts from 1981 to 1994, the novel's plot begins to unfold, through their connection to each other, its separate accounts of the lives of Dot and Jack. In Part Three of the novel, Erdrich uses the device of the night of storytelling to fold into her plot the stories of Eleanor, Candice, and Marlis, the other principal characters who have "tales of burning love" to tell.

In addition to its central characters, *Tales of Burning Love* portrays many others, including several figures who are already familiar to readers of Erdrich's other books. Up until the moment of her fiery assumption, Sister Leopolda remains the ferocious nun who watches for a miracle. It therefore seems fitting that the ambiguities that surround her in her life are reflected in the manner of her death and disappearance. Interestingly, just before she prays that her torment be ended, Leopolda speaks in the old language, the tongue that she avowed in *Tracks* she would never use. Dot's family is also represented in the novel, in the characters of Mary and Celestine. Aunt Mary remains Dot's stalwart supporter, and Celestine is still the loving mother who is for Dot the embodiment of home. Lyman, another familiar character, continues to make his way by plotting and scheming, and readers are told that he is aging "carefully, not to wisdom but to power" (407).

Anna and Lawrence Schlick, Eleanor's parents, are two other significant characters, for their story, as Eleanor relates it, is yet another example of a tale of burning love. Lawrence and Anna are both featured in the novel's central plot, but when Eleanor recounts their history as part of her own story, the account of their lives becomes a tale within a tale within a tale. The Schlicks' story, in fact, gives shape to a subplot within the novel, for Jack is implicated in events that figure in their lives—just as he is also part of the other characters' stories. Anna, once an acrobat, is a woman who has courageously saved lives: She saved her daughter from a death by fire and Jack from a death by ice. In saving Jack, however, Anna ignited flames of jealousy in her husband Lawrence, who readily assumed that Jack was his wife's secret lover. Lawrence disowned Anna, who then survived years of impoverishment through her own fortitude. Like Jack, however, Lawrence never forgot his first love and at last returned to her. Near the end of the novel, when the stout-hearted Anna's greatly weakened heart gives out, Lawrence Schlick cremates himself along with the body of his wife.

Erdrich often provides her readers psychological insights into the behavior of her characters, and this is indeed the case in her depiction of Jack, a figure who clearly experiences difficulty in his repeated efforts to locate a center in his life. Although his first marriage is inspired by an impulse, in the brief interval before it ends, Jack entertains the idea that in his relationship with a woman like June there could be the chance that he might feel "safe" and even "whole." Later, with Dot, he expresses a similar desire when he thinks of her as a safe haven, as someone who will surely "stick by him in his ruin." He is a character who longs to "protect him[self]" (9) through the love of a woman.

Readers' first hint of the likely source of Jack's need for security appears in the first chapter of the book, when he fears that revealing the name of his Ojibwa family might give June cause to be "wary of him" (6). Clearly, this character is troubled by some experience from his past, and, although the full story of his childhood is never unfolded, readers are afforded revealing glimpses of his history in scenes of flashback and reverie. A mixed-blood, Jack's father was German and his mother Ojibwa. During his early childhood he lived on the reservation, but, because his mother regularly suffered catatonic spells, he spent many lonely hours in the house of his strict German aunt. Orphaned early in his life, Jack, like Lipsha, misses the love of his mother. He thinks of her during the night of the blizzard, and, when he envisions her "as a protective arm," he realizes that he has indeed "missed her like a child" (384).

Although the passages in which Eleanor, Candice, and Marlis tell their stories are presented in the first person, Dot is the only character in the novel who narrates complete chapters in a first-person voice. In the fifth novel, readers find her struggling to make a life for herself and Shawn in the absence of Gerry, and it is therefore understandable that she is tempted to accept her boss's unexpected proposal of marriage. In "A Wedge of Shade," a chapter narrated by Dot, readers learn that she is nevertheless troubled by doubts about the marriage from its very beginning, and, in fact, asks herself, "how real is this marriage, anyway?" (30). It is not long, therefore, before she understands that she does not wish to protect and mother Jack; through the mistake she has made, she is forced to confront the truth of her loyalty to Gerry, the man who remains her "real husband" despite her marriage to another.

Eleanor is an inquisitive, "brainy" (39), bookish woman, equally committed to her solitary pursuits of philosophical conundrums and to her long-standing habits of self-indulgence in her pleasures. Indeed, she did capriciously seduce a student in her class. The product of a happy childhood and thus completely free of care "up until the catastrophe of her parents' separation," she is forced as an adult to recognize that her sheltered upbringing failed to prepare her to confront disappointments and confusions—that nothing in her adult life can match "her early childhood perfection" (37). After she burns her bridges by seducing the student, Eleanor turns herself to the task of discovering what it is she wants and needs in her life. To her surprise, she finds that she wants Jack as well as the solitude she needs for her work. She does not know, at the end of the novel, whether she and Jack can live together, but she is satisfied with the thought that they might "move in harmony until the music stops."

Candice, the consummate professional woman, is also devoted to her work and regularly attends seminars in dentistry to make certain that she is aware of new developments in her field. Her story reveals that she brought to her marriage the same attention to detail that she brings to her work, for she made a concentrated effort to share her husband's interests—even when, as in the instance of Jack's fondness for hunting, they were repugnant to her. Candice's attempts to share her husband's life did not, however, seem to her to truly serve to draw him closer, and when her beloved dog was killed through Jack's careless inattention, she at last acknowledged that her marriage could not last.

As her story further reveals, the idea of becoming Marlis's lover did not occur to Candice until someone else mistakenly assumed that the two were lesbians. Shocked, at first, she nonetheless began to consider the possibility that she might indeed love another woman, and, after experiencing a "sympathetic pregnancy" (351) and then attending the birth of the baby, she recognized that she had quite naturally fallen in love with both Marlis and the child. When readers last encounter Candice, near the end of the novel, she tells Jack of her great happiness while she works on his teeth.

Marlis, the youngest and the "most problematic" (141) of the wives, is also, not surprisingly, the least secure in her sense of herself. Like Jack, she has lost her parents and has had to struggle to make her way in the world. As she confides in her story, she was once forced to live underneath her sister's trailer. She readily admits, when she tells the tale of her life with Jack, that after their accidental meeting she purposefully schemed to seduce and entrap him. She then goes on to explain that it was only after they were married that she came to understand that she wanted him to love her. Desperate to claim his affection, she watched over him and tried in every way to attend to his needs. Finally, when she could see that he took her "adoration" (318) for granted, she began to grow weary of his constant fault-finding. Marlis's marriage came abruptly to an end when she was no longer able to bear her husband's indifference.

Diagnosed as a "bipolar" (107) personality, Marlis suffers extreme shifts in mood and is subject to sudden fits of fury. Indeed, Jack was the victim of her wrath after he refused to answer her final demand that he promise to love both her and their baby. It is when she becomes a mother that she at last realizes her desire to experience "true love given and returned" (325), and it is through their shared motherhood that she and Candice discover their love for each other. Her unpredictable outbursts notwithstanding, Marlis is not one, as she says, to ever "hold grudges" (313). That she has forgiven Jack his unkind treatment of her is made apparent near the end of the novel: When Jack comes to visit with his son, Marlis once again seduces him.

THEMES

In *Tales of Burning Love* Erdrich expresses her familiar homecoming theme in her portrayals of lovers' ultimate recognition of each other. Indeed, this idea is elaborated in her memoir, *The Blue Jay's Dance*, in her observation that "our peculiar ability to be at home in the arms of one person, while always a stranger in the presence of another, is an ongoing human mystery" (*TBJD* 106). Like the lovers of *A Midsummer Night's Dream*, those in *Tales of Burning Love* fall under the spell of ephemeral enchantment before they at last find themselves "at home" with someone they truly love. By the end of the novel, when Dot has been paired with Gerry, Candice with Marlis, Lawrence with Anna, and Eleanor with Jack, each of these characters has completed a journey of self-discovery that has led to affirmation of a love that is shared with another. In its celebration of its characters' coming home to those they love, the novel echoes a theme repeatedly sounded in Shakespearean comedy.

If homecoming is, on one hand, the recognition of the beloved, it is, on the other, the return to the place that holds the memories of childhood. Both Dot and Jack experience this return: Dot when she goes home to Argus, and Jack when he returns, after many years away, to the reservation. In describing these returns, Erdrich shows how her characters' sense of belonging is evoked by their recognition of what was once familiar. While Dot is certain that any place she could mention "has better things about it than Argus" (16), nonetheless its soil and air speak to her, and she cannot resist savoring the stale taste of its water. Jack, too, knows that he is home when he can breathe the "difference" in the air on the reservation. He had, before his arrangement with Lyman, always intended to go back to the place his mother had "loved" (401), and when he does return, he welcomes his memories of her and of the world that they shared.

Erdrich's novels all raise questions about land and its use, and *Tales of Burning Love* is by no means an exception. The title of the first section, "Jack of Sunflowers," makes reference to a rich parcel of land near Fargo that Jack leases to his Uncle Chuck, a sunflower farmer. It is Chuck's "circus bright" (151) field of flowers that Jack intends to reclaim for a development project that will transform the spacious landscape into an extension of the city. Like Lyman, Jack has lost his "old-time Ojibwa sense" of the land and no longer understands that it belongs "to nobody and nothing but itself." As the old Ojibwas know, the "land lasts" (153), but Jack's use of it clearly does not, for edifices he constructs upon it in due course cave in, crumble, or burn down.

Gambling is another motif that runs through Erdrich's novels, appearing in specific references to games of chance or presented as a metaphor. Lost in the blizzard and thus gambling with his life, Jack imagines the "other world" (384) of the Ojibwa, the western world where the dead are skeletons who gamble. Jack's own business is itself a gamble, one in which he dares not "bid too high" or "bid too low" (151) for his construction contracts—and readers are told that he acquired his business techniques playing at the gaming tables. On the occasion when Jack's wives play cards, *Tales of Burning Love* offers a meditation on the "unenlightened" (169) game of blackjack, a mesmerizing game that many play well but that no one ever wins. The novel's many references to gambling call attention to the fact that marriage, too, is obviously a risk, a kind of game of both chance and skill. All of the novel's main characters take the risk and suffer losses, but, in Erdrich's fifth novel, "big losses always make big winners" (420), and, by the end of the book, each character indeed finally stakes claim to a winning hand.

ALTERNATIVE PERSPECTIVE: FEMINIST CRITICISM

Ever since the publication of *Love Medicine*, critics and reviewers have repeatedly noted and remarked Erdrich's memorable characterizations of the women in her books. Indeed, because women and their stories play a central role in all of Erdrich's fiction, her work has especially attracted the attention of feminist literary critics, who have written about her powerful and resilient female characters, her representation of her fictional world as the site of community, and her treatment of numerous themes relevant to women's experiences. In *Tales of Burning Love*, for example, where four of the five central characters are women, Erdrich finds occasion to explore a variety of issues that are pertinent to women's interests and concerns. The novel portrays women at work and women in love, and in doing so examines women's ambitions as well as their desires. It reflects on questions of motherhood, and, in fact, it presents a birthing scene—a vivid scene in which Marlis and Candice bark and howl like dogs to stave off the pains of labor. The novel also considers women's sexuality, both in its scenes of love-making between women and men and in the scenes that portray the love of lesbians.

As part of a larger social movement whose ultimate goal is to improve the conditions of women's lives, feminist literary critics and theorists look to literature to consider how its expression of cultural experience accounts for women's public and private circumstances. Along with other art forms, literature provides a useful means to examine cultural experience, for, as Mary Anne Ferguson points out, "Literary images do not exist in a vacuum . . . Literature both reflects and helps create our views of reality; it is through their preservation in works of art that we know what the stereotypes and archetypes have been and are" (Ferguson 3). In studying the images of women encoded in literary texts, feminist critics find an angle of focus from which they can address assumptions that underlie and shape a society's conceptions of gender.

Interested in exploring the ways women and their experiences are represented in literary texts, feminist critics respond to the work of both men and women writers. Studies of texts produced by men usefully afford insights into men's visions of women—both how men regard women and what they desire women to be. In studying what women themselves have written, feminist critics directly address questions of what it means to be a woman. The images of themselves that women writers produce reveal how they respond to the social and political circumstances of their lives, and, as Mary Anne Ferguson observes, "The greatest change in literary images of women over the past two decades is the degree to which women writers have attempted to construct a womanly perspective and make women central in their works" (Ferguson 5). Erdrich is indeed one of these writers, a writer who explores women's goals, fears, needs, and choices, and who portrays how women come to define new identities for themselves.

While representations of gender in literary texts often reaffirm a society's cultural stereotypes, they can, as well, challenge stereotypical images of the roles and behavior of women and men. In *Tales of Burning Love*, Jack Mauser is at first portrayed as a man who is (stereotypically) indifferent to—or ignorant of—the needs of the people in his life. From the moment when he fails to speak (or even remember) the name of his first wife up until the closing chapters of the book, Jack shows no sign that he is able to empathize with others. It is only after he has "died" to all those who know him that he begins to slowly awaken to an understanding of the interests and perceptions of other people. At long last, on the night of the blizzard, he comes to feel the "protective love" (380) of a parent for a child, and, later, when he sees in Candice's eyes "the depth of her feeling for Marlis" (428), he is truly ashamed that he in fact responded to Marlis's sexual advances. In the last scene of the novel, Jack expresses his change of heart in a comical moment: He and Eleanor are making love on the stairs, and he abruptly pauses, "worried and absurd." As it turns out, he is the concerned lover, thinking only of Eleanor, and he has suddenly realized that she "could get a splinter" (451).

In *Tales of Burning Love*, Erdrich uses the occasion of Jack's staged death to mark his symbolic death as the stereotypical figure of the uncaring and self-centered male. Although it finally requires the accumulated crises in his life to propel Jack toward a sympathetic recognition of the identities of the women he married, the stories of the women themselves show that each tried, in her own way, to reveal herself to her husband. It was, of course, Marlis who expressed most dramatically her frustration over her spouse's inattention, and when Jack refused to commit himself to his marriage or his child, she conceived a plan to punish him.

Erdrich's depiction of Marlis's revenge is the comic vision of the spurned woman's fantasy come true. Marlis is determined to impress upon Jack the indignities and pain she has suffered on his behalf, and to this end she ties him to his bed while he is asleep. When she wakes him up, she first informs him that " 'It hurts to be a girl,' " and then she proceeds to demonstrate what her comment means. Marlis plucks Jack's eyebrows, spending a great deal of time "evening and straightening the line" (333) she carefully shapes upon his brow. She then uses a hot wax kit to remove the hairs on his legs. She goes on to pierce his ears and to set his hair in rollers, and then, as her *coup de grâce*, she uses Super Glue to attach to his feet a huge pair of "red and spiked" (334) high heels.

Erdrich's expressed desire to depict her fictional characters as human beings rather than stereotypical figures is reflected in her portrayals of both females and males. The women of *Tales of Burning Love*, all flawed human beings who make their share of mistakes, are nonetheless resourceful and resilient characters, able to survive a blizzard as well as their marriages to Jack. Jack, also a survivor, proves his resilience by overcoming his conditioned impulses to enact stereotypical male roles. In her portrayals of characters who do not conform to ingrained gender roles, Erdrich presents her readers with a form of cultural critique; characteristically, however, her social criticism is leavened by humor, and in her tale of Marlis's revenge, readers can see once again an expression of "survival humor" (Moyers 144). As Bill Ott observes, *Tales of Burning Love* is "a wise ... and wickedly funny novel" (Ott 1075).

NOTES

1. The telling of the story from Jack's point of view reveals that he has not passed out, as the account in *Love Medicine* suggests.

2. In a brief chapter cast in the form of a radio bulletin, readers are informed that on January 5, 1995, a small plane carrying federal prisoner Gerry Nanapush crashes near the Mississippi River. Readers of *The Bingo Palace* already know that Gerry survives the crash.

8

The Antelope Wife
(1998)

In *The Antelope Wife* Louise Erdrich introduces her readers to both a new setting and a new family of characters, but, at the same time, she returns to the use of narrative strategies she first employed in *Love Medicine* and *The Beet Queen*. Like the first two novels, *The Antelope Wife* recounts the interconnected stories of the lives of several generations of characters. Once again, too, Erdrich returns to the use of multiple narrators, including five first-person speakers (one of whom is Almost Soup, a wise and witty dog). In the first and last chapters, the first-person voice is that of an unknown storyteller, a speaker who can see in the intricately bead-worked pattern of events the web of stitching that links the present to the past.

The Antelope Wife's twenty-three chapters are divided among four sections, each of which opens with a reference to the haunting myth that frames the tale. The myth, like that of the Greek Moirai (the Fates), accounts for the spinning out of destiny. In this myth, twin sisters compete with one another as they stitch the patterns of fate. As readers are told in the introduction to Part One, "Ever since the beginning these twins are sewing. One sews with light and one with dark . . . each trying to set one more bead into the pattern than her sister, each trying to upset the balance of the world" (1). In this short passage Erdrich introduces two of the motifs that recur throughout the novel: *The Antelope Wife* tells the

stories of several sets of twins, and it draws upon the metaphor of beading to link together the many strands of its plot.

The scenes in the novel that occur in the present are mainly set in
Minneapolis (Gakahbekong in Ojibwa), and those that occur in the past
take place in the wide-skied prairie lands that lie to the west of Minnesota. As is characteristic of Erdrich's fiction, the plot features no central
protagonist but rather weaves together the lots and lives of many remarkable characters. At the heart of the plot lie two cautionary tales that
unfold the tragic consequences of characters' entrapment within the form
of love that is essentially obsessive and possessive. As these stories show,
this kind of love inspires its own quality of madness, wherein sense of
selfhood assumes the condition of a perpetual state of longing. As the
stories further show, loss of identity is not the only price paid by someone who would willfully possess another, for the obsessive lover also
has a will to cause injury to others. In *The Antelope Wife* Erdrich once
again tells "tales of burning love"; in this novel, however, two of the
stories are those of unrequited love.

Essentially a comic writer, Erdrich balances her accounts of tragedy
and loss against the stories of the survivors, the characters who find ways
to live with their grievous losses and, indeed, to celebrate renewal of
their capacities to love. In *The Antelope Wife*, the occasions for renewal
often take the form of family celebrations; in scenes of a wedding party,
a Christmas dinner, and a surprise anniversary celebration, characters
gather together to affirm the bonds of love and friendship that knit their
lives to one another. The family celebrations are the occasions for feast-
ing, and in Erdrich's detailed descriptions of various dishes and their
preparation, readers find variations played out on yet another of the
novel's central images—that of cookery and food.

PLOT

While *The Antelope Wife* is framed by the legend of the beading twins,
the roots of its central plot reach back into events of the past. In "Father's
Milk," the novel's first chapter, the rhythmically cadenced, annunciatory
voice[1] of a bardic storyteller recounts a little-known history that is in
danger of "fading in the larger memory." The history is that of Scranton
Teodorus Roy, the youngest son of intelligent and reserved Pennsylvania
Quakers. As a young man, Scranton falls under the spell of a traveling

thespian and follows her path as it leads to the west. When he fails to locate her, he enlists in the U.S. Cavalry, and that is how he comes to take part in a "spectacular cruel raid" (1) upon an unprotected Ojibwa village. Women and children are slaughtered in the raid, and Scranton himself uses the bayonet attached to his rifle to viciously murder an elderly woman. In her dying eyes he sees a vision of his mother, and that is when he flees the scene of carnage. Scranton once again heads to the west, this time following a dog that carries an infant strapped upon its back.

Three days pass before Scranton is able to approach the dog and discover that the baby is a little girl who is mesmerized by the necklace of blue beads that hangs from her cradle. Because he must, he finds that he is able to suckle the infant, to nourish her with "father's milk." He claims the child as his daughter and names her Matilda, in honor of his mother. For six years Scranton and Matilda live in a small sod house where they raise guinea fowl. Then, when Scranton marries Peace McKnight, the community's young schoolteacher, the Roy family grows to three. One night, however, Matilda's mother, Blue Prairie Woman, comes at last to reclaim her daughter. Carrying her necklace of blue beads, the child sets out on her journey homeward. After Matilda has disappeared, the time comes for Peace to give birth to her baby. The young woman spends three long days in difficult labor, and then, weakened by her recent bout with the mottled skin sickness, dies just after her son Augustus is born. Once again Scranton answers the call of necessity by suckling a motherless infant.

"Father's Milk" is divided into independent passages that serve to fully detail the aftermath of the raid on the Ojibwa village. In the passages that focus on the village itself, readers learn that Blue Prairie Woman is unable to recover from the loss of her child. In a special naming ceremony, she is given a new name, Other Side of the Earth, a name that allows her to be in two places at once: at home with her husband Shawano she conceives her twin daughters, and, with another part of herself, she looks to the west to trace the path of her first-born daughter. Finally, after she gives birth to the twins, Blue Prairie Woman sets out on her quest. On their journey home, Matilda and her mother both fall prey to the mottled skin fever that claimed the life of Peace McKnight. When she can see that she is going to die and that her daughter will live, Blue Prairie Woman boils her dog Sorrow to provide food for the child. Later, when her mother is gone, the child renamed Other Side of the Earth roams with a herd of antelope. When the "dreamlike" creatures run, she sprints along with them, "naked, graceful, the blue beads around her neck" (20).

The characters introduced in the novel's second chapter belong to the fourth generation of survivors of the massacre. Klaus Shawano, a sanitation engineer who lives in Minneapolis, tells of how he spends his free time traveling as a trader along the circuit of Montana's many powwows. It is on one of these occasions that Klaus spots the woman he believes he cannot live without, and, in the chapter entitled "The Antelope Wife," he relates the story of how he schemed to ensnare Sweetheart Calico, the woman of his dreams. Klaus first sees his wife-to-be as she strolls the powwow grounds in the company of her three daughters. Elegant in their simple dance clothes, the women are "light steppers with a gravity of sure grace" (24). When Klaus makes inquiries of Jimmy Badger, an old medicine man, readers learn that these women are descendents of a woman who spent her summers living with the antelope. Jimmy warns Klaus to avoid these women, for the men who make love to them are somehow "never the same" (29) thereafter. Klaus, however, ignores this advice, and, leaving her daughters behind, makes off with his antelope wife.

Klaus carries Sweetheart Calico, named for the fabric which binds their wrists together, back to Minneapolis. There readers are introduced to several more of the novel's characters. Rozina Roy Whiteheart Beads, who lost her twin sister to diphtheria during their childhood, is the daughter of twins descended from Blue Prairie Woman's twins, and also the mother of twins, Cally and Deanna. Rozin is devoted to her daughters and tells, in "Seaweed Marshmallows," of her many joyful hours spent playing with them. In this instance, the young daughters provide the food for the mother when they draw from their "imaginary store" great quantities of "airsweet" marshmallows all made of seaweed. Rozin eats each one until she is filled with an "invisible, light happiness" (39).

Rozin's life is troubled, though, for she has a secret lover. Although she still loves her husband, Richard Whiteheart Beads, with the old, familiar, and guilty sense of loyalty that she cannot deny after years of life together, her great passion is for Frank Shawano, Klaus's brother. It is, in fact, in Frank's bakery shop that she encounters Sweetheart Calico, a mysterious woman who never speaks but gazes fiercely at the world with hungry and searching eyes. Rozin does not know where Klaus has gone, for four years have passed since she last saw him. Readers learn that after Klaus's antelope wife "proceeded to drive him crazy" (34), Frank took her in and gave her a room above his bakery shop.

Rozin lies to Richard about Frank because she knows that he wants to be deceived. In this fashion, her marriage continues until she learns that Frank has been diagnosed with terminal cancer and has little time to live. Although Rozin has twice during her years with Richard attempted unsuccessfully to leave her husband, she is determined, on the third occasion, that she will end their marriage. Richard responds to Rozin's decision with anger, dismay, and then finally self-pity, and it is out of his monstrous self-pity that he makes an attempt to end his life. He seals the doors of the garage, starts up his engine, and waits in his yellow truck for the exhaust fumes to thicken. After a time he decides that he needs a last drink. Leaving his engine running, he slips into the house, and, when he discovers that he has locked his keys inside the truck, he decides to abandon his efforts at suicide and simply let the truck run out of gas. What Richard does not know is that his eleven-year-old daughter Deanna has sneaked into the truck and is waiting there for his return. With this unspeakable catastrophe, Part One of the novel comes to a close.

Part Two of the novel, a fairly short section, accounts for the passage of the years immediately following Deanna's death. Frank survives his cancer scare, but Rozin, devastated by the loss of her daughter (and haunted by her guilt and regret), abandons thoughts of love. She and Cally move north to the Ojibwa reservation and live there with her twin mothers, Mary and Zosie. Zosie and Mary both think of themselves as Rozin's mother and refuse to reveal which one of them actually carried the baby. The first two chapters of this section are narrated by Almost Soup, Cally's dog, and offer readers further insights into the relationship between animals and people. As Almost Soup notes, while Rozin sits at her beadwork, "Though I live the dog's life ... I am connected in the beadwork. I live in the beadwork too" (91). In "Nibi," the last chapter of Part Two, readers learn that Klaus and Richard have both become drunken bums who live on the city's streets and resort to drinking Listerine when they cannot pay for wine.

In Part Three of *The Antelope Wife*, Cally Roy, eighteen and uncertain of what she would like to do with her life, moves back to Gakahbekong, the big city of Minneapolis. Her grandmothers, Zosie Roy and Mary Shawano, are both in the city, but they move frequently from place to place and cannot be found, so Rozin arranges for Cally to move into

Frank's bakery shop. Cally finds that Frank is still affable and helpful, but he is no longer funny, for during his struggle with cancer he forgot how to laugh. His sister Cecille, who also lives in the shop, tries to find ways to restore his lost sense of humor. Cecille runs a kung fu studio and likes to lecture Cally on the restorative properties of the healthful foods she eats. The shop's other resident is, of course, Sweetheart Calico, the disconcertingly silent woman who grins her "frightful" (105) smile and wanders aimlessly through the streets of the city.

Cally spends her days working in Frank's shop, pondering ambitions that she cannot give a name, and trying to find her grandmothers, for she has many questions to ask of them. She remembers her naming ceremony and knows, for example, that her spirit name is Ozhawashkwa-mashkodeykway, but she yearns to know the meaning of the name. Her grandmothers are namers, those who dream people's spirit names, and they will surely know the answer to her question. The grandmothers, however, are mysterious and elusive figures. While everyone who visits the shop seems to know them, or at least to have heard rumors about them, no one can give Cally their address. She therefore waits and thinks about her many questions.

Klaus, in moments of drunken stupor, is visited by a *windigo* dog, a clever creature who likes to stand on his chest and tell the latest dog jokes. One day the dog asks Klaus for a story and he responds with the tale of his naming. As it happened, Klaus's father returned from World War II troubled by the thought that he had not adequately avenged the loss of his brother in the war. Following the advice of tribal elders, the father kidnapped a former German soldier from a nearby state work camp. When the German recognized that his life was in danger, he offered to bake a cake that he hoped would save his skin. Indeed, Klaus the German's *blitzkuchen* turned out to be the stuff of legend, and from him Klaus Shawano inherited a name. Frank, the older brother, tasted that cake and at once decided he would be a baker: Frank spends his whole career trying to recreate the *blitzkuchen* he tasted in his youth.

Rozin eventually returns to Minneapolis and resumes her love affair with Frank, and Part Three closes with an account of their wedding. Friends and family gather, and a feast is prepared. For their wedding cake, the groom bakes his most recent version of the *blitzkuchen*. The ceremony is held in a cliffside park that overlooks the Mississippi River, and just as it begins, Richard Whiteheart Beads makes an unexpected appearance. Rozin's former husband once again has suicide in mind, and this time he plans to leap from the cliff in full view of the wedding party.

It is only through the reverend's quick-witted action that a dreadful tragedy is averted. After an ambulance has carried Richard away, and the reverend has consumed a bracing glass of champagne, Rozin and Frank are married at last.

The wedding party, however, has not seen the last of Richard, for he appears again during the reception. To attract Rozin's attention, Richard tells her that he has secretly poisoned the wedding cake. He soon retracts his words, but after he is gone, and the time has come to cut the cake, the guests are all loath to bite into a slice. Frank himself, therefore, takes the very first bite, and as he does so he is struck with amazement, for he has finally discovered his cake's "missing ingredient" (178). Frank now knows that it was fear that added extra spice to Klaus's *blitzkuchen*. When the wedding guests taste of the magical cake, they can all see visions of their loved ones. Although it appears, as the afternoon draws to a close, that they have successfully eluded disaster, Frank and Rozin's wedding day does end in tragedy. Richard comes to the newlyweds' honeymoon hotel, and just outside their door, he shoots himself in the head.

The final section of the novel opens with a chapter entitled "Food of the Dead." In solitude, Rozin waits to discover "what she will feel next," for she knows that she must somehow confront the spirits of the dead. She first hears Deanna's voice, asking "Are you coming too?" (186). While she waits to learn what her daughter wants, she painstakingly prepares an elaborate meal and sets two "spirit plates" on the western side of the table "because that is the death direction" (188). Rozin spends ten days alone, revisiting her memories and nourishing the dead. One night a stranger appears in her dreams, stands before her, and "unzips his body" (189). When she sees that he is "all frost inside, all ravenous snow," she knows that he is the "ice spirit of awful hunger" (190), the figure of the *windigo*. Haunted by Richard's hungry spirit, Rozin considers entering the gaping maw of the *windigo*. When it occurs to her, though, that Richard will be waiting for her at the "western gate" (192), she resolves that she will try instead to live with her ghosts.

"Northwest Trader Blue," narrated by Cally, depicts her coming of age. The chapter unfolds during the course of a Christmas dinner, and by the time the feast is over, Cally realizes that the "part of my life where I have to wander and pray is done" (220). Through conversation with her grandmother Zosie, she learns the meaning and origin of her name, and, indeed, she discovers as well that she is herself a namer. As it turns out, Cally was named Blue Prairie Woman, and her twin sister Deanna was given Blue Prairie Woman's second name, Other Side of the Earth. As Zosie explains, she won these names gambling with a woman who possessed a necklace of blue beads. Called "northwest trader blue," the beads were the "blueness of time," and when Zosie gambled lives for the beads, she understood that she was seeking "to hold time" (215). Cally wishes that she could see the beads, and her desire is indeed realized when Sweetheart Calico draws them from underneath her tongue. Able to speak again, the antelope wife's first words are "Let me go" (218).

A recurring motif in Erdrich's work features the image of a woman going home. *Love Medicine*'s June Kashpaw is one instance of this figure, and, in the closing pages of *The Antelope Wife*, Sweetheart Calico comes at last to represent another. The antelope wife belongs to the land "where sky meets earth" (222), and, in a peculiar moment of epiphany, Klaus acknowledges this truth. His insight comes after a lawn mower runs over his head: Suddenly his thoughts are clear and he knows both that he will never drink again and that he will release his sweetheart bride. Klaus once again binds Sweetheart Calico's wrist to his, and then he leads her to the western outskirts of the city. He does not dare look at her while he unties the strip of calico, but he does remain to watch the figure of his "longing" (227) fade into the western horizon.

"The Surprise Party" offers a comic retelling of O. Henry's well-known short story, "The Gift of the Magi,"[2] for in this chapter Rozin and Frank both attempt to surprise the other with the perfect anniversary gift. Frank would prefer a private celebration, but, knowing that Rozin has dreamed of once again gathering together the family and friends who attended the ill-fated wedding, he secretly makes the arrangements for a party. Rozin, on the other hand, plans to surprise her husband with the gift of herself. Each attends to necessary preparations, and, on the evening of their day Rozin comes down the dark stairway when she hears her husband's call. When Frank turns on the lights and the guests cry out "surprise!" Rozin stands before them wearing only her high heels and three stick-on bows. After an interval of horrified silence, the guests are startled by the "bold crack" (236) of Rozin's sudden laughter. When everyone joins in, Frank does too—and in this surprising fashion his sense of humor is restored.

The Antelope Wife is brought to a close when the voice of the storyteller reveals how it happened that Scranton Roy's grandson married the Shawano from whose cabin he would later disappear. Readers learn that in his old age, Scranton found himself haunted by a vision of the old woman he had murdered, and, on the "hundredth night that she visited him" (238), he promised her that he would return to the land of her people. He indeed made that last journey and took along with him his grandson Augustus. Augustus traded his ruby red whiteheart beads for the Shawano girl he desired, and those very beads were woven into a blanket for a child. The child adored his blanket, and out of this attachment grew his name, Whiteheart Beads. Richard Whiteheart Beads then grew into a man who "would have died in his sleep on his eighty-fifth birthday" had he aimed his pistol a mere "centimeter higher" (240).

CHARACTERS

Among *The Antelope Wife*'s large cast of characters are the several dogs who repeatedly demonstrate the truth of Almost Soup's observation that the history of his "old race" is inextricably bound to that of the human race. Indeed, as he points out, "Original Dog walked alongside Wena-bojo,"[3] the Ojibwa's trickster creator. Almost Soup owes his life to the love of Cally—who loves him, as he says, "up there with her human loves" (81). He finds occasion to return this love when Cally falls ill and suffers convulsions. During her delirium, Almost Soup takes her life inside himself just "to keep it safe" (90), and when her fever finally breaks, he puts it back again. Along with the other dogs, Blue Prairie Woman's Sorrow and Klaus's *windigo* Dog, Almost Soup is indeed "connected in the beadwork" of the novel's plot.

Near the end of the novel, after the encounter with a lawn mower has cleared Klaus's mind, he meditates on the question of longing, a condition that he believes all people are subject to unless they are "half dead or lucky." Longing, he comes to understand—and even longing for something good, like love—is what "makes us do the things that we should not" (227). Both Klaus and Sweetheart Calico are depicted as characters engulfed by their longing: Klaus by his longing to possess the woman he hunted and ensnared, and Sweetheart Calico by her longing for her daughters and the freedom of the wide spaces to the west. Both characters are trapped, immobilized by the spell of their unfulfilled desires and thus live their days in a state of waiting. Klaus's drunken visions are always of his sweetheart, the elusive figure he sees as his Blue Fairy and therefore the one who has the power to grant him his wish.

Because they do not know her story or her desires, Sweetheart Calico's silent presence seems sinister to others; both Rozin and Cally are frightened by the ferocity of her unspoken longing.

Whereas Klaus quite simply wants to have the object of his love, Richard's will to possess is inflamed by his unwillingness to give up something he once had. By the time of Rozin's remarriage, he cannot bear the thought that the woman with whom he once made love could desire to make love to someone else. Richard's first response, when the affair begins, is simply to deny it, and Rozin accommodates this position with her ready lies. Later, when she decides to leave him, his denial turns to anger, and his behavior grows increasingly reckless and self-indulgent. Readers, of course, will recognize that these traits were in fact part of his character long before the divorce, for Klaus tells of the risks he took in his business when he illegally dumped toxic waste. After Deanna's death, Richard's feelings of guilt are once again expressed in the form of denial: He forbids Klaus to make reference to the tragedy and instead invents stories he can tell of other children and other losses.

Frank Shawano is the emblem of the nurturing lover, the man who relishes "every hour . . . every solid, aching minute" (233) of his life with his beloved. With Richard, Rozin was clumsy, somehow made inept by her constant awareness of his hungry needs (even her beading went wrong, and he was not pleased with the loomed watchband she made for him one Christmas). Rozin's marriages, then, offer a study in contrasts, for with Frank she always feels at ease, even after he has unquestionably "lost his funny bone" (143). In this partnership, where the lovers share their interests in family and cultural tradition, each also pursues an independent interest: Frank's career is in fact his "calling," and he spends many happy hours perfecting his *blitzkuchen*, while Rozin, who is studying to be a lawyer, pores over her books. Although Rozin sometimes wishes she could undo the past, could "unweave the pattern of destruction" (36), neither she nor Frank, who goes on with his life during her long absence, is paralyzed by longing, as are other characters in the book.

Zosie and Mary, the wise and powerful Shawano twins, embody echoes of the myth of the beading sisters. In the sections of the novel entitled "Windigo Story," readers catch glimpses of these women stitching into their beadwork the fate of Augustus Roy. At first the two compete for the love of Zosie's husband, but then they grow resentful of his separation of them. Instead of trying to win his attention, each twin tries to confound him by making herself indistinguishable from her sister. Augustus grows more and more apprehensive, fearful that he will address one of his lovers by the wrong name. It is after he bites a chunk from Zosie's ear to permanently mark her that he mysteriously vanishes, and when the twins are later asked if they in fact ate him, and which of them it was who took the first bite, it is Mary who glances at her sister's ear and answers merely, "He did" (212).

Cally Roy, the young woman who has inherited her grandmothers' ability to name, assumes a role in *The Antelope Wife* that is in many ways similar to the role Albertine Johnson plays in *Love Medicine* and *The Bingo Palace*. That is to say that Cally is the perceptive observer, the one who recognizes, for example, that her mother still loves Frank after her many years of separation from him. Diana Postlethwaite, in her review of the novel, offers an apt observation when she notes that Cally is much like Louise Erdrich herself, someone "who looks unflinchingly at the secrets of the human heart" (Postlethwaite 6). Appropriately, Sweetheart Calico gives to Cally the necklace of beads that are the color of time, and then Cally accompanies her while she rambles through the city. The two walk through the night, and the antelope wife spins out for her listener "all the words she's stored up" (218) over the years. It is when morning comes, and Cally is once again alone, that she realizes that she now knows her vocation. As she expresses it herself, "I see this: I was sent here to understand and report" (220).

THEMES

In *The Bingo Palace* Erdrich poses questions about the relationship between chance and design, and she returns to that theme in *The Antelope Wife* with her use of the recurring metaphor of beading. Indeed, the images of beading express the pattern of design, the pattern that Rozin realizes she cannot "unweave." When she looks closely at that pattern, however, she sees that within it there are "strands" (36) that she might have changed as well as those she could not. In other words, she sees in her life both chance and design at work and understands that the two are woven together. In *Writing Tricksters*, Jeanne Rosier Smith argues that "in *The Bingo Palace* Erdrich constantly reiterates the interplay between chance and design" (Smith 107), and this point appears to hold true for *The Antelope Wife* as well. In fact, on the last page of the novel, Erdrich leaves her readers with questions about chance and design that imply that neither one alone is sufficient to explain the intricate patterns that finally shape a life. The questions posed in the voice of the storyteller ask the reader to consider the relationship between destiny and luck— and then, the storyteller wonders, "who is beading us?" (240).

If chance and destiny are woven together, so too are lives and events, and in *The Antelope Wife* Erdrich explores the interconnectedness of all the bits of "colored glass sewn onto the fabric of this earth" (240). The lives of the characters are connected across time and space, through the bloodlines of generations and through the chance events that link families together. Animals, too, are part of the design, for the lives of the dogs and the antelope intersect with those of the humans. Erdrich also shows how the living are connected to the dead. Cally, for example, lives her life with the thought that her lost twin is present with her; she can often hear Deanna speaking in "her little-girl voice . . . in the whisper of leaves" (122). Rozin honors her connection to the dead when she prepares a feast for the spirits, and when the wedding guests eat Frank's *blitzkuchen*, they save a few morsels for the dead to taste.

Like others of Erdrich's novels, *The Antelope Wife* relates stories of characters' survival of catastrophe, and, as one of its central themes, it celebrates the life-affirming power of the will to survive. It is, of course, out of some fierce instinct for survival that Scranton Roy produces "father's milk" when he must; Erdrich uses this startling occurrence to create a fable that offers an extraordinary measure of the human will to survive. Almost Soup demonstrates his will to survive by exercising guile and cunning when he faces the threat of the stewpot; to avoid being eaten, he must win the heart of a little girl by exhibiting all the irresistible charms of a puppy—floppy ears, big feet, "puppy drool, joy . . . the head cock and puppy grin" (78). Through his resourcefulness, Almost Soup averts imminent disaster, and his story echoes that of Klaus the German soldier, whose strong survival instinct tells him that to save his own life, he must draw upon the special magic of his baker's art.

Among the several stories of characters who indeed suffer catastrophic loss, those that tell of Rozin's and Klaus's survival are perhaps the most poignant. Rozin's desire to endure is severely tested during her ten days of solitary communion with the dead, and the appearance of the *windigo* represents her great temptation to succumb to the hunger of her grief. In the last days of her vigil she indeed waits for the *windigo*'s return. On the tenth day, when she thinks that he has come, she sees instead the image of Frank, the man whom she loves. After she falls into his arms, she realizes that he is only a figure in a dream, but she also understands that he has given her the "gift" of his strong body as her protection and that she can "hide" in the warmth of that body "from now on as she walks forward in the world" (191). It is when she chooses to accept the gift of Frank's love that Rozin finds a way to survive her despair. Ironically, Klaus's survival too depends upon the giving and acceptance of a gift, for if he and Sweetheart Calico are to break the spells cast over them by their longing, he must give and she must take the gift of her freedom.

In addition to its accounts of characters' personal survival, *The Antelope Wife* celebrates the endurance of Ojibwa cultural tradition. Like Erdrich's other novels, this one traces the cultural legacy that is passed from one generation to another. In *The Antelope Wife*, for example, readers are witness to the preservation of the Ojibwa tongue, for not only do the elders speak the old language, but so too does Cally, the figure who represents the sixth generation of characters in the novel. Traditional names, too, are passed along by families, and when Zosie tells Cally that her spirit name is Blue Prairie Woman, she notes that this is a "stubborn" and "long-lasting" (217) name, one that will not disappear. Indeed, Cally's name is as "long-lasting" as the stories that are also passed down through the ages, for through the voice of its storyteller and the tales its characters tell, the novel invokes the Ojibwa's oral tradition. Needless to say, Indian survival humor, the Indian's "seventh sense" (115), is yet another of the legacies important in the novel, and when Frank temporarily loses his funny bone, readers are informed that he is the only Indian alive who has no sense of humor.

ALTERNATIVE PERSPECTIVE: FEMINIST CRITICISM

As part of the modern women's movement, feminist literary theorists seek to understand women's positions in society and to challenge conventions or traditions that circumscribe the choices available to women. Recognizing that both language and literature have traditionally been dominated by men, feminist critics welcome the voices of writers whose uses of linguistic and literary forms give expression to women's perspectives and experiences. Feminist critics indeed argue that it is through the voices of these writers, both women and men, that literary art can play a significant role in helping to redefine women's social positions and, in so doing, work to redress the imbalance of power that has traditionally divided the genders. Louise Erdrich, whose novels present what reviewer Vince Passaro describes as "a leading and profoundly redemptive role for women" (Passaro 163), is one of these writers, one who, in *The Antelope Wife*, depicts women's power to defy traditions of masculine authority.

In a 1987 interview with Joseph Bruchac, Erdrich gives voice to the very questions about women's power that she later explores more fully in *The Antelope Wife*. Erdrich observes that although women have been taught to present to the world their "demure" faces, these faces often hide the "wild energy" (Bruchac 100) that transforms women into something other than what they seem to be. In her work, Erdrich goes on to explain, she uses those occasions when women take the form of animals to symbolically represent their transformation; when a woman takes the form of an animal, she is enacting "her own power." Readers of *Tracks* and *The Bingo Palace* know that Fleur Pillager possesses magical power when she assumes the form of the bear, and, in *The Antelope Wife*, Sweetheart Calico commands the power to be free when she lives at one with the antelope. When women recognize and express their power, they find their "honest nature" hidden beneath the "socialized nature" that is reflected in "demure" faces. Erdrich goes on to explain that when women realize their power, they come to understand that they can say "No" (Bruchac 101), a word that they are generally not taught to use.

While *The Antelope Wife* addresses women's experiences in a variety of ways, in its characterizations of women, for example, or in its repeated references to beading and cooking, at the heart of its complicated plot lie the stories of women who have found in themselves the power to say "no." In their quite different ways, the bayoneted grandmother, Matilda/Other Side of the Earth, Sweetheart Calico, Mary and Zosie, and, of course, Rozin all resist the efforts of men to impose their will on women, to claim women as the objects of their desire or to define for women the conditions of their being. All of these women are in some sense the "antelope wife," the figure of the woman who draws upon her own power to realize her "honest nature."

The bayoneted grandmother is the old woman only briefly described in the novel's opening pages, the figure whose murder brings home to Scranton Roy the full horror of his deeds. It appears to readers, through most of the novel, that with his slaughter of this woman, Scranton Roy has taken it upon himself to determine her fate, but, when the storyteller reintroduces the woman in the last chapter of the book, it becomes clear that she is in fact not simply dead to Scranton but rather is transformed into a woman who has the power to shape his own family's destiny through the person of his grandson Augustus. When she assumes the form of a ghost, and thus resists her obliteration, she defies the will of the man who imposed upon her the condition of death.

Matilda, too, rejects Scranton Roy's designs for her life, for although she thinks of him as her father, indeed loves him "like nothing else" (11), and remembers with gratitude how he nourished her when she was small, she somehow knows, when her mother comes, that she can no longer be Matilda Roy, daughter to Scranton. She therefore pens a brief note in handwriting that resembles his own and sets out for home. Erdrich once observed that "the women in my books are lighting out for home" (Pearlman 153), and, although Other Side of the Earth is at first uncertain of the direction of her home, she soon discovers that it lies in the land of the antelope.

Zosie and Mary both love the same man, and, in return, they are both loved by Augustus Roy, who is fascinated by the puzzle of his wife's double identity. After Mary confesses to Zosie that she too is Augustus's lover (a circumstance that Zosie has in fact already discerned), the twins offer the husband the persona they share as they take turns visiting his bed. (After all, it was his excitement over the novelty of their confusing sameness that led him to first become unfaithful to Zosie.) This arrangement, perhaps, could have continued indefinitely, but each twin asks, when she visits Augustus, to be called by her own name, and, indeed, Augustus himself desires to possess both of the women. It is when he imposes his will upon the twins by scheming to find a means to imprint upon one of their bodies a mark of the difference they wish to hide that they (in some unexplained way) resist the authority he has assumed.

Sweetheart Calico and Rozin are both the objects of men's desires, and both resist the efforts of men to claim possession of them. Sweetheart Calico, of course, is bodily captured and transported from her home in Montana to the alien environs of the city, but she herself, nameless, mute, and transfigured by her longing, is not to be owned. Klaus always uses the possessive pronoun "my" when he thinks of her, but what he owns is a figment of his imagination, an idea or dream of the object of his longing. Richard's claims on Rozin are, as he well knows, complicated for her by their past together, by the children that they share, and by her own sense of guilt, but she rejects the authority of all these claims when she makes it clear that her husband does not own her. Both Rozin and Sweetheart Calico pay a steep price for resisting the men who would impose their wills upon them, but so do the men, who are, after all, changed into bums. Female characters in all of Erdrich's novels are strong and resilient women; those presented in *The Antelope Wife* represent women's power to say "no."

NOTES

1. This effect is in part achieved through Erdrich's use of sweeping, cumulative sentences punctuated by short, declarative statements.

2. In this story, a young wife sells her beautiful hair to purchase a watch fob for her husband. The husband, in turn, sells his watch to buy combs to decorate his wife's remarkable hair.

3. Wenabojo is a variant spelling of Nanabozho, the trickster after whom *Tracks*'s Nanapush is named.

Bibliography

WORKS BY LOUISE ERDRICH

Books by Louise Erdrich

Novels

The Antelope Wife. New York: HarperCollins, 1998.
The Beet Queen. New York: Bantam Books, 1986. (Cited as *BQ*.)
The Bingo Palace. New York: HarperCollins, 1994.
Love Medicine. New York: Bantam Books, 1984.
Love Medicine (New and Expanded Edition). New York: HarperCollins, 1993. (Cited as *LM*.)
Tales of Burning Love. New York: HarperCollins, 1996.
Tracks. New York: Harper & Row, 1988.

Memoir

The Blue Jay's Dance: A Birth Year. New York: HarperCollins, 1995. (Cited as *TBJD*.)

Children's Book

Grandmother's Pigeon. New York: Hyperion Books for Children, 1996.

Poetry Collections

Baptism of Desire. New York: HarperCollins, 1989.
Jacklight. New York: Henry Holt and Company, 1984.

Textbook

Imagination. Westerville, Ohio: Charles Merrill Company, 1981.

Edited Collection

Best American Short Stories 1993 (Guest Editor). Boston: Houghton Mifflin, 1993.

Books by Louise Erdrich and Michael Dorris

The Crown of Columbus. New York: HarperCollins, 1991. (Cited as *CC*.)
Route Two. Northridge, Calif.: Lord John Press, 1991.

Uncollected Articles and Short Stories

"The Air Seeder." *Anteus,* Fall 1985.
"American Horse." In *Earth Power Coming: An Anthology of Native American Fiction,* edited by Simon J. Ortiz. Tsaile, Ariz.: Navajo Community College Press, 1983, 59–72.
"The Ballad of Moustache Maud." *Frontiers,* September 1984.
"The Beads." *North Dakota Quarterly,* Fall-Winter 1984.
"*The Beet Queen.*" *Paris Review,* Spring 1985, 10–26.
"Best Western." *Vogue,* May 1990, 288–292.
"The Bingo Van." *The New Yorker,* February 19, 1990, 39–47.
"*Chez Sita.*" *Minneapolis-St. Paul Magazine,* September 1986, 14.
"Christmas Lights." *Seventeen,* December 1987, 128.
"Crown of Thorns." *Chicago,* September 1984.
"Crown of Thorns." In *The Invisible Enemy,* edited by Miriam Dow and Jennifer Regan. St. Paul, Minn.: Graywolf Press, 1989, 156–170.
"Destiny." *The Atlantic Monthly,* January 1985, 64–68.
"The Dress." *Mother Jones,* July-August 1990, 50–55.
"Flesh and Blood." *Ms.,* October 1984.
"Flesh and Blood." In *Buying Time,* edited by Scott Walker. St. Paul, Minn.: Graywolf Press, 1985.
"Fleur." *Esquire,* August 1986, 52–55.
"Fleur." In *Prize Stories 1987,* edited by William Abrahams. New York: Doubleday, 1987, 1–14.
"Fleur's Luck." *Georgia Review,* Winter 1993, 659–662.
"Foxglove." *Georgia Review,* Fall 1992, 473–478.
"Freight." *American Voice,* Summer 1986.
"The Garden Path." *The New York Times Magazine,* July 21, 1996, 37.
"Happy Valentine's Day, Monsieur Ducharme." *Ladies Home Journal,* February 1990, 84, 91, 171.
"The Island." *Ms.,* January-February 1991, 38–42.
"Knives." *Chicago,* August 1986.
"Knives." *Granta,* Fall 1986, 135–149.

"The Leap." *Harper's*, March 1990, 65–68.
"The Little Book." *Formations*, Summer 1985.
"Lulu's Boys." *Kenyon Review*, Summer 1984, 1–10.
"Mary Adare." *New England Review*, Fall 1986.
"Matchimanito." *The Atlantic Monthly*, July 1988, 66–74.
"Matchimanito." In *The Best of the West 2*, edited by James Thomas and Denise Thomas. Layton, Ut.: Peregrine Smith, 1989, 98–119.
"Mauser." *The New Yorker*, April 8, 1991, 38–42.
"Mister Argus." *Georgia Review*, Summer 1985, 10–26.
"Naked Woman Playing Chopin." *The New Yorker*, July 27, 1998, 62–67.
"Nuclear Detergent." *New England Review*, Spring 1982.
"The Plunge of the Brave." *New England Review*, Winter 1993, 57–70.
"Pounding the Dog." *Kenyon Review*, Fall 1985, 18–28.
"The Red Convertible." *Mississippi Valley Review*, Summer 1981.
"Resurrection." *Glimmer Train*, Winter 1994, 7–22.
"Saint Marie." *The Atlantic Monthly*, March 1984, 78–84.
"Saint Marie." In *Prize Stories 1985*, edited by William Abrahams. New York: Doubleday, 1985, 103–115.
"Satan: Hijacker of a Planet." *The Atlantic Monthly*, August 1997, 64–68.
"Scales." *North American Review*, March 1982, 22–27.
"Scales." In *The Best American Short Stories 1983*, edited by Shannon Ravenel and Anne Tyler. Boston: Houghton Mifflin, 1983, 141–154.
"Scales." In *The Year's Best American Short Stories*. London: Severn House, 1984, 141–154.
"Scars." *Boston Globe Magazine*, August 31, 1986.
"Sita Kozka." *Ms.*, August 15, 1986.
"Skunk Dreams." *Georgia Review*, Spring 1993, 85–94.
"Snares." *Harper's*, May 1987, 60–64.
"Snares." In *The Best American Short Stories 1988*, edited by Shannon Ravenel and Mark Helprin. Boston: Houghton Mifflin, 1988, 121–131.
"Snow Houses." *Architectural Digest*, December 1994, 40–42.
"Square Lake." *Working Woman*, November 1987.
"A Wedge of Shade." *The New Yorker*, March 6, 1989, 35–40.
"A Wedge of Shade." In *Louder than Words*, edited by William Shore. New York: Vintage, 1989, 136–148.
"Wild Geese." *Mother Jones*, October 1984, 21–22.
"The World's Greatest Fishermen." *Chicago*, October 1982.
"The World's Greatest Fishermen." In *Reinventing the Enemy's Language*, edited by Joy Harjo and Gloria Bird. New York: W. W. Norton & Company, 1997, 411–446.

Articles and Reviews

"Excellence Has Always Made Me Fill with Fright When It Is Demanded by Other People, But Fills Me with Pleasure When I Am Left Alone." *Ms.*, January 1985.

"My Urban Aunt." *New York Woman*, November 1986.

"The Names of Women." In *Sacred Ground: Writing about Home*, edited by Barbara Bonner. Minneapolis, Minn.: Milkweed Editions, 1996: 86–91.

Review of *Texasville*, by Larry McMurtry. *The New York Times Book Review*, April 19, 1987, 1.

"Where I Ought to Be: A Writer's Sense of Place." *The New York Times Book Review*, July 28, 1985, 1, 23–24.

"A Woman's Work: Too Many Demands and Not Enough Selves." *Harper's*, 35–44.

Poems

"All the Comforts of Home"; "His Deathmap"; "Certain Fields." *Decotah Territory*, Autumn 1977.

"Fooling God." *Poetry*, July 1989, 223–224.

"Fooling God." In *Reinventing the Enemy's Language*, edited by Joy Harjo and Gloria Bird. New York: W. W. Norton and Company, 1997, 463–464.

"In the Midlands." *Ms.*, August 1979.

"Jacklight"; "Indian Boarding School: The Runaways"; "Painting of a White Gate and Sky"; "The Strange People." *Frontiers*, Fall 1981.

"The Lesky Girls." *Carolina Quarterly*, Fall 1975.

"Maiden Sister"; "Insomniac's Journey." *Bloodroot*, Spring 1978.

"People." *Frontiers*, Fall 1982.

"Portrait of the Town Leonard"; "Leonard Commits Redeeming Adulteries with all the Women in Town." *Ms.*, Spring 1981.

"The Red Sleep of Beasts." *Ellipsis*, Spring 1979.

"The Rhubarb"; "Lise"; "From a Sentence in a Book of Italian Grammar"; "Tree Prayer." In *Tilt: An Anthology of New England Women's Writing*. Lebanon, N.H.: New Victoria Publishers, 1978.

"Stripper." *Webster Review*, Summer 1979.

"To Otto, in Forgetfulness"; "Here's a Good Word for Step-and-a-Half Waleski"; "My Name Repeated on the Lips of the Dead." *Louisville Review*, Fall 1978.

"Tree Dweller"; "The Book of Water." *Decotah Arts Quarterly*, Summer 1977.

"Turtle Mountain Reservation." *Shenandoah*, Spring 1979.

Articles and Stories Written with Michael Dorris

"Alternate Life Styles"; "Music to His Ears." *Woman*, 1983.

"Bangs and Whimpers: Novelists at Armageddon." *The New York Times Book Review*, March 13, 1988, 1.

"Cows, Colleges and Contentment." *The New York Times*, August 3, 1986, sec. 10, p. 37.

"The Crown of Columbus." *Mother Jones*, May-June 1991, 24–29.

"The Days after Tomorrow: Novelists at Armageddon." In *The Nightmare Considered: Critical Essays on Nuclear War Literature*, edited by Nancy Anisfield. Bowling Green, Ohio: Popular Press, 1991, 52–57.

"Manitoulin Island." *Anteus*, Spring-Autumn 1990, 381–389.

"On the Road with the Kids." *The Boston Globe Travel Magazine*, March 1987.

"Sea to Sea on Route 2." *The New York Times Magazine*, March 15, 1987, 31–32, 43–48.

Article Written with Heid Erdrich

"Listeners Unite." *Redbook*, March 1981.

WORKS ABOUT LOUISE ERDRICH

General Information and Interviews

Alsdurf, Phyllis. "Out of the Garden: Women Writers on the Bible." *Christianity Today*, October 2, 1995, 42–45.

"American Indian Louise Erdrich Plumbs Her Heritage to Produce a Prize-winning First Novel." *People Weekly*, February 18, 1985, 75.

A.S.A.I.L. Bibliography #9. *Studies in American Indian Literature: The Newsletter of the Association for the Study of American Indian Literature*, Winter 1985, 37–41.

Baumgaertner, Jill Palaez. "Upholding Mystery: An Anthology of Contemporary Christian Poetry." *The Christian Century*, June 4, 1997, 569–571.

Berkley, Miriam. *"Publishers Weekly* Interviews." *Publishers Weekly*, August 15, 1986, 58.

"Best Sellers." *Maclean's*, May 13, 1996, 17.

Blaeser, Kimberly M. "Pagans Rewriting the Bible: Heterodoxy and the Representation of Spirituality in Native American Literature." *ARIEL*, January 1994, 12–31.

Bly, Robert. "Another World Breaks Through." *The New York Times Book Review*, August 21, 1986, 2.

Bonetti, Kay. "An Interview with Louise Erdrich and Michael Dorris." *The Missouri Review* 11, no. 2 (1988): 79–99.

Brady, Laura A. "Collaboration as Conversation: Literary Cases." *Essays in Literature*, Fall 1992, 298–311.

Bruchac, Joseph. "Whatever Is Really Yours: An Interview with Louise Erdrich." *Survival This Way: Interviews with American Indian Poets.* Tucson: Sun Tracks and University of Arizona Press, 1987, 73–86; reprinted in *Conversations with Louise Erdrich and Michael Dorris*, edited by Allan Chavkin and

Nancy Feyl Chavkin. Jackson: University Press of Mississippi, 1994, 94–104.

Caldwell, Gail. "Writers and Partners." *The Boston Globe*, September 26, 1986, 15; reprinted in *Conversations with Louise Erdrich and Michael Dorris*, edited by Allan Chavkin and Nancy Feyl Chavkin. Jackson: University Press of Mississippi, 1994, 64–69.

Chavkin, Nancy Feyl, and Allan Chavkin. "An Interview with Louise Erdrich." In *Conversations with Louise Erdrich and Michael Dorris*, edited by Allan Chavkin and Nancy Feyl Chavkin. Jackson: University Press of Mississippi, 1994, 220–253.

Coltelli, Laura. "Louise Erdrich and Michael Dorris." *Winged Words: American Indian Writers Speak*. Lincoln: University of Nebraska Press, 1990, 40–52; reprinted in *Conversations with Louise Erdrich and Michael Dorris*, edited by Allan Chavkin and Nancy Feyl Chavkin. Jackson: University Press of Mississippi, 1994, 19–29.

Contemporary Authors. Detroit: Gale Research Company, 1985.

Contemporary Literary Criticism Yearbook, 1985. Detroit: Gale Research Company, 1986, 128–134.

Cowin, Dana. "Speak Previews." *Vogue*, February 1985, 236–237.

Croft, Georgia. "Something Ventured." *Valley News*, April 28, 1987, 1–2; reprinted in *Conversations with Louise Erdrich and Michael Dorris*, edited by Allan Chavkin and Nancy Feyl Chavkin. Jackson: University Press of Mississippi, 1994, 86–93.

Cryer, Dan. "A Novel Arrangement." *Newsday*, November 30, 1986, 19–23; reprinted in *Conversations with Louise Erdrich and Michael Dorris*, edited by Allan Chavkin and Nancy Feyl Chavkin. Jackson: University Press of Mississippi, 1994, 80–85.

Cunningham, Valerie. "A Right Old Battle-Axe." *Observer*, February 24, 1985, 27.

Desmond, John F. "Catholicism in Contemporary American Fiction." *America*, May 14, 1994, 7–11.

Dunbar, Helen. "A Novel Partnership." *Wall Street Journal*, October 24, 1984, 28–29.

"The Eighties and Me; Writers Reflect on How Their Books Helped Shape a Decade." *Publishers Weekly*, January 5, 1990, 21–23.

Foster, Douglas. "Double Vision: An Interview with the Authors." *Mother Jones*, May–June 1991, 26, 78–80.

Frenkiel, Nora. "Louise Erdrich." *Baltimore Sun*, November 17, 1986, 1B, 5B; reprinted in *Conversations with Louise Erdrich and Michael Dorris*, edited by Allan Chavkin and Nancy Feyl Chavkin. Jackson: University Press of Mississippi, 1994, 75–79.

George, Jan. "Interview with Louise Erdrich." *North Dakota Quarterly*, Spring 1985, 240–246.

Gleick, Elizabeth. "An Imperfect Union." *Time*, April 28, 1997, 68–69.

Grantham, Shelby. "Intimate Collaboration or 'A Novel Partnership' " *Dartmouth Alumni Magazine,* March 1985, 43–47; reprinted in *Conversations with Louise Erdrich and Michael Dorris,* edited by Allan Chavkin and Nancy Feyl Chavkin. Jackson: University Press of Mississippi, 1994, 10–18.

Harvey, Andrew. "The Voice of America: New Fiction from Our Most Talked-About Writers." *Vogue,* September 1986, 410–412.

Howard, Jane. "Louise Erdrich: A Dartmouth Chippewa Writes a Great Native American Novel." *Life,* April 1985, 27+.

Huey, Michael. "Two Native American Voices." *The Christian Science Monitor,* March 2, 1989, 16; reprinted in *Conversations with Louise Erdrich and Michael Dorris,* edited by Allan Chavkin and Nancy Feyl Chavkin. Jackson: University Press of Mississippi, 1994, 122–127.

Jones, Malcolm. "Life, Art Are One for Prize Novelist." *St. Petersburg Times,* February 10, 1985, 1D, 7D; reprinted in *Conversations with Louise Erdrich and Michael Dorris,* edited by Allan Chavkin and Nancy Feyl Chavkin. Jackson: University Press of Mississippi, 1994, 3–9.

Jones, Malcolm, and Brad Stone. "The Death of a Native Son." *Newsweek,* April 28, 1997, 82–83.

"Let Us Now Praise Unsung Writers." *Mother Jones,* January 1986, 27.

"Louise Erdrich." *Current Biography,* April 1989, 13–17.

"Louise Erdrich." In *American Diversity, American Identity: The Lives and Works of 145 Writers Who Define the American Experience,* edited by John K. Roth. New York: Henry Holt and Company, 1995, 7–11.

"Louise Erdrich." In *The Reading List: Contemporary Fiction,* edited by David Rubel. New York: Henry Holt and Company, 1998, 108–111.

Lovenheim, Barbara. "Hearing Echoes (Childhood Memories of Louise Erdrich)." *The New York Times Book Review,* August 31, 1986, 2.

Lyman, Rick. "Michael Dorris Dies at 52; Wrote of His Son's Suffering." *The New York Times,* Obituaries, April 15, 1997, C24.

———. "Writer Who Committed Suicide Faced Sex-Abuse Complaint." *The New York Times,* April 16, 1997, A10.

———. "Troubling Death Brings Plea for Respect, Not Sensation." *The New York Times,* April 18, 1997, A14.

Maynard, Joyce. "Reads for Ladies of Leisure." *Mademoiselle,* July 1985, 158–160.

McDowell, Edwin. "National Book Critics Circle Picks Winners." *The New York Times,* January 15, 1985, 20.

McGrath, Anne. "National Book Critics Circle Awards." *Wilson Library Bulletin,* April 1985, 537.

Morace, Robert A. "Erdrich, (Karen) Louise." In *Contemporary Popular Writers,* edited by Dave Mote. Detroit: St. James Press, 1997, 138–139.

Moyers, Bill. "Louise Erdrich and Michael Dorris." *A World of Ideas.* New York: Doubleday, 1989, 460–469; reprinted in *Conversations with Louise Erdrich and Michael Dorris*, edited by Allan Chavkin and Nancy Feyl Chavkin. Jackson: University Press of Mississippi, 1994, 138–150.

Nathan, P. S. "Offbeat Auction." *Publishers Weekly*, November 13, 1987, 40.

"National Book Critics Circle Announces 1984 Award Winners." *Publishers Weekly*, January 25, 1985, 27.

"Novelist Who Found Her Native Voice." *The New York Times Book Review*, December 23, 1984, 6.

Nowick, Nan. "Interview with Louise Erdrich." *Belles Letters*, November/ December 1986, 9; reprinted in *Conversations with Louise Erdrich and Michael Dorris*, edited by Allan Chavkin and Nancy Feyl Chavkin. Jackson: University Press of Mississippi, 1994, 70–74.

Passaro, Vince. "Tales from a Literary Marriage." *The New York Times Magazine*, April 21, 1991, 34–36, 38–39, 42–43, 76; reprinted in *Conversations with Louise Erdrich and Michael Dorris*, edited by Allan Chavkin and Nancy Feyl Chavkin. Jackson: University Press of Mississippi, 1994, 157–167.

Pearlman, Mickey. "Louise Erdrich." In *Inter/View: Talks with America's Writing Women*, edited by Mickey Pearlman and Katherine Usher Henderson. Lexington: University Press of Kentucky, 1989, 143–148; reprinted in *Conversations with Louise Erdrich and Michael Dorris*, edited by Allan Chavkin and Nancy Feyl Chavkin. Jackson: University Press of Mississippi, 1994, 151–156.

Peck, Claude. "Author Profile." *Minneapolis–St. Paul Magazine*, September 1986, 84+.

Portales, Marco. "People with Holes in Their Lives." *The New York Times Book Review*, December 23, 1984, 6.

Reuter, Madalynne. "National Book Critics Circle Celebrates 10th Year in New, Scholarly Atmosphere." *Publishers Weekly*, February 15, 1985, 24.

Rothstein, Mervyn. "Louise Erdrich, Partner in a Conspiracy to Write; Michael Dorris Is Her Husband and Collaborator, Too." *The New York Times*, October 13, 1986, 17+.

Schumacher, Michael. "Louise Erdrich, Michael Dorris: A Marriage of Minds." *Writer's Digest*, June 1991, 28–31, 59; reprinted in *Conversations with Louise Erdrich and Michael Dorris*, edited by Allan Chavkin and Nancy Feyl Chavkin. Jackson: University Press of Mississippi, 1994, 173–183.

Selwyn, Laurie. "Louise Erdrich." *Library Journal*, July 1988, 70.

Stead, Deborah. "Unlocking the Tale." *The New York Times Book Review*, October 2, 1988, 41.

Stokes, Geoffrey. "Behind Every Great Woman . . . ? Louise Erdrich's True-Life Adventures." *Voice Literary Supplement*, September 1, 1986, 7–9; reprinted in *Conversations with Louise Erdrich and Michael Dorris*, edited by Allan Chavkin and Nancy Feyl Chavkin. Jackson: University Press of Mississippi, 1994, 54–63.

Stone, Brad. "In the Best of Families." *Newsweek*, June 16, 1997, 54.

Streitfeld, David. "A Writer's Descent." *The Seattle Times*, July 29, 1997, E1, E4–E5.

Strouse, Jean. "In the Heart of the Heartland." *The New York Times Book Review*, October 2, 1988, 1, 41–42.

Tompkins, J. H. "Louise Erdrich: Looking for the Ties That Bind," *Calendar Magazine*, Oct., 1986, 15.

Towers, Robert. "Roughing It." *The New York Review of Books*, November 19, 1988, 40–41.

Trueheart, Charles. "Marriage for Better or Words." *The Washington Post*, October 19, 1988, B1, B8–B9; reprinted in *Conversations with Louise Erdrich and Michael Dorris*, edited by Allan Chavkin and Nancy Feyl Chavkin. Jackson: University Press of Mississippi, 1994, 115–121.

Ward, A. Joseph. "Prayers Shrieked to Heaven: Humor and Folklore in Contemporary American Indian Literature." *Western Folklore*, Summer-Fall 1997, 267–280.

"What Next? Bestselling Authors Talk about Works in Progress." *Publishers Weekly*, January 9, 1987, 62.

White, Sharon, and Glenda Burnside. "On Native Ground: An Interview with Louise Erdrich and Michael Dorris." *The Bloomsbury Review*, July/August 1988, 16–18.

Wickenden, Dorothy. "Off the Reservation." *The New Republic*, October 6, 1986, 46–48.

Wong, Hertha D. "An Interview with Louise Erdrich and Michael Dorris." *North Dakota Quarterly*, Winter 1987, 196–218; reprinted in *Conversations with Louise Erdrich and Michael Dorris*, edited by Allan Chavkin and Nancy Feyl Chavkin. Jackson: University Press of Mississippi, 1994, 30–53.

REVIEWS AND ARTICLES

Love Medicine

Alabaster, Carol. "Indian Voices Flow Together to Indict Tribal Life." *The Arizona Republic*, February 10, 1985.

Barnett, Marianne. "Dreamstuff: Erdrich's *Love Medicine*." *North Dakota Quarterly*, Winter 1988, 82–93.

Barry, Nora, and Mary Prescott. "The Triumph of the Brave: *Love Medicine*'s Holistic Vision." *CRITIQUE: Studies in Contemporary Fiction*, Winter 1989, 123–138.

Beddow, Reid. "*Medicine* Fiction Winner; First Novel Runaway Choice of Critics Circle." *The Washington Post*, January 15, 1985, C2.

Beidler, Peter G. "Three Student Guides to Louise Erdrich's *Love Medicine*." *American Indian Culture and Research Journal*, Fall 1992, 167–173.

Blaustein, Arthur I. "*Love Medicine*." *Mother Jones*, December 1988, 49.

———. "*Love Medicine.*" *Tikkun*, January-February 1990, 67.

Bruckner, D.J.R. "*Love Medicine.*" *The New York Times*, December 20, 1984, C21.

Cox, Karen Castellucci. "Magic and Memory in the Contemporary Story Cycle: Gloria Naylor and Louise Erdrich." *College English*, February 1998, 150–172.

Crabtree, Claire. "Salvific Oneness and the Fragmented Self in Louise Erdrich's *Love Medicine.*" In *Contemporary Native American Cultural Issues: Proceedings from the Native American Studies Conference at Lake Superior University, October 16–17, 1987*, edited by Thomas E. Schirer. Sault Ste. Marie, Ont.: Lake Superior University Press, 1991.

DeCandido, GraceAnne A. "*Love Medicine.*" *Library Journal*, November 1, 1990, 139.

Devereaux, Elizabeth. "*Love Medicine* Redux: New and Improved, But Why?" *Publishers Weekly*, November 23, 1992, 30.

Farrell, Susan. "Erdrich's *Love Medicine.*" *The Explicator*, Winter 1988, 109–112.

Flavin, Louise. "Louise Erdrich's *Love Medicine*: Loving Over Time and Distance." *CRITIQUE: Studies in Contemporary Fiction*, Fall 1989, 55–64.

Fraser, Gerald. "*Love Medicine.*" *The New York Times Book Review*, December 15, 1985, 32.

Gilbert, Harriet. "Mixed Feelings: *Love Medicine.*" *New Statesman*, February 8, 1985, 31.

Gleason, William. " 'Her Laugh an Ace': The Function of Humor in Louise Erdrich's *Love Medicine.*" *American Indian Culture and Research Journal* 11, no. 3 (1987): 51–73.

Hanson, Elizabeth I. "Louise Erdrich: Making a World Anew." *Forever There: Race and Gender in Contemporary Native American Fiction*. New York: Peter Lang, 1989, 79–104.

Hunter, Carol. "*Love Medicine.*" *World Literature Today*, Summer 1985, 474.

Jahner, Elaine. "*Love Medicine.*" *Parabola*, May 1985, 96, 98, 100.

Jaskoski, Helen. "From the Time Immemorial: Native American Traditions in Contemporary Short Fiction." In *Since Flannery O'Connor: Essays on the Contemporary American Short Story*, edited by Loren Logsdon and Charles W. Mayer. Macomb: Western Illinois University Press, 1987, 54–71.

Johnson, Bonnie. "Selected from *Love Medicine.*" *Library Journal*, May 1, 1989, 88B.

Kendall, Elaine. "*Love Medicine.*" *The Los Angeles Times*, December 20, 1984, 34.

Kinney, Jeanne. "*Love Medicine.*" *Best Sellers*, December 1984, 324–325.

Kooi, Cynthia. "*Love Medicine.*" *Booklist*, September 1, 1984, 24.

Kroeber, Karl, ed. "Louise Erdrich: *Love Medicine.*" *Studies in American Indian Literature: The Newsletter of the Association for the Study of American Indian Literature*, Winter 1985, 1–29.

Kroeber, Karl, Dee Brown, Ursula K. Le Guin, Scott R. Sanders, and Kathleen M. Sands. "Louise Erdrich's *Love Medicine.*" In *Critical Perspectives on Native American Fiction*, edited by Richard F. Fleck. Washington, D.C.: Three Continents Press, 1993, 263–276.

Lansky, Ellen. "Spirits and Salvation in Louise Erdrich's *Love Medicine.*" *Dionysos: The Literature and Addiction Tri-Quarterly* 5, no. 3 (1994): 39–44.

Littlefield, D. F. "*Love Medicine.*" *American Indian Quarterly*, Winter 1987, 71–73.

Love, Barbara. "*Love Medicine.*" *Library Journal*, October 15, 1993, 87.

"*Love Medicine.*" *Kirkus Reviews*, August 15, 1984, 765–766.

"*Love Medicine.*" *The New York Times Book Review*, December 8, 1985, 3.

Lyons, Gene. "In Indian Territory." *Newsweek*, February 11, 1985, 70–71.

MacDougall, Ruth Doan. "*Love Medicine.*" *Christian Science Monitor*, November 27, 1984, 33.

Magalaner, Marvin. "Of Cars, Time, and the River." In *American Women Writing Fiction: Memory, Identity, Family, Space*, edited by Mickey Pearlman. Lexington: University Press of Kentucky, 1989, 95–108.

Matchie, Thomas. "*Love Medicine*: A Female *Moby Dick.*" *Midwest Quarterly: A Journal of Contemporary Thought* 30 (1989): 478–491.

McKenzie, James. "Lipsha's Good Road Home: The Revival of Chippewa Culture in *Love Medicine.*" *American Indian Culture and Research Journal* 10, no. 3 (1986): 58.

McKinney, Karen Janet. "False Miracles and Failed Visions in Louise Erdrich's *Love Medicine.*" *CRITIQUE: Studies in Contemporary Fiction*, Winter 1999, 152.

Medeiros, Paulo. "Cannibalism and Starvation: The Parameters of Eating Disorders in Literature." In *Disorderly Eaters: Texts in Self-Empowerment*, edited by Lilian R. Furst and Peter W. Graham. University Park: Pennsylvania State University Press, 1992.

Mitchell, David. "A Bridge to the Past: Cultural Hegemony and the Native American Past in Louise Erdrich's *Love Medicine.*" In *Entering the 90's: The North American Experience: Proceedings from the Native American Studies Conference at Lake Superior University, October 27–28, 1989*, edited by Thomas E. Schirer. Saulte Ste. Marie, Ont.: Lake Superior University Press, 1991.

O'Conner, Patricia T. "*Love Medicine.*" *The New York Times Book Review*, December 7, 1986, 84.

Parini, Jay. "*Love Medicine.*" *Saturday Review*, November/December 1984, 83.

Pittman, Barbara L. "Cross-Cultural Reading and Generic Transformations: The Chronotope of the Road in Erdrich's *Love Medicine.*" *American Literature*, December 1995, 777–792.

Purdy, John. "Building Bridges: Crossing the Waters to a *Love Medicine.*" In *Teaching American Ethnic Literatures*, edited by John R. Maitino and David R. Peck. Albuquerque: University of New Mexico Press, 1996, 83–100.

Ruppert, James. "Celebrating Culture: *Love Medicine.*" *Mediation in Contemporary Native American Fiction*. Norman: University of Oklahoma Press, 1995, 131–150.

———. "Mediation and Multiple Narrative in *Love Medicine.*" *North Dakota Quarterly* 59, no. 4 (1991): 229–241.

Sands, Kathleen Mullen. "Love Medicine." *Studies in American Indian Literatures* 9, no. 1 (1985): 12–24.

Sarris, Greg. "Reading Louise Erdrich: *Love Medicine* as Home Medicine." *Keeping Slug Woman Alive: A Holistic Approach to American Indian Texts*. Berkeley: University of California Press, 1993, 115–145.

Schneider, Lissa. "*Love Medicine*: A Metaphor for Forgiveness." *Studies in American Indian Literatures*, Spring 1992, 1–13.

Schreiber, Le Anne. "*Love Medicine*." *Vogue*, March 1985, 330.

Schultz, Lydia A. "Fragments and Ojibwe Stories: Narrative Strategies in Louise Erdrich's *Love Medicine*." *College Literature*, October 1991, 80–95.

Silberman, Robert. "Opening the Text: *Love Medicine* and the Return of the Native American Woman." In *Narrative Chance: Postmodern Discourse on Native American Indian Literatures*, edited by Gerald Vizenor. Albuquerque: University of New Mexico Press, 1989: 101–120.

Smith, Jeanne. "Transpersonal Selfhood: The Boundaries of Identity in Louise Erdrich's *Love Medicine*." *Studies in American Indian Literature* 3, no. 4 (1991): 13–26.

Stripes, James D. "The Problem(s) of (Anishinaabe) History in the Fiction of Louise Erdrich: Voices and Contexts." *Wicazo Sa Review* 7, no. 2 (1991): 26–33.

Towers, Robert. "Uprooted: *Love Medicine*." *New York Review of Books*, April 11, 1985, 36–37.

Van Dyke, Annette. "Questions of the Spirit: Bloodlines in Louise Erdrich's Chippewa Landscape." *Studies in American Indian Literature*, Spring 1992, 15–27.

Velie, Alan. "The Trickster Novel." In *Narrative Chance: Postmodern Discourse on Native American Indian Literatures*, edited by Gerald Vizenor. Albuquerque: University of New Mexico Press, 1989, 121–139.

Wong, Hertha D. "Louise Erdrich's *Love Medicine*: Narrative Communities and the Short Story Sequence." In *Modern American Short Story Sequences*, edited by J. Gerald Kennedy. Cambridge: Cambridge University Press, 1995, 170–193.

Woolman, Lee J. "*Love Medicine*." *English Journal*, October 1990, 83.

Yardley, Jonathan. "*Love Medicine*." *The Washington Post*, November 14, 1984, D2.

Zeck, Jeanne-Marie. "Erdrich's *Love Medicine*." *The Explicator*, Fall 1995, 58–60.

The Beet Queen

Aldridge, John W. "Medium Without Message." *Talents and Technicians: Literary Chic and the New Assembly-Line Fiction*. New York: Charles Scribner's Sons, 1992, 92–100.

Bak, Hans. "Toward a Native American 'Realism': The Amphibious Fiction of Louise Erdrich." In *Neo-Realism in Contemporary American Fiction*, edited by Kristiaan Versluys. Amsterdam: Rodopi, 1992.

Banks, Russell. *"The Beet Queen."* *The Nation*, November 1, 1986, 460–463.

Bataille, Gretchen M. "Louise Erdrich's *The Beet Queen*: Images of the Grotesque on the Northern Plains." In *Critical Perspectives on Native American Fiction*, edited by Richard F. Fleck. Washington, D.C.: Three Continents Press, 1993, 277–285.

"The Beet Queen." *Library Journal*, January 1987, 55.

"The Beet Queen." *The New Yorker*, January 12, 1987, 102.

Bly, Robert. "Another World Breaks Through." *The New York Times Book Review*, August 31, 1986, 2.

Castillo, Susan Perez. "Postmodernism, Native American Literature and the Real: The Silko-Erdrich Controversy." *The Massachusetts Review*, Summer 1991, 285–294.

Chase, Elise. *"The Beet Queen."* *Library Journal*, August 1986, 168–170.

Friedman, Susan Stanford. "Identity Politics, Syncretism, Catholicism, and Anishinabe Religion in Louise Erdrich's *Tracks*." *Religion and Literature* 26, no. 1 (Spring 1994).

Geeslin, Campbell. *"The Beet Queen."* *People Weekly*, September 29, 1986, 12–14.

Gorra, M. *"The Beet Queen."* *Hudson Review*, Spring 1987, 136–148.

Harvey, Andrew. "The Voice of America; New Fiction From Our Most-Talked About Writers." *Vogue*, September 1986, 410–411.

Kakutani, Michiko. *"The Beet Queen."* *The New York Times*, August 20, 1986, 19, 21.

Meisenhelder, Susan. "Race and Gender in Louise Erdrich's *The Beet Queen*." *ARIEL*, January 1994, 45–57.

Palmer, Jean B. *"The Beet Queen."* *Library Journal*, December 1990, 182.

Rubins, Josh. *"The Beet Queen."* *The New York Review of Books*, January 15, 1987, 14–15.

Schumacher, Michael. *"The Beet Queen."* *Writer's Digest*, December 1987, 62.

Silko, Leslie Marmon. "Here's an Odd Artifact for the Fairy-Tale Shelf." *Impact/Albuquerque Journal*, October 17, 1986, 10–11; reprinted in *Studies in American Indian Literatures* 10, no. 4 (1986): 177–184.

Simon, Linda. *"The Beet Queen."* *Commonweal*, October 24, 1986, 565+.

Sokolov, Raymond. *"The Beet Queen."* *The Wall Street Journal*, September 2, 1986, 24, 28.

Steinberg, Sybil. *"The Beet Queen."* *Publishers Weekly*, July 4, 1986, 60.

Storhoff, Gary. "Family Systems in Louise Erdrich's *The Beet Queen*." *CRITIQUE: Studies in Contemporary Fiction*, Summer 1998, 341–352.

Stuewe, Paul. *"The Beet Queen."* *Quill Quire*, October 1986, 49.

Walsh, Dennis M., and Ann Braley. "The Indianness of Louise Erdrich's *The Beet Queen: Latency as Presence*." *American Indian Culture and Research Journal*, Summer 1994, 1–16.

Wickenden, Dorothy. "The Beet Question." *The New Republic*, October 6, 1986, 46–48.

Tracks

Bird, Gloria. "Searching for Evidence of Colonialism at Work: A Reading of Louise Erdrich's *Tracks*." *Wicazo Sa Review* 8, no. 2 (1992): 40–47.

Brogan, Kathleen. "Haunted by History: Louise Erdrich's *Tracks*." *Prospects*, 1996, 169–192.

Clarke, Joni Adamson. "Why Bears Are Good to Think and Theory Doesn't Have to Be Murder: Transformation and Oral Tradition in Louise Erdrich's *Tracks*." *Studies in American Indian Literatures* 4, no. 1 (Spring 1992): 28–48.

Clute, John. "*Tracks*." *Times Literary Supplement*, October 28, 1988, 1211.

Cornell, Daniel. "Woman Looking: Revis(ion)ing Pauline's Subject Position in Louise Erdrich's *Tracks*." *Studies in American Indian Literatures* 4, no. 1 (Spring 1992): 49–64.

Flavin, James. "The Novel as Performance: Communication in Louise Erdrich's *Tracks*." *Studies in American Indian Literatures* 3, no. 4 (1991): 1–12.

Flower, Dean. "*Tracks*." *The Hudson Review*, Spring 1989, 136–137.

Gerrard, Nicci. "*Tracks*." *New Statesman & Society*, October 28, 1988, 37.

Hessler, Michelle R. "Catholic Nuns and Ojibwa Shamans: Pauline and Fleur in Louise Erdrich's *Tracks*." *Wicazo Sa Review*, Spring 1995, 40–45.

Hoffert, Barbara. "*Tracks*." *Library Journal*, September 1, 1988, 182.

Kaufman, Joanne. "*Tracks*." *People Weekly*, December 5, 1988, 30–32.

Kiely, Robert. "The Aesthetics of Solitude, the Politics of Exclusion: Thomas Hardy's *The Woodlanders* after Louise Erdrich's *Tracks*." *Reverse Tradition: Postmodern Fictions and the Nineteenth Century Novel*. Cambridge, Mass.: Harvard University Press, 1993, 235–256.

Kolmar, Wendy K. "Dialectics of Connectedness: Supernatural Elements in Novels by Bambara, Cisneros, Grahn, and Erdrich." In *Haunting the House of Fiction: Feminist Perspectives on Ghost Stories by American Women*, edited by Lynette Carpenter and Wendy Kolmar. Knoxville: University of Tennessee Press, 1991.

Larson, Sidner. "The Fragmentation of a Tribal People in Louise Erdrich's *Tracks*." *American Indian Culture and Research Journal* 17, no. 2 (1993): 1–13.

MacRae, Cathi. "*Tracks*." *Wilson Library Bulletin*, March 1989, 88–89.

Milton, Edith. "*Tracks*." *The Massachusetts Review*, Spring 1989, 118–119.

Narveson, Robert D. "*Tracks*." *Prairie Schooner*, Fall 1990, 132–136.

Nelson-Born, Katherine A. "Trace of a Woman: Narrative Voice and Decentered Power in the Fiction of Toni Morrison, Margaret Atwood, and Louise Erdrich." *L I T: Literature Interpretation Theory*, January 1996, 1–11.

Peterson, Nancy J. "History, Postmodernism, and Louise Erdrich's *Tracks*." *Publication of the Modern Language Association*, October 1994, 982–994.

Quinlan, Eileen. "New Catholic Literature Sails in Open Sea." *National Catholic Reporter*, May 24, 1996, 31–32.

Schweninger, Lee. "A Skin of Lakeweed: An Ecofeminist Approach to Erdrich and Silko." In *Multicultural Literatures through Feminist/Poststructuralist Lenses*, edited by Barbara Frey Waxman. Knoxville: University of Tennessee Press, 1993, 37–56.

Sergi, Jennifer. "Storytelling: Tradition and Preservation in Louise Erdrich's *Tracks*." *World Literature Today*, Spring 1992, 279–282.

Shaddock, Jennifer. "Mixed Blood Women: The Dynamic of Women's Relations in the Novels of Louise Erdrich and Leslie Silko." In *Feminist Nightmares: Women at Odds: Feminism and the Problem of Sisterhood*, edited by Susan Ostrov Weisser and Jennifer Fleischner. New York: New York University Press, 1994, 106–121.

Sheppard, R. Z. "*Tracks*." *Time*, September 12, 1988, 80–81.

Stead, Deborah. "Unlocking the Tale." *The New York Times Book Review*, October 2, 1988, 41.

Steinberg, Sybil. "*Tracks*." *Publishers Weekly*, July 22, 1988, 41.

Strouse, Jean. "*Tracks*." *The New York Times Book Review*, October 2, 1988, 1.

Tanner, Laura E. " 'Known in the Brain and Known in the Flesh': Gender, Race, and the Vulnerable Body in *Tracks*." *Intimate Violence: Reading Rape and Torture in Twentieth-Century Fiction*. Bloomington: Indiana University Press, 1994, 115–141, 147.

Towers, Robert. "*Tracks*." *The New York Review of Books*, November 10, 1988, 40.

"*Tracks*." *The Antioch Review*, Winter 1989, 116.

Vecsey, Christopher. "*Tracks*." *Commonweal*, November 4, 1988, 596–597.

Vizenor, Gerald. "Authored Animals: Creature Tropes in Native American Fiction." *Social Research*, Fall 1995, 661–683.

Walker, Victoria. "A Note on Perspective in *Tracks*." *Studies in American Indian Literatures* 3, no. 4 (1991): 37–40.

Welsh-Huggins, Andrew. "*Tracks*." *The Progressive*, February 1989, 44–45.

Zinsser, John. "*Tracks*." *Publishers Weekly*, September 1, 1989, 50.

The Bingo Palace

Beidler, Peter G. "*The Bingo Palace*." *American Indian Culture and Research Journal*, Summer 1994, 271.

"*The Bingo Palace*." *Publishers Weekly*, November 15, 1993, 72.

"*The Bingo Palace*." *The New Yorker*, March 14, 1994, 95.

Brehm, Victoria. "The Metamorphoses of an Ojibwa *Manido*." *American Literature*, December 1996, 677–706.

Huntington, Lee. "*The Bingo Palace*." *The Antioch Review*, Spring 1994, 366.

Meredith, Howard. "*The Bingo Palace*." *World Literature Today*, Summer 1994, 614.

Messud, Claire. "*The Bingo Palace*." *Times Literary Supplement*, June 17, 1994, 23.

Ott, Bill. "*The Bingo Palace*." *Booklist*, Dec. 15, 1993, 723.

Ross, Patricia. "*The Bingo Palace*." *Library Journal*, January 1994, 159.

Rounds, Kate. "*The Bingo Palace.*" *Ms.*, January-February 1994, 72.
Skow, John. "*The Bingo Palace.*" *Time*, February 7, 1994, 71.
Thornton, Lawrence. "*The Bingo Palace.*" *The New York Times Book Review*, January 16, 1994, 7.

Tales of Burning Love

Childress, Mark. "*Tales of Burning Love.*" *The New York Times Book Review*, May 12, 1996, 10.
Curwen, Thomas. "*Tales of Burning Love.*" *People Weekly*, May 27, 1996, 38–39.
Greenlaw, Lavinia. "*Tales of Burning Love.*" *Times Literary Supplement*, February 14, 1997, 21.
Hoffert, Barbara. "*Tales of Burning Love.*" *Library Journal*, April 15, 1996, 121.
Kirn, Walter. "*Tales of Burning Love.*" *New York*, July 8, 1996, 48–49.
Lee, Michael. "*Tales of Burning Love.*" *National Catholic Reporter*, May 24, 1996, 21–22.
Shechner, Mark. "*Tales of Burning Love.*" *Salmagundi*, Winter 1997, 220–238.
Siegal, Lee. "De Sade's Daughters." *Atlantic Monthly*, February 1997, 97–101.
Smith, Jeanne R. "*Tales of Burning Love.*" *MELUS*, Spring 1998, 200.
"*Tales of Burning Love.*" *Publishers Weekly*, February 19, 1996, 202.

The Antelope Wife

Hoffert, Barbara. "*The Antelope Wife.*" *Library Journal*, March 15, 1998, 92.
Kakutani, Michiko. "*The Antelope Wife.*" *The New York Times*, March 24, 1998, C18.
Ott, Bill. "*The Antelope Wife.*" *Booklist*, March 1, 1998, 1044.
Peterson, V. R. "*The Antelope Wife.*" *People Weekly*, April 13, 1998, 31.
Postlethwaite, Diana. "*The Antelope Wife.*" *The New York Times Book Review*, April 12, 1998, 6.
Stone, Brad. "Scenes from a Marriage: Louise Erdrich's New Novel—And Her Life." *Newsweek*, March 23, 1998, 69.

REVIEWS AND ARTICLES FEATURING TWO OR MORE NOVELS

Burdick, Debra. "Louise Erdrich's *Love Medicine, The Beet Queen*, and *Tracks*: An Annotated Survey of Criticism Through 1994." *American Indian Culture and Research Journal*, Summer 1996, 137–166.
Catt, Catherine M. "Ancient Myth in Modern America: The Trickster in the Fiction of Louise Erdrich." *Platte Valley Review*, Winter 1991, 71–81.
Desmond, John F. "Catholicism in Contemporary American Fiction." *America*, May 14, 1994, 7–11.

Ferguson, Suzanne. "The Short Stories of Louise Erdrich's Novels." *Studies in Short Fiction,* Fall 1996, 541–555.

Hansen, Elaine Tuttle. "What if Your Mother Never Meant to? The Novels of Louise Erdrich and Michael Dorris." *Mother Without Child: Contemporary Fiction and the Crisis of Motherhood.* Berkeley: University of California Press, 1977, 115–157.

Holt, Debra C. "Transformation and Continuance: Native American Tradition in the Novels of Louise Erdrich." In *Entering the 90's: The North American Experience: Proceedings from the Native American Studies Conference at Lake Superior University, October 27–28, 1989,* edited by Thomas E. Schirer. Sault Ste. Marie, Ontario: Lake Superior University Press, 1991.

Kiely, Robert. "Illegitimate Histories: Ghost Stories and Family Secrets by Toni Morrison, Louise Erdrich, and Maxine Hong Kingston." *Reverse Tradition: Postmodern Fictions and the Nineteenth Century Novel.* Cambridge, Mass.: Harvard University Press, 1993, 179–213.

Lee, Robert A. "Ethnic Renaissance: Rudolfo Anaya, Louise Erdrich, and Maxine Hong Kingston." In *The New American Writing: Essays on American Literature Since 1970,* edited by Graham Clarke. New York: St. Martin's Press, 1990.

Lincoln, Kenneth. " 'Bring Her Home': Louise Erdrich." *Indi'n Humor: Bicultural Play in Native America.* Oxford: Oxford University Press, 1993, 205–253.

Manley, Kathleen E. B. "Decreasing the Distance: Contemporary Native American Texts, Hypertext, and the Concept of Audience." *Southern Folklore* 51, no. 2 (1994): 121–135.

Maristuen-Rodakowski, Julie. "The Turtle Mountain Reservation in North Dakota: Its History as Depicted in Louise Erdrich's *Love Medicine* and *Beet Queen.*" *American Indian Culture and Research Journal* 12, no. 3 (1988): 33–48.

McCay, Mary A. "Cooper's Indians, Erdrich's Native Americans." In *Global Perspectives on Teaching Literature: Shared Visions and Distinctive Visions,* edited by Sandra Ward Lott, Maureen S. G. Hawkins, and Norman McMillan. Urbana: National Council of Teachers of English, 1993.

Moyer, L. L. "*Love Medicine* and *The Beet Queen.*" *Christianity and Crisis,* May 18, 1987, 198–199.

Nelson-Born, Katherine A. "Trace of a Woman: Narrative Voice and Decentered Power in the Fiction of Toni Morrison, Margaret Atwood, and Louise Erdrich." *L I T: Literature Interpretation Theory,* Jan. 1996, 1–11.

Owens, Louis. "Erdrich and Dorris's Mixedbloods and Multiple Narratives." *Other Destinies: Understanding the American Indian Novel.* Norman: University of Oklahoma Press, 1992, 192–224.

Rainwater, Catherine. "Reading between Worlds: Narrativity in the Fiction of Louise Erdrich." *American Literature,* September 1990, 405–422.

Rayson, Ann. "Shifting Identity in the Works of Louise Erdrich and Michael Dorris." *Studies in American Indian Literatures* 3, no. 4 (1991): 27–36.

Ruoff, A. LaVonne Brown. *American Indian Literatures: An Introduction, Bibliographic Review, and Selected Bibliography.* New York: Modern Language Association, 1990.

Sarvé-Gorham, Kristan. "Power Lines: The Motif of Twins and the Medicine Women of *Tracks* and *Love Medicine.*" In *Having Our Way: Women Rewriting Tradition in Twentieth-Century America*, edited by Harriet Pollack. Lewisburg, Penn.: Bucknell University Press, 1995, 167–190.

Smith, Jeanne Rosier. "Comic Liberators and Word-Healers: The Interwoven Trickster Narratives of Louise Erdrich." *Writing Tricksters: Mythic Gambols in American Ethnic Literature.* Berkeley: University of California Press, 1997: 71–110.

Tanrisal, Meldan. "Mother and Child Relationships in the Novels of Louise Erdrich." *American Studies International*, October 1997, 67–79.

Tharp, Julie. "Women's Community and Survival in the Novels of Louise Erdrich." In *Communication and Women's Friendships*, edited by Janet Doubler Ward and JoAnna Stephens Mink. Bowling Green, Ohio: Bowling Green State University Press, 1993.

Towery, Margie. "Continuity and Connection: Characters in Louise Erdrich's Fiction." *American Indian Culture and Research Journal* 16, no. 4 (1992): 99–122.

Wong, Hertha D. "Adoptive Mothers and Thrown-Away Children in the Novels of Louise Erdrich." In *Narrating Mothers: Theorizing Maternal Subjectivities*, edited by Brenda O. Daly and Maureen T. Reddy. Knoxville: University of Tennessee Press, 1991, 174–192.

OTHER SECONDARY SOURCES

Narrative Theory

Bakhtin, M. M. *Rabelais and His World*, trans. Helene Iswolsky. Bloomington: Indiana University Press, 1984.

Carter, Angela. "Notes from the Front Line." In *On Gender and Writing*, edited by Michelene Wandor. London: Pandora Press, 1983, 69–77.

Carter, Susanne. *Mothers and Daughters in American Short Fiction: An Annotated Bibliography of Twentieth-Century Women's Literature.* Westport, Conn.: Greenwood Press, 1993.

Ferguson, Mary Anne. *Images of Women in Literature*, 5th ed. Boston: Houghton Mifflin, 1991.

Gerhart, Mary. *Genre Choices, Gender Questions.* Norman: University of Oklahoma Press, 1992.

Ingram, Forrest L. *Representative Short Story Cycles of the Twentieth Century.* The Hague: Mouton, 1971.

Kelley, Margot. "Gender and Genre: The Case of the Novel-in-Stories." In *American Women Short Story Writers: A Collection of Critical Essays*, edited by Julie Brown. New York: Garland Publishing, 1995, 295–310.

Luscher, Robert M. "The Short Story Sequence: An Open Book." In *Short Story Theory at Crossroads*, edited by Susan Lohafer and Jo Ellyn Clarey. Baton Rouge: Louisiana State University Press, 1989, 148–167.

Mann, Susan Garland. *The Short Story Cycle: A Genre Companion and Reference Guide*. Westport, Conn.: Greenwood Press, 1989.

Young, David, and Keith Hollaman, eds. *Magical Realist Fiction: An Anthology*. New York: Longman, 1984.

Native American and Ojibwa Tradition

Allen, Paula Gunn, ed. *Studies in American Indian Literature: Critical Essays and Course Designs*. New York: Modern Language Association, 1983.

Barnouw, Victor. *Wisconsin Chippewa Myths & Tales and Their Relation to Chippewa Life*. Madison: University of Wisconsin Press, 1977.

Benton-Banai, Edward. *The Mishomis Book: The Voice of the Ojibway*. Saint Paul, Minn.: Indiana Country Press, 1979.

Bevis, William. "Native American Novels: Homing In." In *Critical Perspectives on Native American Fiction*, edited by Richard F. Fleck. Washington, D.C.: Three Continents Press, 1993, 15–45.

Bloom, Harold, ed. *Native American Writers*. Philadelphia: Chelsea House Publishers, 1998.

The Buffalo Hunters. Alexandria, Va.: Time-Life Books, 1993.

Danziger, Edmund Jefferson. *The Chippewas of Lake Superior*. Norman: University of Oklahoma Press, 1978.

Hyde, Lewis. *Trickster Makes This World*. New York: Farrar, Straus and Giroux, 1998.

Johnston, Basil H. *The Manitous: The Spiritual World of the Ojibway*. New York: HarperCollins, 1995.

———. *Ojibway Heritage*. New York: Columbia University Press, 1976.

———. *Tales of the Anishinaubaek*. Toronto: Royal Ontario Museum, 1993.

Landes, Ruth. *Ojibwa Religion and the Midéwiwin*. Madison: University of Wisconsin Press, 1968.

Smith, Dinitia. "The Indian in Literature Is Growing Up." *The New York Times*, April 21, 1997, C11–C12.

Vecsey, Christopher. *Traditional Ojibwa Religion and Its Historical Changes*. Philadelphia: The American Philosophical Society, 1983.

Vizenor, Gerald. *Fugitive Poses: Native American Indian Scenes of Absence and Presence*. Lincoln: University of Nebraska Press, 1998.

———. *The People Named the Chippewa: Narrative Histories*. Minneapolis: University of Minnesota Press, 1984.

Other Writers

Alexie, Sherman. *Indian Killer*. New York: Atlantic Monthly Press, 1996.
————. *The Lone Ranger and Tonto Fistfight in Heaven*. Atlantic Monthly Press, 1993.
————. *Reservation Blues*. Atlantic Monthly Press, 1995.
Carr, Aaron. *Eye Killers: A Novel*. Norman: University of Oklahoma Press, 1995.
Dorris, Michael. *The Broken Cord*. New York: Harper & Row, 1989. (With a Foreword by Louise Erdrich.)
————. *A Yellow Raft in Blue Water*. New York: Henry Holt, 1987.
Moore, Marianne. "Poetry." In *The Norton Anthology of Poetry*, edited by Alexander W. Allison et al. New York: W. W. Norton & Company, 1983, 986–987.
Power, Susan. *The Grass Dancer*. New York: Putnam's, 1994.
Sarris, Greg. *Grand Avenue*. New York: Hyperion, 1994.
————. *Watermelon Nights*. New York: Hyperion, 1998.
Treuer, David. *Little*. Saint Paul, Minn.: Graywolf Press, 1995.

Index

Adare, Adelaide (*The Beet Queen*), 54, 59, 60, 63–65, 67–68; as fairy-tale figure, 56; as mother without child, 25, 53, 84

Adare, Dot (*The Beet Queen, Love Medicine, Tales of Burning Love*), 2, 10, 15, 39, 55–59, 63, 65, 104, 111–15, 116–17, 118, 121; as Beet Queen, 2, 59; as child, 52, 57; as Cinderella, 56, 58–59; as narrator, 56, 59, 119

Adare, Karl (*The Beet Queen*), 18, 53–57, 59, 60–61, 63–65, 84; as fairy-tale figure, 56; Oedipal crisis of, 66–68; as trickster, 55, 66; as wanderer, 26, 55, 61, 66

Adare, Mary (*The Beet Queen, Tales of Burning Love*), 18, 20–21, 53–59, 61–63, 65, 67, 111–12, 117, 118; as child, 53–54; as namer, 56

Alexie, Sherman, 15

Almost Soup (*The Antelope Wife*), 131, 135; as narrator, 127; as survivor, 138

Alvarez, Julia, 87

Andy (*Love Medicine*), 17, 110

Anishinabe, 9, 11 n.2, 33, 73, 85. *See also* Ojibwa

The Antelope Wife, 2, 8, 17, 22, 31; acknowledgments, 2, 7; characters in, 135–37; feminist reading of, 139–42; humor in, 21, 134, 139; imagery of, 18, 128, 134, 137–38; narrative technique of, 16, 127–28; plot of, 128–37; setting of, 15, 128; themes in, 17, 137–39

The Arabian Nights, 110

Assimilation, 72, 76–77, 86, 87

Baez, Joan, 2

Bakhtin, Mikhail, 52, 68 n.1

Beads, Deana Whiteheart (*The Antelope Wife*), 130, 133–34, 138; death of, 131

Beads, Richard Whiteheart, (*The Antelope Wife*), 130–33, 135, 136, 141; suicide of, 133, 135

The Beet Queen, 4, 6, 26, 30, 70, 84, 91; characters in, 10, 51–53, 60–63; fairy tales in, 16, 55–56; Freudian literary analysis of, 66–68; humor in, 20–21, 52–53; imagery of, 10, 17, 18, 65; narrative strategies of, 52, 127; plot of, 52, 53–59; setting of, 2, 51, 75, 92; themes in, 25, 63–65

The Bingo Palace, 8, 26, 30, 84, 109, 115, 116; characters in, 102–4; ghosts in, 15, 93, 96, 101, 107; imagery of, 18, 97; narrative technique of, 91–92; plot of, 93–102; psychoanalytic perspective of, 106–8; setting of, 91; themes in, 25, 93, 97, 104–6, 137

Bjornson, Zelda Kashpaw Johnson (*The Bingo Palace*, *Love Medicine*), 46, 93, 94–96, 97, 100, 103, 105, 106–8

The Blue Jay's Dance, 6–7, 121

Blue Prairie Woman (*The Antelope Wife*), 129, 133

The Broken Cord (Michael Dorris), 5, 7

Calico, Sweatheart (*The Antelope Wife*), 130, 132, 134, 135–36, 137, 140–41

The Canterbury Tales (Geoffrey Chaucer), 110

Carnival, 51–52, 53, 56, 64–65, 68 n.1

Castillo, Ana, 33

Ceremony (Leslie Marmon Silko), 14

Characters: in *The Antelope Wife*, 135–37; in *The Beet Queen*, 51–53, 60–63; in *The Bingo Palace*, 102–4; ethnic background of, 9–10; as fairy-tale figures, 16, 55–56; as ghosts, 15, 93, 96; in *Love Medicine*, 36, 41–45; metaphoric depiction of, 18; as missionized Catholics, 9; as mothers without child, 25, 42; as orphans, 15, 25, 52, 63; reading tastes of, 62–63; as survivors, 46, 70, 125; in *Tales of Burning Love*, 117–21; in *Tracks*,
74, 82–84; as tricksters, 22–24; as twins, 22, 127–28, 136

Chaucer, Geoffrey, 32

Chippewa, 9, 11, 33, 73. *See also* Ojibwa

Cook, Marlis (*Tales of Burning Love*), 113–15, 118–21, 123–25

Critical perspectives: feminist criticism, 122–25, 139–42; Freudian literary analysis, 66–68; multicultural criticism, 86–88; psychoanalytic criticism, 106–8; reader-response theory, 47–49

The Crown of Columbus, 5, 8, 17

Culture hero, 23, 24, 44, 102

Dawes Allotment Act, 72

Dartmouth College, 2–3, 4; as setting, 5

The Death of Jim Loney (James Welch), 14

Dorris, Michael, 3, 4, 6, 8; books, 5; suicide of, 3, 7

Dubliners (James Joyce), 32

Erdrich, Louise: awards received, 6, 29; Catholic background of, 9, 14, 16; childhood and adolescence, 1–2; children of, 4, 6–7; collaboration with Michael Dorris, 4–5; education, 3; family of, 1–2; as feminist writer, 14, 15, 42, 122–24, 139–40; interests of, 7; love of Great Plains, 8–9; marriage of, 4, 7; memoir, 6–7; as novelist, 8, 13–14; Ojibwa heritage, 2, 3, 7, 9, 15, 21–24, 26; personal losses suffered, 7; as poet, 2, 3, 8, 13, 17–18; as short story writer, 6, 8, 13, 19, 31–32; work experience, 3, 4; as writer of children's books, 7; writer's voice of, 1, 13, 18–19, 127, 134, 138; writing habits, 2, 5, 10, 19, 70–71

Faulkner, William, 13, 14, 29, 32
Fowles, John, 30
Freud, Sigmund, 66–67, 106–7

Genre, 10, 13, 14, 21; of *The Crown of Columbus*, 5; of *Love Medicine*, 31–35; narrative poetry, 8, 13, 19; novel, 8, 13–14, 19, 20, 21, 31; short story, 5, 8, 13, 19, 30, 31–32; short story sequence, 5, 13, 14, 32–33
"The Gift of the Magi" (O. Henry), 134
Go Down, Moses (William Faulkner), 32
The Golden Apples (Eudora Welty), 32
Gourneau, Patrick, 2, 9
Grand Avenue (Greg Sarris), 15
Grandmother's Pigeon, 7
The Grass Dancer (Susan Power), 15
Graves, Robert, 30
The Great Omar (*The Beet Queen*), 53, 56, 60, 68

Hamlet, 67
Homer, 32
The House Made of Dawn (N. Scott Nomaday), 14
Humor, 15, 20–21, 24, 26, 29, 37, 39, 45, 52–53, 83, 94, 113, 124–25, 134, 139

Immigrants, 9, 71
Indian Killer (Sherman Alexie), 15
Intertextuality, 8, 10, 17, 30–31, 32, 91, 109

Jacklight, 2, 3, 6
James, Celestine (*The Beet Queen, Tales of Burning Love*), 55–56, 57–59, 63, 111–12, 117; as mother, 57, 59, 63, 103, 118; as narrator, 54
James, Henry, 30
Johns Hopkins University, 3, 70

Johnson, Albertine (*The Bingo Palace, Love Medicine*), 15, 37, 39, 64, 101, 106; as Four Soul, 93, 105; as narrator, 37, 39; as observer, 10–11 n.1, 102–3, 137; as survivor, 45–46; as trickster, 44

Kashpaw, Eli (*The Beet Queen, Love Medicine, Tracks*), 37, 42, 46, 70, 77–78, 82–83; as survivor, 46
Kashpaw, Gordie (*Love Medicine*), 39–40, 49
Kashpaw, June Morrissey (*The Bingo Palace, Love Medicine, Tales of Burning Love*), 15, 34, 39, 41–42, 43, 46, 60, 83, 95, 117, 118, 119, 134; as a child, 42, 102; death of, 17, 31, 35, 48, 109, 110–111; as deer, 40, 49; as ghost, 93, 96, 101, 116; as mother without child, 25, 42, 64, 84, 92, 103
Kashpaw, King (*Love Medicine*), 37, 46, 96
Kashpaw, Marie Lazarre (*The Bingo Palace, Love Medicine, Tracks*), 37–38, 43, 45, 81, 94, 97; birth of, 79; as mother, 40, 42, 103; as survivor, 46; as traditional grandmother, 40, 42, 85, 105
Kashpaw, Nector (*Love Medicine, Tracks*), 18, 20, 37–38, 40, 42, 43, 45, 73, 77, 81, 94; as survivor, 46
Kashpaw, Rushes Bear (Margaret) (*Love Medicine, Tracks*), 72, 73, 77–79, 80, 84, 92; as survivor, 46, 70
Kashpaw, Russell (*The Beet Queen, The Bingo Palace, Tracks*), 55, 59, 65, 75, 76, 104
Kingston, Maxine Hong, 24, 87
Kozka, Sita (*The Beet Queen*), 54, 56, 59, 61–65

Lamartine, Henry, Junior (*Love Medicine*), 38–39, 41, 49; as ghost, 98

Lamartine, Lulu Nanapush (*The Bingo Palace, Love Medicine, Tracks*), 15, 37–39, 77, 80–85, 101–2; as enchanter, 39, 45, 93, 101–2, 104, 116; as gambler, 43; as listener, 69, 71, 73, 81; as mother, 38, 42, 193; naming of, 77; as survivor, 46; as traditional grandmother, 40, 42, 85, 105; as trickster, 23, 42–43

Lamartine, Lyman (*The Bingo Palace, Love Medicine, Tales of Burning Love*), 39, 40, 43–44, 92, 94–95, 97–98, 103–4, 110, 114, 117, 118, 122; as gambler, 97; as survivor, 46–47; as vision quester, 93, 98–99, 107–8

Love Medicine, 4, 17, 22, 51, 70, 83, 84, 85, 91–92, 94, 95, 102, 109–10, 122, 134; awards, 6, 29; characters in, 10, 34, 36, 41–45, 100, 102, 137; comic vision of, 45, 53; expanded edition of, 30–31, 84; genre of, 14, 19, 31–35; ghosts in, 15, 42; humor in, 20, 39, 45; imagery of, 17, 32, 43; narrative strategies of, 8, 31–35, 127; plot of, 34, 35–41; reader-response perspective of, 47–49; setting of, 2, 35; short stories in, 5, 6, 8, 31–32; themes in, 14, 25, 29, 31, 45–47, 84; trickster tradition in, 23–24, 42–43, 44–45

Magical realism, 15–16
The Magus (John Fowles), 30
Manitou, 21, 22, 23, 79, 84, 86
Márquez, Gabriel García, 15
Mauser, Eleanor Schlick (*Tales of Burning Love*), 112–17, 118–20, 121, 124
Mauser, Jack (*Tales of Burning Love*), 21, 110–17, 118–22, 124; as survivor, 125. *See also* Andy
McNickle, D'Arcy, 14, 25
A Midsummer Night's Dream (William Shakespeare), 121

Miller, Jude (*The Beet Queen*), 57, 59, 64–65, 67, 109
Misshepeshu, 21, 75, 77, 81, 86, 93, 99
Momaday, N. Scott, 14–15, 25
Moore, Marianne ("Poetry"), 88
Morrison, Toni, 14, 19, 24, 87
Morrissey, Lipsha (*The Bingo Palace, Love Medicine, Tales of Burning Love*), 15, 17, 18, 26, 34, 38, 40, 43, 84, 85, 92, 93–108, 109–10, 119; as gambler, 24, 41, 44, 96; as narrator, 91, 101; as quester, 23, 41, 96; as survivor, 45–46, 116; as trickster, 24, 44–45, 94; as vision quester, 93, 98–99, 101
Multiculturalism, 21, 24, 48–49, 86–88

Nanabozho, 23, 27 n.4, 42, 44, 82, 135
Nanapush, Gerry (*The Bingo Palace, Love Medicine, Tales of Burning Love*), 40, 41, 95, 111, 116, 119, 121; as culture hero, 24, 44, 70; as fugitive, 39, 41, 44, 93, 100, 101, 109, 114; as survivor, 46, 109, 125 n.2; as trickster, 23–24, 42, 44
Narrative technique, 8, 13–14; of *The Antelope Wife*, 127–28; of *The Beet Queen*, 52; of *The Bingo Palace*, 91–92; of *Love Medicine*, 32–34, 41; story within story, 16–17, 38, 110, 118; of *Tales of Burning Love*, 110, 119; of *Tracks*, 69, 71
Naylor, Gloria, 33
North, Milou (pseudonym), 4, 5, 6
North Dakota, 1, 8, 9, 17, 69, 110
North Dakota novels, 8, 10, 16, 17, 24, 29, 32, 92, 110

O'Connor, Flannery, 14
Ojibwa, 9, 11 n.2, 70, 72, 92, 106, 122. *See also* Anishinabe; Chippewa
Ojibwa oral tradition, 13, 16, 21, 31, 33, 88, 139

Old Nanapush (*The Bingo Palace, Tracks*), 9, 72–73, 76–82, 84, 85, 91–92, 98; as narrator, 69–71; as storyteller, 69, 73, 82, 84; as survivor, 46, 82; as trickster, 21, 23, 82–83

Other Side of the Earth (*The Antelope Wife*), 129–30, 134, 141

Ovid, 32

Pantamounty, Candice (*Tales of Burning Love*), 113–15, 117, 118–21, 123, 124

Pfef, Wallace (*The Beet Queen*), 55–56, 57–59, 61–62

Pillager, Fleur (*The Beet Queen, The Bingo Palace, Love Medicine, Tracks*), 15, 20, 72–82, 93–94; as bear, 16, 83, 98, 102; disappearance of, 102; as gambler, 75–76, 80, 98, 140; as medicine woman, 18, 45, 54–55, 83–84, 85, 98; as mother without child, 25, 73; as survivor, 46, 70, 84–85; as trickster, 75

Pillager, Moses (*Love Medicine, Tracks*), 43, 45, 77, 84; as survivor, 46

Plot, 14, 16, 19, 31, 34, 52, 118, 128; of *The Angelope Wife*, 128–37; of *The Beet Queen*, 53–59; of *The Bingo Palace*, 93–102; of *The Crown of Columbus*, 5; of *Love Medicine*, 35–41; of *Tales of Burning Love*, 110–17; of *Tracks*, 73–82

Power, Susan, 15

Puyat, Pauline (*Tracks*), 71, 73–82; as mother without child, 25, 79; as narrator, 69, 71, 81; as observer, 75–76, 83; as outsider, 75, 83, 88; as seeker of power, 76, 78, 79, 83, 86; as Sister Leopolda, 81, 83; as survivor, 84–85. *See also* Sister Leopolda

Remembrance of Things Past (Marcel Proust), 25

Roy, Cally (*The Antelope Wife*), 131–33, 135, 138–39; as Blue Prairie Woman, 133, 139; as namer, 133, 137; as observer, 10–11 n.1, 137; as twin, 130, 138

Roy, Matilda (*The Antelope Wife*), 129–30, 140–41

Roy, Scranton Teodorus (*The Antelope Wife*), 128–29, 135, 138, 140–41

Roy, Zosie (*The Antelope Wife*), 131–34, 136–37, 140–41

Sarris, Greg, 15

Setting, 8–9, 17; of *The Antelope Wife*, 128; of *The Beet Queen*, 51; of *The Bingo Palace*, 91; butcher shop, 2, 53, 75, 109; of *The Crown of Columbus*, 5; the Great Depression, 2; of *Love Medicine*, 35; of *Tales of Burning Love*, 110; of *Tracks*, 69–70; urban, 15

Shawano, Frank (*The Antelope Wife*), 17, 130–34, 136

Shawano, Klaus (*The Antelope Wife*), 16–17, 130–32, 134, 135–36, 141; as survivor, 138–39

Shawano, Mary (*The Antelope Wife*), 131–32, 136–37, 140–41

Shawano, Rozina Roy Whiteheart Beads (*The Antelope Wife*), 21, 22, 130–33, 136, 137, 138–39, 140–41; as mother, 130; as survivor, 138–39

Story cycle, 32–33, 92

Silko, Leslie Marmon, 14–15, 25

Sister Leopolda (*The Beet Queen, Love Medicine, Tales of Burning Love, Tracks*), 14, 37, 38, 54, 81, 83, 109, 117; disappearance of, 112, 118; as ghost, 116. *See also* Puyat, Pauline

Sorrow (*The Antelope Wife*), 129, 135

Storytelling, 16, 71, 84; as beadwork, 96, 127; by characters, 13, 57, 69, 82, 95, 114–15; by Erdrich, 10, 21, 24, 45; in Erdrich's family, 1, 2; as oral

tradition, 19, 31, 33; purpose of, 16–
  17, 18, 45, 115, 118, 138
The Surrounded (D'Arcy McNickle), 14

Tales of Burning Love, 2, 16, 17, 26, 30,
  75; characters in, 109–10, 117–21;
  feminist reading of, 122–25; humor
  in, 21, 113, 124–25; imagery of, 18,
  109; narrative technique of, 110, 117–
  18, 119; plot of, 110–17; setting of,
  110; themes in, 25, 121–22
Tan, Amy, 33
Themes, 10 n.1, 14, 24–26, 29, 45–47;
  in *The Antelope Wife*, 137–39; in *The
  Beet Queen*, 63–65; in *The Bingo Palace*, 104–6; community, 1, 10, 25, 47;
  feminist, 14–15, 42, 123, 140; gambling, 43–44, 92, 105, 122; homecoming, 8–9, 14–15, 25–26, 32, 46,
  59, 84, 104–5, 122; in *Love Medicine*,
  45–47; mother without child, 25, 42;
  naming, 16–17, 105, 132, 137; survival, 20, 24, 26, 45–46, 84–85, 105–
  6, 128, 138–39; in *Tales of Burning
  Love*, 121–22; in *Tracks*, 84–86
Toose, Shawnee Ray (*The Bingo Palace*), 94–95, 101, 105; as mother, 25,
  103, 105

Tracks, 2, 9, 15–16, 19, 21, 23, 30, 32,
  92; characters in, 26, 74, 82–84; historical background of, 71–73;
  humor in, 20, 83; imagery of, 17–18,
  71; multicultural perspective of, 86–
  88; narrative technique of, 69–71;
  plot of, 73–82; as political novel, 70–
  71; setting of, 69–70, 87; themes in,
  25, 71, 84–86; trickster tradition in,
  24, 83; writing of, 3–4, 70–71
Treuer, David, 15
Trickster, 21, 22–24, 26, 42, 44–45, 82, 94
Turtle Mountain Reservation, 2
Twostar, Vivian (*The Crown of Columbus*), 5

Vidal, Gore, 30
Vision quest, 92, 93, 98–99, 101

Welch, James, 14–15, 25
Williams, Roger (*The Crown of Colum-
  bus*), 5
Windigo, 22, 23, 132, 133, 138
Winter in the Blood (James Welch), 14

Yeats, William Butler, 30
A Yellow Raft in Blue Water (Michael
  Dorris), 5, 8

About the Author

LORENA L. STOOKEY is Lecturer in the English Department at the University of Nevada, Reno, where she teaches courses in mythology, poetry, and British literature. She is the author of *Robin Cook: A Critical Companion* (Greenwood, 1996).